Jung and Rorschach

Jung and Rorschach

A STUDY IN THE ARCHETYPE OF PERCEPTION

ROBERT S. McCULLY

Spring Publications, Inc.   Dallas, Texas

Published by Spring Publications, Inc.; P.O. Box 222069; Dallas, TX 75222. Printed in the United States of America. Cover designed and produced by Allison Esposito

The first edition of this book was titled *Rorschach Theory and Symbolism* and was published by The Williams & Wilkins Company, Library of Congress Catalog Card Number 74-160437, SBN 683-05749-9. The appendix originally appeared as an article — "A Commentary on Adolf Eichmann's Rorschach," *Journal of Personality Assessment* 44 (1980): 311-18 — and is here reprinted with the kind permission of the Society for Personality Assessment. Eichmann's Rorschach itself is reprinted by permission of Michael Selzer.

International distributors:
Spring; Postfach; 8800 Thalwil; Switzerland
Japan Spring Sha, Inc.; 1-2-4, Nishisakaidani-Cho; Ohharano, Nishikyo-Ku;
   Kyoto, 610-11, Japan
Element Books Ltd; Longmead Shaftesbury; Dorset SP7 8PL; England

Library of Congress Cataloging-in-Publication Data

McCully, Robert S., 1921–
   Jung and Rorschach.

   Reprint. Originally published: Rorschach theory
and symbolism. Baltimore : Williams & Wilkins, 1971.
With new appendix.
   Includes index.
   1. Rorschach test.   2. Archetype (Psychology)
3. Jung, C. G. (Carl Gustav), 1875–1961.   I. Title.
BF698.8.R5M23   1987   155.2'842   87-16570
ISBN 0-88214-332-8

Each has its lesson; for our dreams in sooth,
Come they in shape of demons, gods, or elves,
Are allegories with deep hearts of truth
That tell us solemn secrets of ourselves.

HENRY TIMROD

Foreword

Dr. Robert S. McCully is a pioneer in the application of Carl G. Jung's concept of the archetype to responses elicited by the Rorschach inkblots. This is not his first publication in this area, but it is certainly his most systematic and extensive contribution. His "wish to extend our grasp of our [Rorschach] data" motivated him "to examine each stimulus plate with a view toward identifying its potentials as an activator of kinds of psychic experiences." These experiences, called "archetypes" by Jung, comprise those which, since the dawn of consciousness and organized group living, everyone experiences at some time. Common and vital experiences are the source of the usually unconscious archetypes, which may reveal themselves to the consciousness in the form of archetypal visual images. Awareness of such imagery is not necessarily synonymous with a realization that the images are archetypal.

"Archetype" is one of the most frequently misunderstood concepts. Archetypes are believed to be related causally to fundamental psycho-social situations which constitute the "human condition." Dr. McCully lists, among the archetypes, such prototypal experiences as food gathering, mother, father, self [the most important], femininity, maleness, sleep, fertility, elimination, childhood, god (good), goddess, devil (evil), circle, square. He points out that Christ and Buddha are also archetypes as two basically different prototypes of life and one's role in it. "For a hundred thousand years, they [primitive men] worked and reworked important themes whose archetypal energy took them beyond where they were when they started," comments the author.

While they are lasting, archetypes are not inalterable. They are fixed patterns of motivation in the sense that they reveal basic problems of human existence. They are the essence of accumulated human experience, including the most frequent and tested ways of handling those problems, and are transmitted from generation to generation by nonverbalized example, often unintended, as well as by direct instruction.

The story of Adam and Eve, as told by Dr. McCully, is an excellent explanation of the concept of the archetype. No one has given a better and more detailed one. It takes the mystery out of the concept. His perceptive analysis of Paleolithic and Neolithic art brings out the relation between archetypes, on the one hand, and psychological maturity, possibilities for organized social actions, and apparent accumulated group experience, on the other hand.

Archetypes appear in religious myths, national attitudes and ideologies, but also in schizophrenic delusions. They are supra-individual or collective, *i.e.*, shared alike by very many despite numerous differences among the individuals of a group. The schizophrenic disease process reduces patients' capacities for effective and contented living in similar ways. The result is the sharing of many grave concerns and threatening experiences, which tends to create archetypal schizophrenic behavior. However, these archetypes are not limited to schizophrenics. They appear in normals, although in an attenuated and unconscious form, when these normals suffer from states of extreme hopelessness and panic.

To explain schizophrenia, Rorschach used the picture of an earthquake which causes deep fissures. The schizophrenic is hurled to the bottom of the crevice where he becomes aware of the oldest, most primitive, pitiless, and destructive human urges, located in the deepest layers, as it were. He is helpless and thus panicky. He cannot climb out at will. The great writer—continued Rorschach—descends into the crevice deliberately, sees similar things as the schizophrenic, then ascends at will and unaided to describe his observations.

The archetypes of most normals remain unconscious, probably because of their low intensity or good realistic and conscious control. By contrast, schizophrenics express their archetypes relatively easily through their original images, often visualizing destructive outcomes.

It is natural to seek archetypal images among Rorschach responses, as Dr. McCully has been doing for some time now. Every Rorschach plate or its part can be interpreted by subjects in a variety of ways, and all of the various responses can be of equal plausibility with equally good form quality. If a subject has several equivalent options but spontaneously chooses one, in an act of free association, his choice is a function of his own subjective attitudes. Since the choice is unconscious, the attitudes revealed are genuine and are not distorted by conscious or semiconscious reasons for disguising or concealing his responses. Archetypes become conscious through freely associated visual images. Responses to the Rorschach plates also are freely associated visual images: visual images, freely associated to ambiguous visual stimuli.

Another circumstance which increases the significance of the archetypal images elicited by the Rorschach plates is their originality. A Rorschach response is called original when it appears in less than 2 per cent of test records. It is well known that every original Rorschach response contains specific and important information about the individual who produced it. That information, however, cannot always be immediately inferred, simply because by definition original responses are very rare and consequently require much time to decipher their specific meaning.

The author offers in this book a new method of content analysis of selected responses, practically all of which are original in the Rorschach sense. The archetypal method complements, but does not take the place of, other systems of interpretation. Dr. McCully proposes his method hypothetically, as a new and pioneering procedure for experimentation and validation, albeit with a hopeful expectation that eventually it will be improved in practice, systematized, and validated with gratifying results. The included case studies with their samples of archetypal Rorschach responses make one share the author's expectations. When the hopes are fulfilled, we shall be able to differentiate between conflicts relating to basic universal human problems and conflicts peculiar to the individual. It seems reasonable to suppose that such a differentiation would help us to make better psychotherapeutic plans and thus make psychotherapy more effective.

In ingenious analyses and commentaries, the author has explored the capacity of each Rorschach plate "to activate archetypal sources." His method has led him, in a number of fascinating illustrative Rorschach records, to conclusions not deducible by means of other interpretive systems. The case studies are sensitive and penetrating, rich in many valuable suggestions. The test evidence in support of the conclusions is, as a rule, indicated.

Sound personality theories, properly applied, widen the range and depth of conclusions inferred from test findings. The interpretation of Rorschach responses can be compared to the interpretation of X-rays. In both tests the human being appears quite different than in direct nontest contacts. Very much depends on the skill and knowledge of the interpreter of test findings. It is a pity that so much still depends on the personal qualities of interpreters of Rorschach test records. This should not be so. Rules of interpretation should be formalized and valid.

Dr. McCully's brave, novel, and unconventional book is a determined step not only toward enriching the Rorschach test but also toward that high aim of objectivity in a very difficult and arresting area of personality research.

His method relies in part on the belief in universal symbols. This does not make the author's enterprise so futile as some may think. A number of universal symbols do exist and their meaning has been well established. There may be many more of them unknown to us today. In grave danger, associated with fundamental life matters that cause deep and lasting anxiety, individual differences in feeling, thoughts, and behavior dwindle drastically. This creates a condition for the production of similar imagery among very many different individuals. Such a condition favors the development of archetypal images. Besides, human imagination is too feeble to create specific images for every variant of fundamental life situations and conflicts, including several possible solutions to the problems. Thus, even human inertia makes a science of universal psychological symbols theoretically possible.

ZYGMUNT A. PIOTROWSKI
May 29, 1971

Preface

There are two major objectives in writing this book. The first is to offer a fresh point of view in interpreting inkblot-mediated imagery. The second is to call attention to the Rorschach experience as a means toward furthering our knowledge about psychic structure. We will present a new theoretical rationale associated with the structure of these plates and thus provide a framework for extending our grasp of those processes which occur through the Rorschach method. Through our first objective we hope to enrich the range of an individual's use of Rorschach material, and by way of the second, to kindle inquiry.

While a central concern about Rorschach pertains to its interpretation, we believe that more emphasis has been put on this method's performance with disturbed patients than on other important potentials which are inherent in the technique. It may be that our emphasis in using the Rorschach to diagnose trouble and as a research tool measuring pathology has obscured our grasp of other facets operating in the emergence of material apart from the routine questions we have put to it.

We expect to make use of a number of ideas found in C. G. Jung's depth psychology as we proceed. Our position is that he has provided the widest grasp of the psyche in Western tradition, and we will use his model of the inner world as a frame for our own position. We are careful to say Western tradition because Eastern ones may include an even wider grasp of psychic sources, in some instances, than those found in Western writings. Some years ago, while studying the *Dhammapada*, a collection of Buddhist teachings, the author was astonished at the correspondence between the stages in Buddhist thought and stages in Jung's individuation process. There are also qualities in common with the work of Abraham Maslow. So it is with aspects of Hermann Rorschach's grasp of life and his interests. The sources were similar. As we proceed, we will draw on sources in literature when we can identify them in the works of creative writers, such as may pertain to the source we wish to amplify.

A chapter will define and illustrate those concepts of Jung's that we will use or apply to our theory. A knowledge of Jung is not presupposed for the reader, nor do we saddle Jung himself with our expositions. In fact, we will take exception to some of Jung's remarks about the Rorschach method. Nevertheless, in the main, we will keep to the approach to symbolism which Jung followed, and not the traditional Freudian one. Jung was influenced by Johann Jakob Bachofen, the Swiss social philosopher, and Jakob Burckhardt in that regard. Jung's model for the psyche was radically different from that of Freud's, and, unlike Freud, Jung did not propose a theory. The absence of a dogma or theory leaves us remarkably free to rove through Jung's writings and select those concepts which seem useful for our purposes. We have not included some of his concepts that he considered crucial, since they do not further our purposes here.

We will spin our own theory in an attempt to explain certain aspects about the reliability associated with Rorschach's plates, and we arrive at our theoretical option through our own empiricism and not Jung's. We will take departures from his thinking, sometimes pushing his concepts further, and at other times we will make use of meanings differently than he might have used them. In general, Jung's psychology has been the inspiration for our task.

From our source material, we expect to distinguish features we will identify tentatively as laws that pertain to subjective processes. We feel this is necessary to give structure inside the subjective world and to provide a means to *objectivity* as one deals with subjective material. This has been generally absent in the work associated with projective data, and it has created problems familiar to all researchers about the Rorschach. Our position is that one cannot apply the laws of conscious logic to many aspects of subjective experience. The tentative laws we suggest are no more than the author's empirical observations about processes in the Rorschach experience over a period of years. Others have doubtless observed the same things. After they were organized in this book (they simply grew; there was no intent behind describing them), their correspondence with aspects of Gestalt theory was rewarding for the author. We arrived at them from an entirely different means than had the Gestaltists. Our means was simply observation through Rorschach data. However, they are no more than guides for us to objectivity, pivots which help orient us.

In essence, we have done little more than arrange what we have observed about Rorschach phenomena in an empirical, but defined frame. We have hoped to break new ground in some areas, and merely amplify known ideas in others, but our plan is to further interest and knowledge about this important method of inquiry at a time when many changes are occurring in the field at large. We are pleased that this writing coincides with the 50th anniversary of the publication of Rorschach's work.

Our definition of Rorschach behavior is those psychological processes which occur as perception is diverted from outer to inner stimuli and experience. We hope to communicate our way so that it may be useful to others apart from their particular level of training. We have devoted considerable attention to problems in interpreting the Rorschach materials of disturbed patients. We have not assumed that others will necessarily use our mode or approach to interpretation, but knowledge about this way can extend anyone's range. Insofar as was possible, we have attempted to explain how we arrived at an interpretative conclusion.

At the same time, we hope to show or underscore how the use of the Rorschach method for diagnostic evaluation has narrowed our understanding of the technique. Apart from clinical problems, it is our most effective way of gathering subjective data in an objective frame. At that point in the future when we can properly assess the contribution of the Rorschach method to human knowledge, we may find that it will have contributed as much to philosophy, or to what we call the embryology of psychic structure, as it will have to clinical problems.

Nevertheless, the clinician has to deal with those qualities that underlie symptoms in patients. All clinicians know how the Rorschach may be exceedingly helpful. This continues regardless of many academicians' bias about the method. Its wide use makes its pragmatic worth obvious. We tend to discard techniques that do not prove their value. This does not mean that criticisms of the method are not valid. In Rorschach, we not infrequently obtain more data than pertains to our clinical questions. Usually, we disregard those data which do not seem to pertain, or which we have failed to observe or grasp. We may find it useful to ask questions of the Rorschach that do not necessarily accompany clinical practice. We hold that the plates activate psychic processes, and that those psychological phenomena flow without regard to the questions in the mind of a particular examiner or researcher. Rorschach behavior is an example of natural phenomena, and nature's values cannot be exclusively human. What flows out from inside carries with it some imprints of the source. The Rorschach plates provide us with a means of studying the nature of the psyche itself and extending our knowledge of those processes that underlie the essential substance that we call human nature. We will suggest that these inkblots activate psychic centers *because* the structure of the blots may be not unlike the nature of the structure of the psyche itself. The Rorschach does not just hold a mirror to the psyche; experience forms around its substance, and images appear through the forces that created them. Consciousness accompanies this and reacts. So may it be with the neural structure that supports waking life and dreams. We have no quarrel with Shakespeare's estimate of us as stuff dreams are made on, but we would have to add the dimension of conscious reaction to dream-making stuff to be inclusive. The Rorschach is a net which catches glimmers from both.

To
My Wife Patricia, Duff, and Nina

Introduction

A sufficient supply of introductory books exists for students who want to learn the Rorschach technique. We do not offer instruction on administration or scoring. However, we do anticipate presenting useful material to a student who has only begun his studies. We aspire to provide the beginner with a way of thinking and information which he can take beyond his first studies. Further, our goals include the effort to offer the experienced clinician an approach which may augment his own fund of knowledge. We welcome as readers anyone who may be seriously interested in studying the nature of subjective behavior. He need not be a student of the Rorschach method at all. It is our hope that our point of view may be fruitful for anyone who deals with patients and psychological data, including the psychotherapist, the researcher, and even the philosopher.

We have made no effort to provide completeness when we have included sources from the literature. We do not even claim to have included all published materials pertinent to our theses. We have tried to include those references which have seemed important, as either a source or a comparison against the point of view we have supplied. This may be considered a serious limitation by some scholars, but we are willing to accept this criticism against our belief that cutting across mountains of vaguely relevant research aids us in attaining clarity. If our ideas stimulate research, we will have been justified in this liberty.

Insofar as we know, at least some of the steps we take in this book have not been taken before. If our approach takes us into controversy, we will feel rewarded. At least in the United States, a certain complacency seems to have settled around the Rorschach method because it has been an elusive mode for research. Complacency usually means something ought to happen, since it often reflects an inaccurate estimate of the state of knowledge about a subject. At the 1965 International Rorschach Congress in Paris, the author observed a participant jump onto the stage in anger, poised to fight because of an exception he took with someone's points. When this happens, we know inquiry is alive.

Through a careful delineation of our position, and a meticulous and direct application of it to clinical material, we hope to communicate to the student the excitement that emerges when the Rorschach experience unfolds aspects of someone's being. It puts in sharp relief what we mean by individual differences in human nature, and the originality inherent in the springs of nature bursts boldly out, leaving us with a deep sense of awe. Complacency always omits awe and this usually puts us off from discovery.

When we look at the confluence of forces that come into play as Rorschach responses happen, we hope to provide the experienced worker with some new tools for amplification and widened scope. We believe that anybody's store of information or frame of reference can be enriched. We certainly have felt this for ourselves, and it can take place alongside quite widely disparate theoretical paths. Our goals are to augment ideas and stimulate new ones, not to impose a particular theoretical stance. No one should be robbed of any theory that puts him in touch with meaningful experience.

Whether any of us be student, scholar, teacher, clinician, believer, or doubter, our personal objectivity may be enhanced by looking closely at our attitudes. Perhaps the teacher should be held most in account in that regard, since he touches youth and shapes its set. In the 50 years Rorschach's method has been available, attitudes toward it have run high. It has seldom been a neutral subject. Some have held it infallible, while others have predicted its doom.

Along the way we will discuss some of the reasons for this cloud of mixed opinions. The potentials our method provides are too important to be judged by the attitudes of the moment. When we extend our grasp of it, we will extend the probability for discovery. We will suggest that the research models applied to the study of the Rorschach have often been misapplied. If we can call attention to the need to identify the range of Rorschach processes, we may thus further the cause of investigation. *How* we ask research questions may be more important than *what* we ask.

Those academicians or clinicians who have expected the Rorschach method to provide precise, simple, short but inclusive information associated with clinical questions *should* be disappointed with this technique as a means of quick solutions. Our modern pace tends to disregard anything that takes time and requires reflection. Yet, if one sets out to unravel or understand the psychological substance of an individual, no short cuts or prescribed blueprints exist. To view the Rorschach as a means to easy solution is to misunderstand the technique on the one hand and human nature on the other. It is surprising sometimes to learn that experts on human behavior have observed so little of how nature works. Discovery has seldom followed the tight bonds which dictate the nature of research design. Apples did not fall up before Newton published his observations, and we are among those who do not doubt that the spider did indeed teach Descartes about order in nature's laws. We are suggesting that our methods of studying the Rorschach have been limited in proportion to our grasp of how the technique works.

The nature of some of the questions we ask of the Rorschach cuts it up into artificial hunks. We may ask it a legitimate clinical question, but if an individual subject is open to an outpouring of complex data, much more data surge forth than pertains to our question. We have yet to discover how much of this fits together and whether findings of the moment have different implications for the past or the future. That we as observers simply want a particular answer does *not* influence the nature or extent of psychological behavior that takes place when inkblots mediate reactions. We suggest that we often allow the urgency of the problems we pose to cloud our grasp of the meaning of what is before us. We do indeed sample the contents of a psychological well with our rustic bucket, but we may not fully grasp the spectrum of what we bring up. It is our grasp that is limited, and we do not yet know enough to indict our method. We have as yet to learn a great deal about how psychic processes work, how they emerged in the evolution of development, the laws that pertain to experiences like dreams that are not under the control of consciousness, how or why symbols form, and the extent to which our models of the psyche are limited.

This state of Rorschach theory need not bog the student down. On the contrary, it should fire his imagination. We do feel it is useful for the beginner to become aware that much is yet to be known. He needs to know the range of what may be involved when he speaks of modifying behavior. We need the student's interest in these matters for it is he who will extend our horizons and guide tomorrow's research.

Our general plan involves beginning with a brief look at the influence C. G. Jung has had on the development of projective techniques and his relationship with Hermann Rorschach. Next, we will outline and define those constructs which Jung has given us which pertain to our task. Following that, we will look at our concept of the nature of Rorschach experience. We will then trace our sources back in time through a kind of *paleopsychology*. That journey augments the meaning of archetypes and sets us well on the way to looking at symbols from our viewpoint. This enables us to trace archetypal sources in each inkplate stimulus. We will take up each plate individually and discuss its stimulus value against the constructs we will propose as useful for analysis. This leads us into a theory about how the blots work. At each step we will use illustrative materials from a single Rorschach record, referring to specific responses for each of the 10 plates. Then, we will outline and illustrate a method for analyzing processes as they happen in the Rorschach experience. From there we move into a study of five sets of case materials. These cases have been selected because they show the kinds of processes and qualities that pertain to our theses. While they are unusual, many facets in their materials are common enough in everyday clinical practice. How we approach them may be used for any kind of case. It was not an analysis of hundreds of papyri that enabled scholars to translate the Egyptian language, but the Rosetta stone. We believe that certain cases teach us more than others, and that they are statistically infrequent. Each case has been selected to amplify our approach and to illustrate our point of view. They were not, though, sorted out from many. The case used to illustrate stimulus qualities in each Rorschach plate simply came along at the time the author was writing about that matter. Any number of cases might illustrate single points, but these particular ones appeared to pertain in a larger sense to our goals for the book. Not every image in each case was considered. Nor would the interpretation we have made be considered either definitive or complete. Our goal in presenting them was to take the issues and questions away from conventional clinical ones and relate the Rorschach's value to the changing professional and social scene. Some of the conventional questions we have raised about patients have tended to become obsolete. *Questions* based on individual data can be more useful for a particular subject than tentative answers about dynamics.

In our final chapter we will pull together an estimate of what we have presented. We will discuss the implications we believe exist around our theory. We will make some predictions about the future of the Rorschach method and we will call attention to those avenues for thought and research planning which seem especially promising to us.

Acknowledgements

The author would like to acknowledge several unseen influences which helped carry the warp and woof of the book into being, specific individuals who aided him personally with the book, and those settings whose aid he used:

To *Elizabeth Elmina McCully*, a boy's aunt, who took him into myth, fairy tale, and to awe in nature; to *Leonore L. Fabisch* and *M. Esther Harding*, who went with the man into his own nature; to his long-time teacher, friend, and fertile inspirational source, *Florence R. Miale*; to another teacher and friend, *Jessie E. Fraser*; and to *Harold J. Isaacson*, through whose vision the author journeyed to the East.

To *Edward F. Edinger* and *Vernon Brooks*, and members of the faculty of the New York Institute of the C. G. Jung Foundation who took an interest in the book in its early stages.

To *Myrtle Guy Coyle* and *Katie Hicks*, and *Edna A. Lerner*, who helped the author or inspired him, as well as others of the faculty of the Department of Psychiatry, Cornell University Medical College—The New York Hospital, who were interested in the task.

To *Margaret P. Schachte* and *Jane Britt*, who aided in the work of assembling the manuscript, cataloguing data, and sundry tasks; and to the Department of Psychiatry of the Medical University of South Carolina, whose support aided in assembling materials necessary for the book.

Appreciation is expressed for generous access to the materials in the *Archive for Research in Archetypal Symbolism*, a Department of the C. G. Jung Foundation in New York City, and for aid rendered by its staff.

Finally, the author and publisher are indebted to *Hans Huber* of Berne, Switzerland for their kind permission to reproduce the Rorschach plates.

Contents

ONE

The Interlacing of Genius: Hermann Rorschach and Carl Jung

Hermann Rorschach, a man 10 years junior to Jung, began his inkblot studies during the same period that Jung's pioneering studies took place. Both men worked outside the contemporary modes of their professions, both were isolated from their colleagues at certain periods of their careers because of their ideas, both were brilliant empiricists, and both have provided us with a profound grasp of human nature, taking us further than their predecessors. That both of these Swiss men of genius did not combine their efforts personally provides us with a remarkable mystery. Ellenberger (2) has remarked that someone 300 years from now might try to prove that Jung and not Rorschach wrote the *Psychodiagnostik*. Ellenberger (2) noted that there is certainly a mystery about how Rorschach's masterpiece sprang up, since it is hardly a manual explaining a method. There is a genuine enigma about the influence Jung had on Rorschach. Rorschach, before his death in 1922, was familiar with Jung's publications, and Jung certainly knew about Rorschach's work. Perhaps neither man grasped how much the other sought the same goals.

We may need to be reminded that Carl Jung was the first psychiatrist in modern times to apply the scientific method to the study of disturbed patients. This may surprise those who associate Jung with an affinity for mysticism, but he *began* the application of the experimental method in the study of psychiatric illness. Nearly 70 years ago, Jung was fully versed in those same research methods that psychiatrists are scurrying to acquire today. Jung and his associates spent more than a half a dozen years of the first decade in this century in their laboratory studying psychological problems similar to those being studied today. They applied the experimental method in the study of reaction time, of the associations of normal and disturbed populations, and of memory. In this period, Jung developed his

1

Association Test, which provided us with the first experimental data on unconscious processes. The Association Test led to the discovery of what he called the "psychological complex." He began his psychophysical experiments through studying memory and associations in 1904, and he and Peterson were the first to report the use of the galvanometer as a measure of psychological reaction in disturbed patients in 1907.[1] How many authors from the great pile of published literature on psychogalvanic response have given Jung credit as the original pioneer in using the method? Many workers would assume that projective techniques grew out of psychoanalysis and Freud's work. As progenitor of the movement, Jung's word association technique earns him the title of father of the indirect way of activating subjective processes, as a means to understanding individuals. Some of the major pioneers worked with Jung personally or knew him. Others were influenced by reading his works. Among those are Bruno Klopfer, Henry A. Murray, Miale and Holsopple, and Hermann Rorschach himself. He trained and influenced some of the major thinkers in the existential approach to symbol interpretation, including Ludwig Binswanger and Medart Boss.

Jung was drawn away from the mainstream in psychological research because he made startling discoveries in the eddies. While Freud concentrated on studying neurotics, Jung tackled the confusing complexities of the psychotic. He considered his experimental studies important, but, as he discovered more and more data which did not lend themselves to investigation based on the methods of conscious logic, he began to discard the experimental method. By 1907, in his book, *Psychology of Dementia Praecox,* Jung (4) remarked that the subjective could only be understood and judged subjectively, and he added that we cannot measure distance in pints. Most of Jung's colleagues did not bother with analyzing psychotic material; Jung not only gathered this material, but also wanted to deal with it and understand it. In his opinion, the experimental method was of little help in that regard. An explorer seldom brings a method applicable to a new discovery with him. We have not reached a more refined way of studying subjective data today than was available in Jung's time. Our state is not dissimilar to that of the astronomer interested in the outer reaches of space prior to the advent of radio techniques. Gifted astronomers saw implications in their empirical data suggestive of certain phenomena, but there was no direct means of study or confirmation. Suddenly, and in our time, radio astronomy has extended our knowledge about the universe manyfold. Data about and from explanatory source material came into being, and this allowed for the validation of many assumptions. We have not reached this point in studying the inner life of man. Both in Jung's time and now, the knowledge about sources for certain kinds of subjective data remains unknown. Jung, as he

---

[1] Jung and his associates published 13 experimental studies between 1905 and 1908.

charted unknown psychological seas, must have behaved quite in the manner of Charles Darwin, as he made his famous Voyage of the Beagle. Both men held to scrupulous objectivity in their bold empirical observations and recorded what they found through their exceptional powers of perception. The implications for the data they gathered came to each one much later.

Hermann Rorschach was equally lonely in his work as he moved into territories about which nothing was known. His isolation peculiarly handicapped him, insofar as the prejudices of his colleagues were concerned. Yet, that same isolation may have been a major source of his creativity. Even so, most of his colleagues believed that no significant scientific work could emerge outside a university. Hermann Rorschach had never trained at the *Burghölzli* in Zurich, the prestige training spot of his day. Worse, he was working in a mental hospital in an obscure Swiss canton, and there was *no senior professor* to guide him. True, he had done his doctoral dissertation under Eugen Bleuler, but professional opinion held that a mere clinician in some outpost was not equipped to make discoveries, much less develop creative work. Like Jung, Rorschach worked with elusive material, but in an atmosphere of rigorous self-demand and meticulous objectivity. What he found often carried him into the reaches of discovery, and there were no precedents and no adequate means to evaluate what he had found. Since the experimental method is based on John Stuart Mill's observations about conscious logic, the method did not bend itself readily to materials from sources outside conscious processes.

When Rorschach (7) published his *Psychodiagnostik* in 1921, the German Society of Experimental Psychology, which met that year, took note of the work by blasting it. Their influence was so great that Rorschach's method dropped into a temporary oblivion, though it lasted almost a decade. Professor William Stern, one of that society's most influential leaders, attacked Rorschach's book so violently that it became unsafe for a researcher to include a publication on Rorschach's inkblots in his credentials if he wished a university post. Such was the influence of the *Professor* in the Germanic university tradition of the time.

It was not only Jung's and Rorschach's work associated with discovery around subjective material that has parallels, but they also showed striking similarities in their *curiosity* about the same qualities in human nature. Neither man was caught up in the materialism of their times as much as some of their other colleagues in psychology. We see this from the manner in which they set their discoveries philosophically.

It is not our purpose here to draw a complete schema about the impact of other pioneers like Freud on Rorschach's work. This has been amply handled by others. That Freud's influence was great is clear enough. It is our point, though, that Jung and Rorschach went to the same sources for the same purpose, that of extending their understanding of human nature. Both men grasped how man's history contains, like fossils in stone, powerful projections that link us together. Hermann Rorschach was keenly interested in folklore as it might enhance understanding, and he was deeply involved in studying the work of the Gnostics. In trying to accommodate Christianity to Plato, Pythagoras, and certain Oriental philosophers during the first six centuries of the Christian era, the Gnostics have left us a rich storehouse of psychological material. Jung viewed Gnostic literature as having sprung directly from unconscious sources and, thus, as a highly valuable source for understanding unconscious processes. Rorschach viewed Gnostic writings in a similar way. It was this kind of approach to recorded human data that Arnold J. Toynbee applied to history. Toynbee (8) credited Jung with having added a new dimension in the picture of the world for him. A grasp about *how* man projects his universal links, and *where* he did it, connects Jung and Rorschach in a way in which neither is connected with some of the other major pioneers in the field. While both men readily acknowledged their great debts to Freud, neither one was inundated by Freud's theories. This took great courage both then and now. Rorschach drew as much on Jung and the theories of John Mourly Vold,[2] a Norwegian philosopher, as he did on Freud in considering a theory of dreams. Mourly Vold knew nothing of Freud's work, and he described a theory of dream imagery apart from libido theory. Neither Rorschach nor Jung was convinced that Freud's libido theory was a complete one.

In a posthumous paper attributed to Rorschach (2), he discussed the personality structure of two leaders of obscure, erotically oriented religious cults in the Swiss Alps. Phallus worship (as in some hippie-drug cults of today) played a dominant role. The author of that paper rejected Freud's libido theory in accounting for the qualities associated with power over participants held by these leaders. According to Ellenberger (2), Rorschach distinguished between cult leaders on the basis of intrapsychic "archetypes," which were described as having high or low status or order. If this paper does express aspects of Rorschach's approach to inner experience, it has some parallels with some of Jung's later work on the collective unconscious.

It is interesting to note that Jung began his experimental studies with "words," in his association test, while Rorschach began his with "colored pictures," his inkblots. Each used different visual modes to catch and examine projections. True to their original means, Jung was able to say at a later time that "the psychological meaning of an epoch" existed in the *words* the Gnostics wrote. Hermann Rorschach believed that one could fathom the "mentality of an epoch" by studying the relation of movement to color in *paintings* (colored pictures) from the past. The notion of a collective reser-

---

[2] 1805–1907.

voir for unconscious processes in conscious products was implicit in both Jung's and Rorschach's work. While both men may have been influenced by Bachofen's[3] (1) ideas in that regard, they both saw beyond their data in a fashion given only to a few.

Perhaps Rorschach's most original contribution centered around his notion of *Erlebnistypus*. This is a cogent example that supports our thesis that the larger value of using the Rorschach technique comes from its application beyond examining pathology. *Erlebnistypus* is a concept which describes the state an individual is in at any one moment due to the proportion of introversion and extraversion in his approach to life. He came to understand this phenomenon through observing order in the data caught by his inkblots.

Ellenberger (2) noted the closeness between Rorschach's idea of *Erlebnistypus* and the Hindu notion of Karma. This was spelled out in the Indian *Vedas,* the oldest body of knowledge in the Western tradition. Karma contains the idea that one's destiny is in the hands of a constant manifestation of inner forces. Jung's ideas about the nature of *individuation,* which came later but had facets like Rorschach's *Erlebnistypus,* closely resemble some of the goals of self-realization of Vedantic philosophy.

Rorschach borrowed the terms "introversion" and "extraversion" from Jung. Rorschach was careful to say in his *Psychodiagnostik* (7) that he was using the terms differently than did Jung. Except for one reference to the Jung-Riklin word association experiments, Rorschach refers to Jung's work in the *Psychodiagnostik* (7) only to differentiate his use of the term from Jung's. Perhaps history would have gained if Rorschach had used different terms altogether. Jung understood those terms differently at different times, and Hermann Rorschach was not around to observe later changes in Jung's grasp of those terms. Through *Erlebnistypus,* Rorschach may have had a wider grasp for the meaning of the terms than Jung did in 1921, though it is really hard to tell fundamental differences in the grasp both men came to, in their understanding of the scope of the two primary perceptual types that Jung first described. How unfortunate for history that the two men did not spend long evening hours discussing theory and data on the subject.

Richard Evans (3) recorded the following comments Jung made about Hermann Rorschach in a personal interview in 1957, 4 years before Jung died. Evans (3) reported that Jung appeared to be in excellent health at the time.

Dr. Evans: You knew Hermann Rorschach, I believe, did you not?
Dr. Jung: No. He has circumvented me as much as possible.
Dr. Evans: But did you get to know him personally?
Dr. Jung: No. I never saw him.
Dr. Evans: In his terms, "introtensive" and "extraversion," of course, he is

---

[3] 1815–1887.

reflecting your conceptions of introversion and extraversion, in my own estimation, that is.

Dr. Jung: Yes, but I was the anathema, because I was the one to first outline the concepts; and that, you know, is unforgivable. I should never have done it.

Dr. Evans: So you really didn't have any personal contact with Rorschach?

Dr. Jung: No personal relations at all.

Dr. Evans: Are you familiar with Rorschach's test which uses ink-blots?

Dr. Jung: Yes, but I never applied it, because later on I didn't even apply the Word Association Test anymore. . . . I learned what I had to learn from the exact examinations of psychic reactions; and that, I think, is a very excellent means.

It would have been a strange touch of fate if there was no evidence of some contact between these two Swiss giants, Jung and Rorschach. Both men were in close contact with Eugen Bleuler at various times in their lives. Rorschach took the major part of his medical training at the medical school of the University of Zurich, and his transcript[4] lists two lecture courses that he attended that were given by Jung, who was a *privatdocent* at that time. They were: *Psychopathologie der Hysteria* in the winter semester 1907/ 1908 (approximately 5½ months), and *Kurs über psychotherapie* in the summer semester of 1908 (approximately 3 months).

This fact establishes that Hermann Rorschach came under Jung's personal influence. However, there was not necessarily any close exchange between professor and medical student in those days. Jung may never have known that Rorschach had attended his classes. We may assume this from Jung's remarks to Evans (3). It does not follow, though, that Jung did not then exert a powerful influence over his young student. If Hermann Rorschach did not have a personal reaction to Jung beyond the ordinary, it would contradict what is known about Jung's personal impact on others. It was powerful enough to make Freud faint and fall into a heap on two widely separated occasions. The 1907–1908 period would have been an exciting time to hear Jung speak since it was a time of tremendous discovery and change in his viewpoints and career. He was leaving off his experimental studies at the Burghölzli, because he had become absorbed in archetypal imagery in disturbed patients and how to deal with these images in treatment. He had just published *The Psychology of Dementia Praecox* (4) in 1907, and this work disclosed his original ideas and means to understanding illness outside Freud's theories. There can be no question that Jung expressed some of his new ideas to his students, and they could not have failed to capture the interest of a serious student in medicine interested in psychiatry. Rorschach was no ordinary student, and, as a creative young man, he was unlikely not to have responded to creativity as it passed near him. We would be inclined to hold to this belief quite apart from what

---

[4] This information was provided the author by Dr. Wolfgang Schwarz.

Rorschach may have held in his conscious attitude about Jung and what he may have said about him. There is indeed a mystery about the absence of further personal contact between these two men who could have been easily accessible to each other. Jung gave us a clue in his remarks to Evans (3). He often spoke in allegory, and it was through allegory that Jung often expressed his keen sense of humor. He was sobered, but often amused by the effect he had on others. He would disclaim any effect on others as being due to something "personal" in him, but he knew about the power he had through contact with archetypal sources in himself. He regarded those qualities as impersonal. His ego could take no credit for them. So, when he said to Evans that Hermann Rorschach "has circumvented me as much as possible," he probably used an allegory. He meant that the powerful effects of what Jung saw in the world of archetypes were aspects of the psyche that Rorschach kept away from or circumvented. He assumed this from the nature of Rorschach's writings. Jung probably did not know about Rorschach's wide grasp and personal interests, and since he had already lost interest in his Word Association Test, he may not have given Rorschach's technique much thought when it was published. Our point is that, through ignorance, Jung may have done Rorschach an injustice. Rorschach may have been much closer to grasping the collective side of the unconscious than Jung thought. Rorschach may have grasped more about the meaning of the relationship between extraversion-introversion and its effect on the subject's life experience than Jung did in the early stages of his thinking on the subject. It is not impossible that Jung himself planted some of the seeds that fluorished later in the unknown student of 1907–1908. We know that Rorschach was fiercely independent in his thinking, and that this was necessary for him, so as not to be inundated by the theories or concepts of others. Unfortunately, we were not allowed the wisdom of Rorschach's maturity.

Whatever may have been Rorschach's thoughts on Carl Jung, the man, Ellenberger (2) has informed us that Hermann Rorschach used Jung's techniques *prior* to his learning about Freud's methods and psychoanalysis. He showed a lifelong interest in the association method Jung devised. Together with a friend, Konrad Gehring, who was a teacher, he showed inkblots to patients and students and compared the results with those obtained by using the Word Association Test. Five years later, in 1916, Rorschach combined three techniques in his studies: inkblots, free association, and word association.

Jung did not find that word association brought enough archetypal material forward, and he was eager to devote all his energies to understanding such material. He leveled the same criticism at the Rorschach method. Jung praised the Rorschach as a means to learning about subjective processes, but he regarded it as limited in associating an individual with his collective material. We will take sharp exception to that observation of Jung's.

Jung's influence on the development of projective techniques went much beyond the way he may have (or may not have) influenced Hermann Rorschach. As a major pioneer, Bruno Klopfer (5) has acknowledged how much his personal association with Jung contributed to his own efforts to extend our knowledge about Rorschach's method. Henry A. Murray (6) has written movingly about the personal impact his experiences with Jung had on his personal life and career. In 1961, at a memorial meeting for Jung in New York City shortly after his death, Murray remarked that Emily Dickinson must have had someone with powers similar to Jung's in mind when she wrote:

> He found my Being—set it up—
> Adjusted it to place—
> Then carved his name—upon it—
> And bade it to the East.

In our opinion, time will show a far closer kinship between Rorschach's and Jung's grasp of human nature than either would have thought, had he been asked. Since Rorschach died at 37, shortly after publishing his major work, he never had the benefit of reflection, refinement, and subsequent discovery through what he had accomplished. The *Psychodiagnostik* (7) shows signs of having been written in great haste; in an effort to crowd so much in, we are certain that he crowded so much out. It was indeed the work of a man who was shortly to die. Magnificent insights about human nature were woven in among pedantic attention to minutiae and nosological facets. Ellenberger (2) has sensitively grasped the impact of the *Psychodiagnostik* (7) by comparing it to what Paul Valéry said of Leonardo da Vinci's works, "the debris of nobody knows what grandiose games." Rorschach's formulations were bold, and the variety and differences among the major sources that influenced him were remarkable. He did indeed grasp the importance of his work beyond the tedium of diagnosis and its use with mental patients. Rorschach viewed his *Psychodiagnostik* (7) as containing a universal key for deciphering and understanding all human culture and civilizations. Both Rorschach and Jung looked through their telescopic modes into the inner reaches of the psyche and discovered some of the essential substance of man. Their discoveries have interlaced them.

REFERENCES

1. Bachofen, Johann J. (1885) 1967. Myth, Religion, and Mother Right. 309 p. Princeton: Princeton University Press.

2. Ellenberger, Henri. 1954. Hermann Rorschach, M.D. 1884–1922. Bull. Menninger Clin., 18: 173–219.
3. Evans, Richard I. 1964. Conversations with Carl Jung. 173 p. Princeton: D. Van Nostrand Co.
4. Jung, Carl G. (1907) 1909. The Psychology of Dementia Praecox (Eng. trans.). 153 p. New York: The Journal of Nervous and Mental Disease Publishing Co. (Vol. III, Collected Works, p. 3–151).
5. Klopfer, Bruno. 1955. Editorial dedication honoring Jung's eightieth birthday. J. Projective Techn., 19.
6. Murray, Henry A. 1962. In: Carl Gustav Jung, 1875–1961, a Memorial Meeting. The Analytical Psychology Club of New York publication, p. 17–22.
7. Rorschach, Hermann. (1921) 1942. Psychodiagnostics. 263 p. Berne: Hans Huber.
8. Toynbee, Arnold. 1962. In: Carl Gustav Jung, 1875–1961, a Memorial Meeting. The Analytical Psychology Club of New York publication, p. 41.

TWO

Jung's Concepts and a Pragmatic Schema

While we will deal with psychopathology, particularly in our case materials, at the same time we hope to lift it into a larger scope. We have been at pains to view Rorschach processes as natural happenings which may or may not be specifically related to pathology. Jung's[1] formulations take the theory and practice of psychotherapy out of the exclusive realm of pathology and relate them to the whole history of the evolution of the human psyche in all its cultural manifestations. Analysis for Jung meant not only a therapy for disturbance, but also a technique for growth for anyone. Defined this way, psychoanalysis could never be the exclusive domain of a medical guild. Medical training alone seldom provides the scope necessary for this skill, insofar as Jung conceived of analytic treatment. Our notion of what emerges in the happenings of a Rorschach experience corresponds with the breadth of view Jung held. We aim to present a viewpoint which may enable us to put a telescopic lens on our inkblot camera, and to look at the picture we obtain alongside the whole man and what he has *become,* perhaps through elements we call pathology, and perhaps not.

Some of the most important or highly personal Rorschach material takes birth through symbol formation. We will view the meaning of a symbol in its universal form, *not* as a manifestation of a complex alone. We will strive toward extracting a symbol's essence, or looking at its intrinsic value. This should be done against the qualities of the individual who produced it.

An outline of Jung's model for the psyche will aid us in understanding *sources* for Rorschach imagery. If this extends our means of grasping processes, it will be useful. We expect to define some of Jung's terms in such a way that they may amplify *what* comes from those sources. We are well aware that sources in the Rorschach may be explained differently. Roy Schafer (5) has looked at and identified processes and sources against Freudian theories. Others have viewed Rorschach data against multideter-

---

[1] An observation made by Dr. Edward F. Edinger.

mined continua. Our frame is simply a different one. Without a doubt, some of the concepts we use here are used elsewhere, though under a different name. This need not deter us or pull us away from our task. Atalanta may drop golden apples at our feet, but we must move on to approach our material consistently alongside the way we have defined our terms. We are in a position not unlike that of Hermann Rorschach himself. We will make use of Jung's terms in a way not always identical with the way he used or applied them. Our means may even amplify or alter their meaning. Jung's concepts took Rorschach into fruitful endeavors. Our aim is to use them in a similar fashion. If this enables us to improve our capacity to predict behavior, it will have been useful quite apart from the intrinsic validity in Jung's model.

The *ego,* as we will use the term, refers to those psychic contents which are in awareness at a given time. It combines awareness and the product of thinking about what is perceived. It has stability insofar as we have individual habits of thinking about what is perceived, and flexibility insofar as the contents of awareness fluctuate. The ego is the result of a constant process, and, while it is the center of conscious activity, it exists also in the unconscious insofar as it becomes projected in the dream as the person of the dreamer. In relation to Karma and *Erlebnistypus,* ego is that which observes the momentary manifestation of psychic processes in us. Inside a given state of consciousness, it is the product of a mixture of psychic processes. The ego tends to be fixed only insofar as an individual uses consistent thinking habits. That mode of dealing with the contents of consciousness emerges as the child moves through the experiences of development. For example, a capacity to feel is the quality of experience when the ego responds to the physiological state we call emotion. A broad range of individual differences exists around an ego's capacities in that regard. Ego is more what we think we are than what we actually may be, insofar as other influences besides thinking shape us. Ego is the mind's conscious eye, and it may contain beams and motes. Much individual difference exists about the extent of clarity and the extent of blind spots in ego functioning. When we become aware of the existence of blind spots, we find clues about the directions we have to take to grow. The psychology of the ego is understood through the term, *persona.* Just like its meaning of a mask from an ancient Greek play, it is the face we show the world audience, or anyone who watches us. Some are vulnerable to the error of being convinced they *are* the same as what they show the world. They have become oblivious to their own blind spots. Hence, in their development, they have wandered from the path of continued growth and sometimes turned to stone. This form of one-sidedness in one's beliefs leaves one vulnerable to sudden collapse. One has no tolerance for any evidence that disputes such a rigid self-belief. Yet, we *need* some form of protection, and our personae provide us with a shield and thus aid us as bridges to relationships. Others may be more apt than we are in recognizing what is false in the way we regard ourselves. At the same time, the belief that we can open ourselves totally to another leaves out an important ingredient in relating. It is a kind of misconception of what relationships can be, because it ignores the necessity for a sense of responsibility about what we reveal. We need to be responsible to ourselves as well as to others. The nature of the persona can provide us with data about what we need to give and what we need to receive as we brush against others. A close look at it can illuminate what our poses for others reveal. Some are swollen and false, some are open and true.

The *unconscious* includes all psychic elements which are outside conscious awareness. It does not represent a simple repository for rejected material or unwelcome debris. It is the larger aspect of what remains unknown to the ego at a given moment of time. Material can come and go from it. The ego is like a coral reef, and the vast sea that surrounds it represents the source, the unconscious, from which unknown material may wash up. Like the sea, the unconscious is a vast container and repository of collective human experience. It is the sleep that surrounds our little lives of consciousness. We seldom know very much about what is in it, but its ebb and flow across the ego makes up our Karma, our *Erlebnistypus*. The contents of the unconscious include a repository of the evolution of human experience. Our destiny *becomes* as it filters imperceptibly across our personal lives.

One may go through life attending to ego processes exclusively and never know anything of the sea within him. When this is the case, one is so out of touch with inner resources one becomes like a shell or stone. Sometimes that has to be, since any deviation outside the ego-persona world throws the person into chaos. It is not our job to judge what is right for a man, but to look at what we find.

Those who seem to become genuine individuals accomplish this through being in touch with *more* in themselves. The man who believes he is identical with what he wants the world to think of him knows nothing about the sea within. He becomes top-heavy, and, though he may appear outwardly successful, when the going gets rough, he topples over. Sometimes, all the king's horses and all the king's men cannot put him together again. It comes from being exclusively glued to the ego. The psychotic no longer attends to what happens in the ego. He is either convinced he is the inner dream or hypnotized by the power of its contents. We usually are not the exclusive product of ego or the unconscious, but a combination. Our Rorschach plates provide us with an image of what *happens* when conscious and unconscious processes meet. How, where, and when the ego and the unconscious *touch* one another become crucial for our purpose in understanding the Rorschach experience. We suggest that these inkblots provide us with a *mirror in which touching points are reflected.* When nothing is kindled by a touch, the individual at hand may be a person with only one psychic dimension, someone who lives wholly in the persona, imprisoned by defense mechanisms. When too much is kindled by a touch, the ego balance may be lost because it may be buffeted by too many dimensions at once. We can see these psychological states come into play before our eyes through our inkblot media.

The *personal unconscious* includes what Freud called id, but it is not identical with it. Usually, its contents are more readily available to consciousness than other products that may be found in those parts of the sea that seldom touch shores of the ego's reef. We recognize the contents of the personal unconscious readily because they come from our experiences associated with family figures and others who provided impact on our development. This aspect of ourselves may be personified by the *shadow.* It means that which our conscious selves must turn around to see. We may be surprised to discover something has been following us all along, parts of ourselves we have not wanted to recognize. The shadow gets us into all manner of trouble because we have ignored its existence. We have left it out in the conscious estimate we have made of what we are. The shadow can be a bridge between the ego and the broader reaches of one's inner nature. A man who shows himself only the face he shows the world has no shadow. He ceases to develop. Like the figure in Alice's dream, he runs as fast as he can to stay where he is. Insofar as we fail to call this part of us by name, our egos are likely to get pulled out of orbit. Some unseen thing pulls us toward itself when we want to go another way. Our defects demand recognition, and unless they get it, we stop growing or start growing the wrong way. We learn of the shadow by watching for its influence.

The *collective unconscious* turned out to be a troublesome term for Jung. As he said, inventors of terms come to be anathemas for others, especially if the terms do not fit against those already in use. Contents of a personal unconscious are easy for people to grasp since one recognizes them, but to speak of contents that do not "belong to the person" upset Jung's colleagues bent on rationalism as a means for accounting for everything. When we cannot recognize something in us because we never saw it before (thus had no term for it), we tend to disbelieve it exists. Material that appeared and reappeared in his researches led Jung to give it a name. At a later point, he discarded the term collective unconscious and replaced it with *objective psyche.* By this he meant that part of our unconscious side that could not be traced as the product of the individual's subjective experience. It is objective, because it *happens to* subjective experience. We will make this concept fundamental to our way of approaching symbol formation.

Anyone who has studied embryology knows that the potentials for structure exist in simpler state. A limb bud in an animal is not a limb, but the bud contains *all* the makings of a limb, provided it is allowed to grow out all its potential. Consciousness as we know it had to grow out of a substrate. It, like all other aspects of us, must have been a product of evolution. If we call all that experience that affected the physical structure that underlies consciousness something that the genus of man experienced together, we can understand our use of the term "collective." Every human embryo has limb buds at some point. All humans share together the collective experience of growing limbs from potentials inherent in embryonic substance. The teleology inside the genetic code that produces a limb must be quite a complex evolutionary product. We may be able to isolate genes and rehook them in the laboratory, but what of the morphology or essential makeup inside the speck that creates so much from its potential?

We are not in a position to define the psyche, much less come to dogmatic opinions about its makeup. We are able to predict that a brain will develop from a neural fold, but we cannot predict anything about what psychic processes may be inherent in a brain. The human psyche is the least tangible product of evolution or collective development, but it is exactly that component that makes us different from all other living forms. We do not even know how the psyche is supported anatomically except in the most general way. While elusiveness about the activities of the psyche may be frustrating, it should not be surprising if a multitude of collectively shared deposits reside in the deeper reaches of ourselves. Potentials exist in some neural fold that get activated in our dreams. Our best knowledge suggests that human consciousness was potentialized only yesterday in the evolution of the human species. Early forms of men may have dreamed before they thought. For some reason, the Pleistocene was a time when nature burst forth with a wide experiment of life forms, and a *capacity* for consciousness emerged then for early men. Collective experience influenced what was laid down in the germ plasm, because all men share a capacity for consciousness today. From ego to collective unconscious, we span man's psychic evolution. We knew almost nothing of our collective psychic heritage until Jung explored some of its reaches with his inner eye. As an empirical frame, we may find this notion useful in explaining the data our inkblots yield.

Jung called the contents of the collective unconscious *archetypes*. We could just as well call these contents imprints, the product of imprinting. We infer the presence of instincts in man because we need to account for recurrent behavior patterns. Instincts seem to be forms of drive-energy that activate physical behavior. Archetypes may serve to activate psychic behavior. We know little about why, how, and where. When something is fed into our visual cortex through visual perception, we do not know anything about the complexity of reverberations that may take place, since they may be outside our awareness. We suggest that certain images have a prototypal power or capacity to send waves across psychic structure. Consciousness or the ego may or may not react or become involved. Some Rorschach happenings may be a product of this wave action. In a later chapter, we will discuss the power of Rorschach's plates to activate archetypal involvement. Our concern with archetypes will be elemental. That is, we will deal only with that aspect of knowledge about archetypes that pertains to understanding Rorschach processes. Man has commonly used the tree as an analogy to picture his psychic life. The root network is a source for the tree's substance. The network has many features associated with how an individual tree rooted and developed. It is the taproot that is its most essential substance. Archetypal material connects us deeply into our substance like the taproot. The rest of the root mat is a product of growth associated with the happenings of the individual.

Jung's notion of the *self* is that it is something that has to be discovered. A youth has to learn to deal with his environment, and the ego and its activity provide him with the power to do so. In the first half of life, ego processes tend to dominate, or become the center of the personality. If one extends one's contact with one's potentials that are not directly related to outer affairs and the concerns of the moment, one builds onto a psychic structure that emerges as opposite to the ego. We call it the self. The task of building a structure we may call the self, as we discover more and more what we are, Jung called *individuation*. When the nature of the self becomes integrated into awareness, it replaces the ego as the center of the personality. Buddhism and other Eastern philosophies are based on similar conceptions. At least insofar as the goals of depth psychology are to remove false ideas in man's conception of himself, Jung's wisdom tends to resemble aspects of the wisdom of the East. Ellenberger (1) noted that Hermann Rorschach died just at that point in time when the second half of life usually begins (Rorschach was 37). We feel certain that Rorschach was moving rapidly along the path we call individuation. Had he lived and had the opportunity to move further toward a grasp of the self, we have no doubt that he would have distilled essences from his *Psychodiagnostik* for us and spun us a new philosophy.

We do not make the point that responses in the human organism associated with archetypal activity are necessarily more profound than those associated with ego activity. They are different and may lead to different things. As we attempt to trace a given type of Rorschach activity to its source, we must also connect it with behavior. For example, psychosis may be defined as behavior which ensues from being overwhelmed by archetypal power. We will describe an extraordinary case to illustrate how this takes place. It is useful to call archetypes the great *connectors,* since they link us with essential human elements. We do not refer to group experiences, but experiences in an individual that link him to his brothers. There are archetypes directly related to mankind's experience *in* a group context, but they are not our concern here.

Perhaps if we could study the embryology of the psyche, we would find that archetypes were the building blocks that led to the development of consciousness itself. Imprinting of essential or taproot experiences finally led to the transformation of experiencer to observer. The moment Adam and Eve could stand aside and *observe* themselves, they became conscious they were naked. In that account, the *Bible* provides us with information about the *archetype of knowing.* Later, we will examine the contents of that archetype.

Jung regarded the sexual instinct as an important determiner of behavior, but no more than other fundamental needs in man. It is our closest link with other animals, and, because it is a powerful activator of types of archetypal responses, it grows out of proportion readily. To say that there is a variety of sexual patternings is also to say that there is a variety of sexual archetypes. Jung would say that the Oedipal complex, which became a keystone in Freud's system, was a description of a certain form of archetypal experience. It may or may not be a dominant experience for a given person. The exposure to an experience, that of a son's competition with his father for his mother's affection, is so common in man's development that it has archetypal significance, but a "complex" in that regard becomes an individual matter. There is a bit of a paradox in Freud's having grasped the "archetypal" significance of the Oedipal romance, and his having used a term of Jung's ("complex") to describe it. Men of genius are still human. Something in Freud may have allowed the consequence of an Oedipal complex to grow out of proportion to its general usefulness. Archetypes work that way. Whatever may be true, Freud's emphasis on the Oedipus complex has been the target for many attacks.

One may say that the experience of being a woman has led to certain archetypes that cannot appear in the psyches belonging to men. The most obvious one is giving birth to a child. Another is the menstrual cycle. Through time, experience in living as a woman has laid down archetypal patterns which constitute what we will call the *feminine principle.* Not only his physical structure, but man's way of projecting himself into the environment, has been different from woman's since the dawn of prehistory. Correspondingly, a *masculine principle* emerged against the necessary psychic structure in men. As the only forms of human beings, men and women have a great collective archetypal heritage together as one. It does not correspond with experience to assume that male and female have essentially the same psychic structure, though they may differ physically. We would certainly agree that the sexes strive for union physically, and psychically too, but their essential difference has been commonly defined as the "facts of life." There, we have an archetype, that is, an archetype surrounding *difference* between male and female. Awareness about these matters has been clear enough ever since man recorded his history. Much of Chinese philosophy, being the oldest of our records, is based on notions of *yin*, the female principle, and *yang*, the masculine principle. A grasp of the importance of these two principles is necessary for our understanding some of our constructs for the Rorschach.

Feminist movements have sprung up all through history. Sometimes women appear to have forgotten that the matriarch dominated in epochs of prehistory. Men had to go through a process of differentiating themselves from the goddesses of the mother cults. The Western woman of today is caught up in differentiating herself from an outworn model of the female. New archetypes may appear, but they are not likely to alter in a radical way what has been built into psychic structure. Imprinting is a function of deposits repeated through long stretches of time. This is, though, the way of change, subtle alterings, and adaptation. There is no reason to think that all psychic structure is fixed or that new archetypes do not appear. Perhaps it is even *because* our psychic substance is so intangible that it remains flexible, and our psychic adaptability has enabled us to become the dominant earth animal. It seems clear that change is a powerful component in the feminine psyche of our time. One may expect a compensatory reaction and change in the masculine psyche alongside it.

A masculine principle is not the same as a masculine psyche. The male psyche may have a dominant masculine matrix and also contain recessive elements of the feminine principle. Opposite counterparts exist in the female psyche. Time has provided the male with characteristic modes of dealing with psychic activity. Probably because intrapsychic patterns differ, males and females tend to handle their responses to psychic activity differently. Thinking and practical adaptation have come to be habitual male modes, while intuitive reasoning and feeling responses are more habitual with females. Many combinations and degrees of those modes may be found in either sex.

The masculine and feminine principles are modes underlying experience. They are activated or energized through the archetypal contents that belong to them. For our purposes, we intend to look primarily at the simple essences that might be associated with them. The activity of an energized principle influences behavior. The chief essence of the feminine principle may be personified by *Eros,* the great relator of human beings. It is the power which relates us to others. Rodin's sculpture, "The Thinker," may personify the essence of the masculine principle as *Logos,* the provider of order and logic in human affairs. We have no prior means of determining how these modes come into play in a given personality, but we may understand how they influence us from their chief or universal quality.

When we refer to male or female, we will refer to psychic substance and to modes of experiencing what emerges in life. Unless we are examining sexual behavior specifically, no connotation about the sexual impulse is associated with generic terms. Even when we do consider sexual behavior, we will emphasize that a woman's way of experiencing sex is different from a man's. Since each sex has different experience, each has had different psychic imprints laid down around that experience. We suggest that some archetypal sources associated with sexual behavior are similar and some are different in males and females.

Essential masculinity is not a matter of a capacity for a display of outer masculine modes, but a function of how a man is related to the power of inner archetypes associated with masculinity. We must split the term "identification" into its component parts if we wish to understand fully what it may mean for a given individual. If we look carefully, we may find that we often use the terms masculine or feminine "identification" to describe no more than ego attitudes in a person. Using the term in that fashion usually yields no further data. We must broaden our grasp of masculinity and femininity, if we wish to comprehend more fully the power of certain Rorschach plates to call forth a person's masculine and feminine underpinnings. Pointing out sexual blot areas is not sufficient in accounting for the startlingly complex imagery that may emerge in association with such areas. This is especially true if we hold that genuine symbol formation in Rorschach provides us with information about how an individual may change, and we do not stop with simply viewing data as descriptive of what happened to him ("problem with identification" and similar generalities). Perhaps we are beginning to realize that a man's goal should not be an identity with his masculine "stuff" alone, but with his wider being insofar as he can grasp what it comprises. We can see around us one aspect of the power our hippie cults have. A member is offered some relative "freedom" from having to "prove" his or her identification through conventional means. While this may be a useful way to get perspective, one cannot acquire from a group what one has not found for onself. Frequently, the group experience provides little more than temporary protection from inner pressures. For a male or female, what counts is the relationship in the individual between his ego and the power of relevant archetypes.

In the East, for centuries sages have defined the "true meaning of manhood" in terms of his grasp of and response to inner forces. An outward display of feminine modes in a male does *not* allow us to presuppose an absence of a productive association with the power of masculine archetypes. When maladaptive behavior occurs (that which is destructive for either the person or others or both), we may assume a strongly negative effect from the power of a particular archetype which has dominated at the expense of the person. Interaction among the strengths of these inner powers influences outer behavior. In any person, the power an archetype holds over the personality may alter as an individual moves away from the rigid stance of dominance by ego attitudes and approaches more wholeness through a search for the self.

Constructive interaction between archetypes of the opposite within us seldom takes place when ego attitudes dominate the personality. Yet, a person may need resilience in order to absorb the impact of the recognition of qualities of an opposite within. The impact of a sudden acquaintance with qualities of the opposite may require violent projection, or the person may destroy himself. It is usually a shadowless man, one glued to ego values, who may suddenly become splintered when material he cannot tolerate springs up. We will suggest that something like this may have happened in our discussion of a case involving double homicide and suicide, in a later chapter. Contact with some elements of the self, dimensions beyond the ego, may provide the necessary buffer or resilience. When we discuss a case of transsexualism, we hope to show that it is the essential relationship between dominant and recessive archetypes, and not surgical alterations that must be considered in understanding those symptoms, if we do not wish to damage psychic structure. In our view, some relationship to the recessive qualities of the opposite within may be necessary for change.

We cannot discuss potentials in an individual's Rorschach materials without some grasp of how we will view the nature of creativity. Inkblots offer the opportunity to stimulate creative sources in a person. Neumann (4) has outlined for us how much creativity is related to the archetypes of the opposite within us. Certain kinds of creativity in the males may spring from modes that are generally more dominant in feminine experience. The reverse may hold for women. Because these modes are recessive, each sex has a different relationship with creativity. Thus, intuition may provide a powerful creative inspiration for a male, and, through the mode of thinking (logos), he may transform his inspiration into a formal structure. In the female, cognition, or the way one knows, may be different in some respects than it is in men. A capacity to structure her form of inspiration through her own mode of cognition opens the way to creativity in the female. A creative woman should be free to fashion her own way and not be bound by attitudes associated with the way men create. Both may need to take the same path in some instances and different routes in others. In general, crea-

tivity has been defined in too narrow a way. It may come and go unnoticed, because it may have come in small packages.

We have not made any attempt to provide a complete view of the ingredients in creativity. We have isolated what we think to be certain essential features. The quality associated with complex thought is an equally
important ingredient of creativity.

Creativity probably cannot be taught *per se*. It does not necessarily grow
out of our educational philosophy, because we see that it springs up in
the most unexpected spots. Pressing children into contact with "creative"
pursuits may often be futile insofar as it is done with an idea of grafting
creativity onto a child. We should examine the responses of children critically,
and observe those who are furthered by creative activities and recognize
those who may be frustrated by exposure and expectations that are inappropriate to them.

We would like to emphasize that falling *under the power* of archetypes
of the opposite sex within us often leads to serious trouble. A false driver
gets into the seat. It seldom leads to creativity in any sustained way. Fascination with the power of the opposite may destroy a man or woman, and his
life may become no more than a restless, obsessive search for something
that is never found. We will see cases of this in our clinical materials. When
we get under the power of an archetype, we are in a negative relationship
with it, and it makes us its pawn. Destructive behavior in obsessive forms of
sexual expression can serve as an example of what we mean by a negative
relationship. In those situations, an individual may take a psychological
pose which leaves him with qualities like an applicant for second class
membership in the opposite sex. In striving for achievement as a "thinker,"
a woman may abandon her feminine nature and live "only to think." We
see this in the type who peels the baby and powders the potatoes while
she reads Kant. These interests may take the person further from creativity and not closer to it, because the power of the attraction of the opposite within is too strong. One loses contact with the taproot source of one's
substance. To subsist on corollary rootage leaves one vulnerable in a
storm. Quite the same may happen to a male, though men are less prone
to abandon wholly some of their masculine modes.

Acts of creativity may be large or small, but we should be free to claim
them for our own. A tremendously creative individual who could never lay
claim to his achievement is known to the author. He had reached a
pinnacle of success insofar as his fellow men were concerned, but not in
his own eyes. He played games with the power of the opposite within, and
he was often very fearful that he would fall under its power. It was, at the
same time, his source of inspiration. When ego values and living on a
one-dimensional plane dominated, he lost inspiration and became de-

pressed. Even though he was exceptionally creative, in some ways he did not live creatively.

Our main point associated with understanding creativity is to call attention to archetypal power as source springs for creativity. We suggest that some aspect of creativity may be different in *form* for women. We base this on some of the differences that exist in archetypal underpinnings in men and women. Some are shared; some are different. The psychology of the ingredients that went into the painting of the *Mona Lisa* is a masculine affair. Whatever Leonardo's relationship to his archetypal opposite within (and we suspect it was powerful), his creativity in relation to it was through masculine perception. We suggest that apperception associated with the recessive opposite within provides each sex with a source for creative expression. *Because* a *recessive* source similar to that existing in one's sexual opposite exists within, the apperception is different, and when an associated creative impulse springs up, creative achievement ensues when a framework is constructed around that experience. Perhaps this is a reason why we have never had many major female composers of music. Music is often the great vehicle for and repository of powerful emotions and apperception through feelings, modes in which women excel over men. Perhaps because they are dominant and not recessive, women have not externalized feelings in a formal structure or container, such as music provides. We do not suggest no great female composers will arise. We simply apply our constructs to explain what exists. A belief that our distaff members have been too preoccupied with domestic affairs to become creative does not explain the statistics one may note about creative achievement in the sexes. Creativity for the woman must not be defined in masculine terms or one may do the potentials associated with feminine creativity a disservice. We need to sharpen our grasp of differences, or be open to them, as we deal with Rorschach material. History has been enriched through time by creative approaches in thinking (logos) offered by women. Her linkage of logos with intuition can put her into possession of as much creativity as a man, but it is not necessarily an identical form of creativity. We will see some of the corollaries between these points and the differential power inherent in the stimulus qualities of some of the Rorschach plates.

The unconscious speaks through *symbols*. A symbol emerges as the end product of complex subjective phenomena. We know little about how this takes place. Some aspects of psychic conditions may not conform to the conditions of outer reality. We know this is true in dreams. Qualities of the laws that apply in dreams seem to apply in symbol formation. At any rate, some confluence of forces creates an image. That image contains the meaning of the summation of those forces. Hence, a symbol is not for us a sign, or something that represents or stands for something else; it is a communication, a form of language expression. It forms around a psychic happening and it is a product of those conditions. If we examine it carefully enough, we may discover the nature of its communication. The Rorschach blots stimulate symbol formation and provide a means for recording them. Visual images, like sound, cannot be stopped in their midst. To review or relisten, the experience must be captured. We learn about sources through analyzing the product. The word "symbol" may be used in several ways. We say the American eagle is a symbol for the United States. Yet, if we examined an image of the American eagle for years, we would not find out anything about the United States from that endeavor alone. Jung has observed that free association is not a reliable way to discover the meaning of symbols. One may free associate to a Hittite inscription for a long period without coming any closer to discovering what it means. We may have provided information about ourselves and our complexes as we free associate, but it is not a method suitable for translation. The meaning of each psychological symbol is unknown until we discover it. We must learn to extract the collective or universal quality in a Rorschach symbol and then apply it to the data we have about the individual at hand. Our personal attitude toward the nature of a symbol *must* be excluded. Our preconceived notions must be discarded, or we contaminate another's material. In this fashion, we apply objectivity to subjective data. Henry A. Murray (3) made an adroit reference to the necessity for this approach to subjective material in his instructions for the Thematic Apperception Test. A detailed and profound treatment of the nature of symbol formation and its relation to Rorschach data may be found in Florence Miale's (2) doctoral dissertation at the New School for Social Research in New York City. As we look at individual images in the materials of our cases, we will apply a similar method to interpretation (based on Jung's view of symbols).

Because we do *not* take a theory with us, we do not have to fit our interpretations into it. Having to do just that limits the scope of a Freudian approach. We see no reason why our method of extracting meanings from symbols through looking at their intrinsic qualities would not extend one's scope, regardless of the theory one uses. At the same time, our concepts may be at variance with assumptions associated with a given theory. Yet, any means to understanding the human psyche is useful so long as it holds up at an empirical level and supports our predictions.

REFERENCES

1. Ellenberger, Henri. 1954. Hermann Rorschach, M.D., 1884–1922. Bull. Menninger Clin., 18: 173–219.
2. Miale, Florence R. 1959. An approach to projective materials. Doctoral dissertation, The New School for Social Research, New York.

3. Murray, Henry A. 1943. Thematic Apperception Test Manual. 20 p. Boston: President and Fellows of Harvard College.
4. Neumann, Erich. (1952) 1956. Amor and Psyche. 181 p. New York: Pantheon Books, Inc.
5. Schafer, Roy. 1954. Psychoanalytic Interpretation in Rorschach Testing. 446 p. New York: Grune & Stratton.

THREE

The Nature of the Rorschach Experience

After Szymon Hens (5) published a study on children's imagination in association with inkblots in 1917, Rorschach worked feverishly to complete his own studies for publication. He was careful to distinguish between his own emphasis on *patterns* of perceptive process and Hens's emphasis on *content* associated with inkblot imagery. Thus, Rorschach's work was launched with a predisposition toward interpretation associated with the relationship among response categories. This has been unfortunate for the subsequent history of his method because the content cannot be separated from patterning, and each has its imprint from the psychic forces that went into their formation. In our efforts to understand Rorschach processes we will focus around the implications associated with content. This does not mean that we disregard the implications for patterns as they appear around scoring. Various works exist for those who prefer to rely on pattern interpretation. This work is not dedicated to uniting the two approaches, content versus pattern analysis, though we recognize such a unity as an important task for the future. In no way do we advocate content analysis alone. This is especially dangerous for the neophyte, since he does not as yet have sufficient experience for an adequate frame of reference. In a later chapter we will discuss patterns as we look at processes that emerge against a frame for analysis. The more one knows about a given set of Rorschach data, the better equipped he is for accuracy in interpretation. To achieve an objective approach in dealing with subjective data, one must draw on guides. Scoring techniques further an objective position in preparation for interpretation. The more absorbed we become in our data the more it comes to mean. Careful scoring puts us in touch with our material in a way that is essential for objectivity. It acts to feed the imagery into our own experience. It becomes our own motor and visual product insofar as the patient has shared it with us. This way, we learn more about what the patient or subject experienced. A highly gifted graphologist once told the author that you have to climb into handwriting and taste it. The more we can achieve something similar with our Rorschach imagery, the more we further the cause of understanding. At the same time, one of our chief purposes is to provide a method of dealing with symbols that may enrich our approach. In doing this, we will attend more to content than patterns amongst the determinants.

Hermann Rorschach (14) likened symbols that appeared in inkblots to those of the dream. His own thinking about dream theory drew on that of John Mourly Vold's. Mourly Vold proposed that kinesthetic perceptions were the fundamental substance in personality structure. These perceptions were repressed by consciousness, but reappeared in dreams. Rorschach believed that the sensorial matter in dreams was identical with Mourly Vold's kinesthetic perceptions. In the construction of a dream, kinesthetic perceptions tend to be organized by the action of symbols and influenced by the existence of complexes. In his view, the symbol appeared at the intersection of kinesthetic material with the presence of a complex.

In his careful application of Freudian theory to the understanding of Rorschach material, Roy Schafer (16) accounted for imagery in the Rorschach as that stimulated by the blot's partial resemblance to real objects but emphasized that images are pushed forward by the subject's "infantile conflicts and tendencies." Both Hermann Rorschach and Schafer viewed the subject's pathology as the organizing principle in Rorschach imagery. We feel that this emphasis on pathology has tended to produce a *set* about Rorschach material which may do it an injustice. It underlies the dilemma that occurs when a Rorschach worker reports an extensive "degree of pathology" in a patient, while the patient's therapist reports having found none in like degree or intensity in his contact with the patient. What happens in Rorschach must be viewed against a frame that is wide enough to include the variety of the component parts inherent in the occurrence. We will view pathology as only one factor which may or may not play a role in what happens at a given moment in the Rorschach experience. Further, it may limit our grasp of what we have caught in our data if we use the dream as a standard for comparing the scope of what we find in Rorschach. Both Hermann Rorschach and Roy Schafer tended to view the dream as providing a wider scope than did Rorschach material. This tends to place too harsh a value judgment on what we find. The meaning inherent in a symbol defines its own scope, and it may be broad or narrow. We should not judge the meaning of a symbol through bias.

At the same time, Schafer (16) has observed what he called "the creative spread of the Rorschach response," which, he remarked, may encompass many psychic levels simultaneously. Our theory will attempt to account for Schafer's observation. We would prefer to call *the response* the end product rather than the spreader, and we will view how this happens as a creative *process*. Inner psychic activation may occur at different "levels," but we prefer to consider end products as coming from different *sources*. There is something about the notion of "layers in the unconscious" that implies a more fixed idea of the structure of the psyche than serves our purposes here. Rorschach data are not dream data. They are not just conscious activity and do not contain a symbol that came from a dream. *They are something new and something different, carrying their own uniqueness.* They are a product of what happens when conscious and unconscious are provided with the opportunity to react with each other. Whatever we catch in our Rorschach nets needs to be viewed that way, and it can give us information which may extend our knowledge beyond what either consciousness or dreaming might provide us alone.

For the purposes here, we have quoted more from Schafer than others primarily because he set out specifically to apply theory (Freud's) to Rorschach data. Other writers on the Rorschach method have not devoted themselves wholly to application via a theory. Schachtel (15) has been the most recent to extend the larger scope of Rorschach interpretation in depth, but both he and other significant authors on the Rorschach method have not been specifically concerned with the application of the method to the frame of theory.

We do not claim to have done more than offer bits of the essence of both Hermann Rorschach's and Schafer's efforts to apply the method to theory; we have called attention to cornerstones that influenced their views. While both Schafer and Rorschach wrote about the more limited quality of a Rorschach image as compared with an image appearing in a dream, their lyrical belief in the method actually carried their pens much beyond the limits of their own cautions. So it always is when we attend to the etxraordinary subtleties of psychic processes. They simply will not sit tight in the rational biases our scientific harnesses require. They have a way of leaving us far behind ourselves, a game often filled with good humor.

It has never been sufficiently clear why Hermann Rorschach's particular inkblot plates functioned to provide us with rich and meaningful psychological material in a consistent way. Quantities of published studies over four decades have yielded precious little to account for the variables that underlie the method. We still lack a clear idea about those factors which contribute to the emergence of a Rorschach image and why images carry significant information. The idea that pathological states primarily produce pathological images takes us no further than that, which is to say, description about results. We may speak of "primary process" material in association with some particular data, but we still know nothing about why or how it happened. A Rorschach image is never "latent," it has *already* happened. If we assume an image contains information about a certain pathology, we may make a judgment about whether the behavior we expect to accompany the pathology is manifest or latent. Experience does not show that the emergence of autistic material necessarily presages the appearance of manifest autistic behavior. We have to try to discover what the appearance of the image means against the inkblot *stimulus* on the one hand, and the *psychology of the person* on the other.

Much has been written about the nature of the stimulus material in Rorschach's inkblots in an effort to account for what is produced. Most standard texts provide accounts of those studies. Ambiguity in the stimuli as impetus to production; the determinants including shading, color, form, and different combinations thereof; and sundry aspects of the inkblots have been studied in different ways. We do not propose either to review this vast body of literature or to account for the results here. While valuable information has emerged from validity and reliability studies, we tend to agree with Holtzman (6) who has remarked that such studies are irrelevant to the empirical, clinical-intuitive method of approach to Rorschach plates. We do hold that not enough is known about the *sources* for Rorschach material, and that we cannot design effective research until we have the appropriate tools. We are going to theorize about Rorschach sources. We will use what we define of them as a means toward objectivity. It is our hope that this may extend the means for research. Our manner of accounting for our data may be incorrect, and it would be surprising if it did not offend some, but it may provide others with vision about new sorts of parameters for research. While we will use intuition as a means in grasping aspects of data, intuition may appear without an objective frame. Our position for interpretation is one that requires an objective frame for observing subjective experience. We make no apology for this approach; it is the chief means by which we can proceed. It has been known to be the way to discovery. It kept Hermann Rorschach to his course.

We are offering a different frame of reference to both the clinician and the concerned researcher. Aspects of our approach have been used by some of the great teachers of the Rorschach method, including Bruno Klopfer, Florence Miale, Camilla Kemple, David Kadinsky, and others.

We do not know the details about what went into Hermann Rorschach's selection and creation of the standard plates we use today. We know he discarded a great many blots as his experiments continued. A publisher arbitrarily lopped off 5 of the 15 plates he wished to publish. The details of any creative process usually remain veiled in mystery, and often to the creator himself. We do know that Rorschach was a man of genius, that he selected his plates from a multitude of experimental ones, that he worked steadily with his technique during several nonconsecutive years, and that he was a brilliant clinician with a wide knowledge of individual patients. Almost no literature existed for him to draw on insofar as work with inkblots was concerned. One may be sure that his intimate knowledge of his patients guided him through stacks of plates and piles of images, and that his insights about material from his blots corresponded with insights about the inner structure of his patients.

In 1920, H. Behn-Eschenburg (1) developed a set of inkblot plates with Hermann Rorschach's personal assistance. Each Behn-Rorschach plate was meant to serve as a direct parallel alongside each of Rorschach's original ones. The Behn-Rorschach was published with a set of norms by Hans Zulliger (21) in 1941. Most clinicians agree that the Behn-Rorschach is not a series that provides a parallel with Rorschach's original ones. The set Behn-Eschenburg developed did not seem to have equivalent stimulus power or to provide the same qualitative features of richness in imagery. This supports our point that the processes that were associated with the development of the original plates may not have been entirely clear to Rorschach himself. At the very least, since Hermann Rorschach assisted Behn-Eschenburg, one may assume that the construction of psychically potent inkplate stimuli requires special gifts associated with special circumstances. Rorschach's plates have never been equalled, even in later attempts by Rorschach himself.

More recently, Holtzman (6) has published two sets of inkblot plates which are said to be parallel. Holtzman has described in detail how his plates were devised, developed, and standardized. Construction and selection of these plates were the product of the judgment of members of a research team, and final choices for individual plates were made through group selections. Holtzman and his co-workers had a particular intent in their work, in part similar, and in part different from that of Hermann Rorschach. Primarily, they intended to develop a psychometric device yielding scores which could be applied easily to research and assessment techniques. Their goal was to provide inkblot data which could be geared to logical analysis. At the same time, they stated their object also was to devise plates which would provide for a "richer variety of material capable of eliciting much more information than may be obtained through Rorschach's original ten plates." After a decade, it seems clear not only that the Holtzman plates have not provided us with the means of obtaining more or richer psychological data, but also that they fall far short of a capacity to potentiate psychic experience in depth. However, Holtzman's work has provided us with a valuable psychometric technique for research.

Insofar as constructing projective techniques is concerned, it appears that logic begets logic and inspiration spawns inspiration. Efforts to develop varieties of thematic picture techniques subsequent to the publication of the Thematic Apperception Test (T.A.T.) (1943) have not been more fruitful than those with inkblots. Murray's picture stimuli have been generally more successful than other sets of stimuli. Making note of the presence of special stimulus qualities associated with particular methods keeps us in touch with the complexities involved in understanding subjective data. Something about them eludes the best efforts of our logic. It is not our logic but how we play it that may trump our ace.

Piotrowski (12) has reminded us that the degree of actual similarity between separate sets of blots is a complicated issue. He noted that it is difficult to distinguish between genuine personality change on retesting when one uses a so-called parallel set of blots, and objective differences between the sets of blots. He suggested that this may account for many clinicians' reluctance to use different sets of blots. We agree with those observations, but we would add that genuine differences in the power to release psychic processes exist in different sets of inkblots as well as thematic pictures. If we look closely, the mark of genuine creativity can always be distinguished from its absence in any given context. Whether it be a work of art, a scientific insight, or a projective technique, if it is a genuine product of spontaneous creativity, different variables probably went into its formation than happens when we set about with a conscious determination to "create" a product. Each may have its own application, but our concern here has to do with possible reasons for the success of Rorschach's plates.

It is interesting for our purposes to note how often a subject really questions whether Rorschach's blots are truly made from ink. We often chalk up such a reaction to suspiciousness or another clinical manifestation. Often, that sort of comment from a subject calls attention to the power of the plates to draw one into experiences. One doubts their face value as inkblots. When a subject humorously says this is an inkblot, he is often touching the base of reality against the power the blots have to draw him away from that base. It seems less likely that a subject would come to doubt that blots like Holtzman's were made from blotting inks. We do not say this to detract from the Holtzman blots, but we use it to illustrate differences in even casual observations about stimulus qualities. It is more *reasonable* to think of Holtzman's as inkblots, whereas Rorschach's immediately suggest there is more there. Both the Behn-Rorschach and Holtzman blots lack the subtlety of construction which may be detected as one observes Rorschach's plates. We see this in the juxtaposition of rich alternatives and the layered depth in Rorschach's blots. The Holtzman blots do not provide cohesiveness between shading and its relation to the whole blot. Contrasts tend to be quite sharp, and there is not the necessary blend of ambiguity and richness of determinants that Miale (10) described as necessary for releasing subjective phenomena. Form is either too clear or not clear enough in some of the Holtzman plates. Perhaps the most fundamental variable associated with the difference between Rorschach's first efforts and his work later with Behn-Eschenburg lay in Hermann Rorschach's intimate knowledge of his own patients. Those patients were his means of standardization. It seems improbable that he was as well acquainted with Behn-Eschenburg's population. Rorschach did not have the same means for study of comparisons of stimulus power when the set with Behn-Eschenburg was developed. Holtzman has told us that his group depended on entirely different means in the selection of their blots. Holtzman (6) has indicated that published studies on the nature of perception guided their judgments. The extraordinary difference between the power of color in Holtzman's and Rorschach's plates may be easily observable. The color intensity in the Holtzman plates is almost the reverse of color power in Rorschach's blots. Emphasis on pasteling with paled, even washed-out qualities tends to dominate in Holtzman's series, while Rorschach's plates offer color boldly and in sharp contrasts. Each would be expected to elicit different response patterns.

For the most part, in our view, many aspects of the Rorschach experience remain shrouded in mystery. While Freud cast a brilliant light into our darkness or lack of enlightenment about the nature of the unconscious, his vision did not seem to stray much beyond where he first looked. His libido theory has not been complex enough to satisfy us in understanding more about complex psychic phenomena that may be observed. There are times when one can see a symbol form around the inkblot stimulus. To understand this in terms of libido theory alone is often not satisfactory. Upon occasion, Rorschach plates catch signs of the occurrence of extraordinary phenomena, comparable perhaps to meteors crossing the sky or particles streaking across a cloud chamber. We have discovered the laws that govern celestial objects (inside our range), but we do not have a sufficient way of understanding certain extraordinary happenings within us. When Rorschach phenomena are multidetermined and highly complex, we must study them in a frame wide enough to allow for comprehension. We do not believe that Freud's theories meet that criterion insofar as our goal about understanding the nature of Rorschach processes is concerned.

Since we are looking at the Rorschach experience through certain modes of depth psychology, we would ask where do we find archetypal influences? We have defined archetypes as activators of psychic behavior; so if the Rorschach experience does indeed involve complex psychic behavior, archetypal influences must be around. We can expect nothing else if our approach is to be consistent.

In 1955, Bruno Klopfer dedicated one of the volumes of the *Journal of Projective Techniques* to C. G. Jung to honor him on his 80th birthday. The articles in that issue were concerned with application of Jung's ideas in work with projective data. In one of those articles, Harvey Mindess (11) concluded that one reason underlying difficulty in applying Jung's approach to the Rorschach was the rarity of material which could be identified with the collective unconscious. The matter tended to rest there. So far as the author knows, no one took those issues up again until the author presented the main ideas in several of these chapters to the International Rorschach Congress in London in 1968. Later, in the fall of that year, the author presented an expanded version in a series of public lectures at the New York Institute of the C. G. Jung Foundation in New York City. A précis (9) of those lectures was published in 1969.

We ask, may it not be *because* Rorschach stimuli do indeed activate sources in the collective reaches of the unconscious that we get such meaningful material? Mindess was looking for a particular kind of image. Jung himself remarked to Evans (4) that neither his Association Test nor the Rorschach technique fished out enough archetypal data to hold his interest. Our point is that Mindess and Jung both overlooked the nature of *processes* in their views about the Rorschach method. If we simply stand by and watch for an archetype to appear, we may overlook its influence as a source. A source is not an end product, though we may identify its imprint *on* the product. We must look for trademarks and decipher them. One never actually sees an archetype in a dream. We see a wheel turn but we do not observe the power that causes its action. Like contents in a supersaturated solution, archetypes contain the power or potential to be filtrated or *form* around something. Until that something comes along, they remain potential as energies. They are nothing more than imprints from prototypal behavior men have shared in common throughout evolution. Their power can only be seen in what has been produced. They remain fixed or flexible insofar as human experience varies in its essence.

In our work of understanding the Rorschach, we do not need to identify material "from the collective unconscious" at all. We need to understand our inkblot stimuli as containing the *potentials* to activate the psyche. We offer hypotheses about how this is mediated. Collective sources may be more or less evident in an individual case, but the power of individual inkblots varies regarding the springs they may tap. We believe that this power underlies the uniqueness of Rorschach's blots. Identifiable features in the stimulus materials may set going processes which cut across the whole spectrum of psychic potentiality. This includes conscious processes, ego reactions, attitudes, judgments, material associated with an individual's development and the construction of his defense shield, and data from commonly shared or collective substance, the repository of man's psychological experiences.

In borderline conditions, the subject is often open to waves of imagery which the ego is unable to recognize as belonging to its realm. In that state (borderline), the ego still retains some power through its hold on the center of consciousness. In psychosis, the ego loses its hold on the center of consciousness and control is taken over by certain energies in the collective unconscious. In borderline states, it often seems as if the ego is at great pains to disclaim any connection with the strange, even "magical shadow shapes" that move in front of it. These images not only look alien to the ego, they *are* alien.

Rapaport (13) described very useful ways of comparing the relation between the ego and foreign forms of images. A given image may be "ego-accepted" or "ego-alien." It will be useful to view important Rorschach images against their probable psychic source. This gives us an idea about what an ego responds to *selectively*. For example, if the images that appear alien to the ego are rather bland, or are related to complexes, we may draw a different conclusion about the nature of an ego state than we would if the imagery bore the clear stamp of collective sources. There are ego states in which material that looks strange and alien to an examiner does not look so through the ego judgment of the subject. Collective material may sustain the ego and not threaten it. This may occur in creative individuals, and in persons not psychologically disturbed. Careful observation about the manner in which an ego responds to sudden confrontation of potentially alien imagery provides us with important clues, as we consider predictions about future behavior for the subject. One may see confrontation between ego and image in the Rorschach. In a dream, the interpreter must infer ego attitudes and states from dream images of the person dreaming.

While it is most certainly evident that an individual may use an automatic means like repression or avoidance to escape recognition of complexes or to bypass infantile yearnings, those *means* must be distinguished from what we refer to here. That is, images occur which had never been discarded through an action of the ego. Most images from collective sources have never been subject to ego rule or to repressive action that may have originated through ego power. That distinction is extremely important in understanding the approach we take as we analyze Rorschach material. Ego consciousness does not have to face any strange dream image *directly*. This is not the case with Rorschach experience. Part of the Rorschach process involves *confrontation* between aspects of the psyche that had never been brought together before in the same way. This is an extremely important function perhaps unique in the Rorschach method.

We are not taken any further in understanding if we chalk up *all* of these strange collective images as being "disguised sexual strivings." Some may be associated with sexual strivings, and some may have only an indirect connection, while others may not be connected with sexual strivings at all. Many of these peculiar visual experiences have *no* meaning to ego consciousness. Hence, the ego develops an attitude as if it *never* had anything like that in its makeup. We must listen impartially and often accept psychic processes at face value. An ego may not have been confronted with certain visual combinations before and not have had anything to do with depositing them in the unconscious. Symbols do not emerge to dissimulate. Their appearance may inform us, if we care to decipher them. At the same time, we are not suggesting that the ego may not be threatened by materials that were repressed through its power. We distinguish images against their likely sources, and the meaning or implication we give them is related to knowledge about an image's source.

If our vision is sufficiently sharpened, we may distinguish between sources. Some imagery is so completely alien and destructive to an ego that its power can smash that ego. The power of the ego gets abandoned or lost to unconscious forces. We must learn to particularize those forces that take over insofar as we have the data to do so. The *strength* of a particular ego is often discussed in overly general terms regards "being attacked" by unconscious forces. We have tended to use the term too narrowly, and that has caused us to exclude useful data. Ego strength is related to the range of conscious dimensions an individual has at his disposal. Ego strength is obviously weak when a one-dimensional personality is toppled by the mere touch of collectively based images. The same individual may be shaken but not toppled when ego-repressed images may recur. Another individual may be sustained through collective images by virtue of the range of dimensions available to consciousness. A study of the zone in which ego and unconscious powers fall into juxtaposition may advance our knowledge about the nature of psychological disturbances as well as provide information about the structure of the psyche. The Rorschach gives us a means for that study in a way we feel has been neglected.

While our point has been that archetypes are a source for particular kinds of Rorschach experience, we must be careful not to assume their influence when they are absent. Spiegelman (17) has considered how Jungian concepts may be applied to the T.A.T. He suggested that the father archetype is activated as an individual responds to a T.A.T. card showing a father and his son. We would not be inclined to expect such to be the case. If we wish to artificially arouse or set going processes that stimulate collective sources, the stimuli must be appropriate and sensitive enough for that purpose. Experience suggests that *only* when the stimulus includes a means of bypassing conscious grasp does it have the power to activate collective sources. This pertains to ordinary states in the psyche, not borderline conditions or psychosis. We would expect that the T.A.T. picture showing an older man with his son would tend to elicit a persona problem or ego attitudes about authority or fathers, and that materials having been repressed through ego pressures might be activated. While the T.A.T. does have the power to activate collective sources (a factor underlying its success), we question that it does so through a one-to-one effort to stimulate them. Spiegelman (17) made a reasonable assumption, but the collective unconscious is often elusive, bending little to expectations associated with logic. His idea was based on laws of reason. Gerald Blum's (3) Blacky Pictures (1949) were constructed on similar assumptions. While archetypal power is often charged against the repressions that tend to center in the personal unconscious, they are not aroused by stimuli which do not include proper qualities needed to arouse them. Stimuli designed to trigger responses about personal complexes do not necessarily extend into collective roots. That may be the reason pictures like Blum's or Symonds's (18) fall short of the arousal range of Murray's T.A.T. Techniques like Jung's Word Association Test and the Blacky Pictures usually carry us no further than complexes. They offer us valuable material, but from a circumscribed source. We hold that Rorschach's plates activate a wider scope of psychic reactions because they potentiate a variety of sources.

Other forms of projective techniques contain structural qualities which may activate archetypal sources. When an individual is open to a range of inner processes, we may see the effects of archetypal activity on drawings. The human figure may be especially potent for activating archetypal sources. A child learns consciousness through discovery of body parts. We may assume the same to have obtained as early forms of men became conscious of body members. It is reasonable to assume that imprints of the consciousness of body parts have a paleo-psychological embryology. We see signs of extraordinary, stylized features in the drawings of psychotics. Some are astonishingly complex, and psychotics lose the ability to draw certain complicated symbols when they recover. We would call attention to Picasso's use of twisted perspective in some of his drawings, which we may also see in children's art. A body may be drawn in profile and head and face in frontal view. Some of the oldest drawings in Paleolithic mural art show an identical portrayal. In the cave at La Gréze,[1] a gigantic bison is shown with his body in profile and his horns spread out in frontal view. It is incorrect to interpret twisted perspectives as being "primitive." Very complicated psychological processes have taken place when they occur. They are the work of archetypal activity and *laws of altered perception.*

When one uses the technique of obtaining a recall Bender after a subject has drawn all nine designs from the Bender Gestalt series, an opportunity occurs to catch the consequences of archetypal activity and effects from the *laws of altered perception* in that subject. In our opinion, the Gestaltists were using archetypal stimuli in some of the experimental work they accomplished in the second and third decades of this century. Lauretta Bender (2) selected her designs from configurations used by Max Wertheimer (19) in his work on visual Gestalt Psychology. There is an astonishing parallel

---

[1] A chart describing all Paleolithic cave sites may be found in the back of this book.

between the Gestalt figures and signs made by prehistoric men in cave art. In his monumental work on prehistoric art, André Leroi-Gourhan (7) studied and classified all the forms of markings or signs that accompanied figures drawn by cave painters. He analyzed and applied statistical means to the study of some 2000 drawings from 66 caves. The signs were intentionally applied by the artist who had drawn an animal or human form. They include rows of dots and circles that look like the recall Benders of some patients, done for Figures 1 and 2. Squares and circles exist, showing the ingredients for Figure A. One of the most frequent signs found was a chevron or arrow form quite like Figure 3. Leroi-Gourhan (7) has drawn a design from the Périgord-Pyrenees art group which is much like a stylized form of Figure 5. At La Meaza, there are full loops like a wave from Figure 6. One finds design contaminations in recall Benders. One may see similar groupings of the signs cave artists drew alongside their paintings. At La Ferrassie, one may see Figures A and 2 combined rather like a contamination. The Bender Gestalt includes some of the shapes that were basic in the consciousness of men as consciousness was being developed. These shapes may activate archetypal processes in modern men.

If we want to decipher intrinsic meanings in Rorschach symbols, we must extend our technique beyond those offered by Freud's libido theory. When that theory is useful, and the material seems appropriate and complete, we apply whatever aspects of Freud's concepts that seem applicable. If Rorschach material contains imagery which libido theory does not decipher, we must have the means to look further. Freud understood all symbols against his libido theory exclusively. Since symbols became elaborately complex, he devised the notion of a "censor" whose work was to obscure meanings on the basis of the discomfort they may initiate for the ego. Jung rejected the idea of a psychic censoring mechanism and remarked that Freud had invented the term to explain material he was not in a position to interpret. We have indicated that one of the conditions peculiar to the emergence of a symbol is that of blocked off awareness while perception remains open, *so that symbols may appear.* Not only do we view them as not having been screened by a censor, we approach the product not as a distortion of related influences, but as a synthesis of those forces that made it into a visual form. Awareness, a conscious function, had to be excluded. Each time we meet a symbol, we have to translate its meaning from inside, *subjective components* into the components of *objective thought.* The language of one neural modality is translated into another one. Space telemetry uses similar principles. In a satellite's fly-by of another planet, instruments record their activity in one form on tapes, and later the data may be translated into a visual picture. In using our means of looking at symbols, we get taken far afield from translation through the means of libido theory. We understand the conditions we have described for symbol formation as defining certain subjective laws.

In research, when we design experiments to *exclude* subjective qualities, we never learn anything about those qualities. The exclusion may be absolutely necessary in a given instance of study, but we are not precise if we exclude subjective qualities when they are a component of the data we are studying, simply because they often elude quantification. While the rationale for exclusion is often useful against a particular hypothesis, exclusion has sometimes become a false *sine qua non*, or a limiting habit. It has led us to neglect research and discovery associated with subjective processes, which remain a legitimate form of psychological behavior for study. We need to include features associated with subjective experience in our hypotheses as a matter of scientific responsibility.

Even though the study of subjective phenomena tends to be neglected at the moment, we are in possession of considerable data about them through the means of various projective methods. The data bank we have about them stems from empirical sources. The body of information is sizable, but few have made any efforts towards viewing these empirical data as a means of extracting knowledge about subjective laws. Most have been content to accept that all subjective experiences follow the guidelines provided by libido theory. We do not feel that such an assumption serves the need to extend our knowledge. We must isolate meaning and repeated patterns against a criterion of prediction. Laws provide such a means. If we do not do this, subjective qualities will continue to hamper experimental design by creeping in when they are unwanted, and our techniques will remain inadequate insofar as we wish to study them.

While workers have observed that subjective behavior goes contrary to the laws of logic, we often proceed as if we had not noted that they behave atypically. Yet, it remains that laws governing subjective behavior seem contrary to laws that govern what we call "logic" in our thinking. A common example would be the dream. We do not dream "as if", it *is* reality for the dreamer. Pain in a dream is not simulated pain; the delights and fears that occur include all the physiological responses that underwrite these sensations in the waking state.

Subjective phenomena happen outside any conscious intent to bring them about. Conditions that further their existence exclude that part of consciousness that makes us aware. Activity in the collective sources of the psyche seems to be necessary for some forms of subjective experience. We may view as tentative laws the essential conditions we can isolate about subjective processes. The laws we intend to describe did not originate from ideas offered by Gestaltists. We have indicated elsewhere that aspects of Gestalt theory often come close to the discovery of archetypal activity. The basis for offering several "laws" here is an empirical one. They have been formulated directly from Rorschach imagery and symbolism through an empirical means of repeated observation and recurrence. We would call one of them the *law of excluded awareness*. A symbol forms when sufficient psychic sources are activated and conscious awareness is excluded from perceptual meanings associated with properties belonging to the stimulus. Hermann Rorschach (14) told us that John Mourly Vold viewed consciousness as that state preventing the dream. This observation is very simple, but a keystone one. We suggest that it may be true because consciousness evolved later through evolution. The neural structure that supports consciousness is in some way antagonistic to the neural structure that supports storage of the vast range of contents that make up the unconscious. This is useful in conceptualization of experimental design. Facets of the methods of investigation used to analyze the contents of consciousness may not be applicable when one wishes to study subjective data.

It is important to distinguish between excluded awareness and Freud's notion of a censor. Both assume that material from the unconscious has a peculiar relationship with awareness. Beyond that, no connection exists between the concepts. Freud's idea of a censoring mechanism was a protective one, in which infantile sexual strivings or guilt-producing memories from the past needed to be kept away from awareness to prevent anxiety and other symptoms. That idea was the most mystical of all of Freud's formulations, and it tacitly recognizes a positive power in the unconscious. In general, it has been accepted without question. That is one of the most remarkable paradoxes in our rationalistic philosophy. The censor served to "fool" the ego into not recognizing material that the ego had discarded. Old wine was put into new bottles.

Not only is no disguise associated with our notion of *the law of excluded awareness*, we suggest that because its source was not connected with material that had been repressed by ego action, the symbol that emerges contains all the qualities necessary for identification. The sources are from the preconscious condition that sustained the psychic life of men prior to consciousness. They must have been remarkable indeed to support the hazards that could have meant extinction in the ages of evolutionary development. We must learn the route best suited to recognizing those forces still alive in us. Through them, we learn a great deal about ourselves against complexes or psychological tasks that may be associated with the meaning of symbols. With this information, we may intervene in our own Karma or destiny.

Archetypal sources are at work when startling perceptual distortions occur through viewing certain picture stimuli. Card I of the T.A.T., showing a boy observing his violin, seems to have provided something powerful in its influence as a stimulus, when the violin is seen as an object other than what it objectively looks like. The power we speak of acts to dissolve the reality of the outer visual form. When the violin is not apprehended in T.A.T. Card I, we suggest that the archetypal roots of *matriarchal power* have been activated in the viewer who is open to influence from that source. It is interesting to note that the shape of a violin is almost identical with that of a stylized female torso. There is a startling resemblance between the violin and stylized fertility figurines from the Paleolithic age. Psychotic patients sometimes draw female figures with torsos identical in form with the stylization of those fertility objects.

When the objective boundaries of a visual object are dissolved, and the light stimuli from that object necessary for visual perception continue unchanged as they are absorbed on the retina, an extraordinary event has taken place. We do not understand its laws. We suggest that similar qualities are associated with perceptual alterations that unquestionably occur in some instances of posthypnotic suggestion. Judgment associated with awareness is changed because the outlines of ordinary visual patterning are experienced *subjectively* as if they were dissolved. We view those phenomena as a function of the work of archetypal forces. Gestalt theorists came close to describing archetypes. Archetypes influence patterns of excitation on neural substance, when the conditions that activate that influence occur. We suggest that the resulting subjective experience came about through the *law of altered visual perception*. Archetypal energy blotted out the original form of excitation coming into the visual cortex and reshaped the form that was recorded. Consciousness apprehends the altered percept.

In such an instance, presumably we would be able to show that the original excitation pattern on the visual cortex corresponded to the objective lines of the outer object. When the percept is apperceived in a sharply different way, phenomena have happened contrary to the laws of conscious logic. It is not an occurrence that is alogical or mystical; it is different and subject to different laws. Perception has been apprehended through what we may call a *subjective consciousness*. The conditions that pertain to subjective consciousness are governed by various laws which we have not understood. Yet, we have had experimental data about the existence of subjective consciousness since Zeigarnik's (20) work on memory for uncompleted tasks in 1927. When an open circle is perceived as closed, the outer object has been perceived as altered through the mode of *subjective consciousness*.

Archetypal power may be the agent through which psychic activity is unified. We suggest it as the agent at work producing what Roy Schafer (16) called the "creative spread" in Rorschach experience. He used the term to account for the range Rorschach images have taken as "several layers of the unconscious are activated simultaneously."

Archetypal power is an essential ingredient in symbol formation. Not all Rorschach protocols contain genuine symbols. When an individual's materials tend to have personal contents as the most prominent feature, sources underlying the personal unconscious may have dominated. No symbols may have appeared. In that case, we would indicate that no collective sources were activated or put into arrangements necessary for symbol formation. We hypothesize that symbols do not form when no corresponding power is activated in the collective side of the unconscious. Our notion of *subjective consciousness* is not the same as "dream consciousness," nor are Rorschach symbols the same as dream symbols. However, they doubtless share qualities in common with each other. But Rorschach images and symbols take place in a context of conscious perception of them. The ego functions alongside the formation of Rorschach material, though what is formed has its roots inside the wide range of unconscious sources. The *laws of symbol formation* come into play against the confluence of diminished awareness alongside open perception *and* a range of unconscious processes which must include active archetypal energy. Unlike dream symbols, the requirements include forms of conscious participation, and the waking state is not eliminated. The ego continues to function, but without a prominent requirement for logical judgment—awareness of meaning about the symbol. In abnormal states, like borderline psychosis, the ego of the subject may have some approximate awareness or vague comprehension of meaning, but that exists under radically changed psychic conditions. In normal conditions, a symbol emerges or forms around a stimulus through the influence of the *law of incomplete understanding*. We hold that, if consciousness is fully active and it is possessed of the meaning which would influence the appearance of a symbol, we would not have a state of psychic conditions in which a symbol could appear. It appears when some part of our nature is calling attention to lack of awareness of certain conditions in another part of it. This does not presuppose anything beyond the conditions that call for its existence. Without the right proportions of the formula for the appearance of symbols, no symbols appear. Like any other kind of indicator of conditions, the symbol is an instrument of communication. Through its special language, that of the visual imprints of the forces that brought it about, it communicates a special condition in the psyche when specific forces come into play.

Examples of this may be seen in sexual symbols, which are common occurrences in Rorschach patterns. We must be careful to define exactly what we mean. It is important to distinguish between important ego attitudes reflected in Rorschach material and genuine symbols. We do this by making a judgment about the source for the material. For example, an individual's comments about the "bisexual" aspects of the human figures on Plate III does not usually indicate visual symbol formation. Those comments may provide us with useful information, but they are reflections of ego attitudes and not verbal reactions to emerging symbols. In such an instance, we would say that an essential ingredient in the *law of symbol formation*, collective sources, has not been activated. Rather, we have gathered information associated with an ego attitude, a persona problem, or possibly a complex associated with faulty development. If one sees a sexual organ attached to a figure on a Rorschach image, it is not a symbol; it *is* the organ. That one's attitude about it may have symbolic implications is an entirely different kettle of fish. Later, we will show the psychological importance of the difference in a subject's perception of sexual organs attached to persons and those separate from other parts of the human body. The stimulus power of a disembodied organ is of a different order than that inherent in sexual organs attached to the body in a natural way. Noting that figures on Plate III have bisexual qualities does not imply that a symbol has crystallized around parts of the inkblot as an image. On the other hand, when a blot area usually associated with a specific sexual shape (objectively looks like it) is experienced as an image of the opposite in sexual shape, then the symbol for sexual reversal has formed. We must not take this as a matter of course; it calls for our sense of wonder. We believe this astonishing kind of visual alteration occurs *only* when archetypal power has been at work. This usually has nothing to do with wish fulfillment. The subjective *law of altered visual perception* has created an image of the opposite. When the same blot area is seen as an object completely unrelated to a sexual organ, and the objective form of the configuration is appropriate to the image reported, we have something else besides symbol formation. The symbol of the sexual opposite calls our interpretation in one direction, while the nature of a wholly different concept emerging from the same area may call us in another. We simply have different patterns due to different inner conditions.

A *law of psychic correspondence* appears to function in some instances when symbolism emerges around altered visual perception. As an image is experienced visually as different or opposite to its natural perceptual state, it is apperceived in *subjective consciousness* in a fashion that *corresponds* psychologically to the visual alteration. Reality for what is perceived has a corresponding psychological reality. Subjective apperception becomes appropriate for the plane on which the image is projected, when the experience is activated through archetypal energy. A function of this law enables us to interpret material with precision. By definition, interpretation is inaccurate when it applies to the plane *from which* the image was displaced through psychological means. When the psyche goes through the process of objectification, we must attend to it objectively. When a non-sexual image forms around what could have been an objectively formed sexual object, a sexual interpretation for the new image is inaccurate. The sexual form was changed psychologically into something else for the subject. We must discover what that change means for the subject. This does not mean that there may be no connection between what happened and a sexual complex in the subject. There may be and there may not be. We lose our sense of awe and wonder when we automatically assume that something sexual was "repressed" or when we view the newly emerged image as a "disguise." In our view, nothing was either repressed or disguised. A source inside the unconscious was activated, and its conditions were communicated through natural laws. The happenings were not a function of ego action, which repression and disguise require. Through subjective laws, phenomena were enabled to objectify themselves. A chief function for repression is to protect the ego against anxiety or guilt. Through experience, we have seen subjects rendered much more anxious and sometimes startlingly disturbed by complex images around which no sexual meanings existed for the patient. The ego gets shaken by material powerful enough to challenge its ability to stay in charge of the subject's consciousness. Subjective phenomena do not necessarily come under any influence from conscious activity. No deference is paid to ego attitudes; that is not the purpose of these phenomena. To assume deference is to assume something mystic. They exist through laws that enable them to objectify themselves. These phenomena are not the same things as mechanisms like repression, displacement, introjection, and others that may energize alongside personal material and its relation to the ego and its action.

It may happen that we may draw a conclusion about a person's sexual adjustment without considering archetypal influences in a Rorschach symbol, and find later that that conclusion was correct. When we do this, we lose data and simultaneously our objectivity about what we have done. We have made a correct deduction through an illegitimate means. Crucial information and the meaning of the symbol remain unused and unknown.

It should be clear by now that we are suggesting that Rorschach's plates may contain stimulus powers with potentials for activating any or all aspects of conscious or unconscious psychic contents. We will examine each stimulus plate with a view toward identifying its potentials as an activator of kinds of psychic experience. We can by no means do an exhaustive analysis of those potentials. If we succeed in recognizing a few of them, and they turn out to lead to the discovery of others, or to aid us in predicting behavior in a reliable way, we will have made a useful excursion. The path we take may be one some will be reluctant to follow. Our only rationale is the wish to extend our grasp of our data. To the author's knowledge, no one has attempted to view Rorschach's plates in just our manner before.

We believe that the way we are applying the concept of archetypal forces takes us further in understanding Rorschach processes *because* it gives us a wide enough frame. Whether our formulations prove to be correct or not makes no difference if we can use them as vehicles to extend our knowledge. Roy Schafer's (16) work based on Freud's libido theory took us a long way toward extending our knowledge about Rorschach processes. No major follow-up work on theory has emerged since. We believe this has been due to insufficient knowledge about a wider frame necessary to extend such a purpose. The effect has been to divert researchers from interest in subjective processes and to leave the area in neglect. This has become so acute that the major journal devoted to publishing studies about projective techniques has changed its name and sought manuscripts from different sources. We hope that work like ours may inspire the development of a new journal devoted to the psychology of subjective experiences. We repeat that some of the processes we wish to describe may never be observed *directly,* and we are going to have to allow for a different sort of schema to explain them.

In order to avoid confusion, we want to emphasize that our concept of "material from collective sources" is not the same thing a Freudian means when he refers to "primary process material." Material from collective sources may or may not have a corresponding pathology. The generally accepted idea of "primary process material" implies the presence of a pathological condition. Usually, the assumption is that either it causes the pathological condition or it should not be present. Exceptions to those assumptions appear and we must account for this. We hold that the ego's relation to other dimensions in the psyche, as well as its response to the alien form of material, determines the extent of pathology. It is our job to recognize and interpret Rorschach correlates with pathology. Nevertheless, in order to interpret the Rorschach experience, we must have a broad understanding of it. We would recognize some forms of "primary process material" as a *destructive* force. When we have identified the source of this material, and it is usually a collective one, we must observe its effect on other qualities in the psyche. We hold that *constructive* forces emanate from the same source. How this material affects ego consciousness and the shield of defenses becomes crucial, since that allows us to judge the *kind* of force we have. The content of an image alone may not tell us. We will illustrate what we mean as we look at "process analysis" in a later chapter. A borderline case is one in which the side that succeeds to power is not yet decided. Rorschach data put us to great advantage in providing us with clues about the probable winner. Our position is that Rorschach plates have the power to stir collective roots in us all, and that this may take place quite aside from pathology. What exactly *is* stirred up depends on the nature of the individual.

In a given Rorschach, the responses may cluster around ego attitudes and ego experiences, and the majority of the sequences may not be any more than a reflection of interplay between ego and its shield of defense. When that is the case, the Rorschach may *not* have failed to go "deeper" or "break through the defense." We simply got reflections in our mirror about where and how the subject lives. We may do his psychic reality a grave injustice when we ask "where is the deeper material so that we can know more about what he is like?" We must not ask for egg in our Rorschach brew. At that time, the individual may simply not have been in contact with much else inside. There are many instances of one-dimensional personalities.

If our assumption is valid that Rorschach's plates contain archetypal potentiating stimuli, and then we find little evidence in our materials that suggests the imagery came from archetypal sources, we may assume that much distance exists between that person's ego experiences and potentials (positive or negative) in his unconscious. This may be a highly useful finding if it is interpreted as a means of understanding the subject. If it does indeed show the nature of his inner state, we will have to decide if it is in the subject's best interests to remain in it. One has to be able to distinguish between meager records due to lack of cooperation, and genuine reflections of one-dimensional living in one-dimensional materials. In some records, collective sources may have a dominant influence on the nature of the material, and data about more personal material in the unconscious may be meager. It is useful to recognize these qualities in the way we handle our data.

Creative individuals seem to be in an active relationship with materials that have emerged from collective sources. The ego functions with the materials, and the person lives among many planes. The psychotic seems to be in a *passive* relationship to flooding from collective sources, and the ego does not function in relationship with them. When we look at our materials in this fashion, we have attempted to understand what Shafer (16) called "the fluctuations of the level of psychic functioning." Individuals differ widely in how open or closed they are to inner processes. When one dreams, one is no longer open to conscious processes. Our Rorschach medium captures something of both, but the proportion of each is a matter for discovery in an individual. The effects of the ego on the unconscious and the effects of the unconscious on the ego help to determine what we call individual differences. It is not always useful or accurate to view "primary process material" as destructive. We must develop a system of understanding Rorschach data that is wide enough to account for the fact that autistic imagery can exist inside a personality that remains intact. It is common to speak of "ego strength" and to view it as antagonistic to "onslaughts from the unconscious." Our effort is to get underneath those terms and analyze

more fully what we may be talking about. The person adept with the Rorschach has the means to do this. What qualities underwrite an ego's capacity to survive an "onslaught" and come out the better for it? That quality
may exist in individuals who live on more than one plane and whose values
do not coincide exclusively with ego-persona ones. This takes us to the
view that unconscious sources may have a positive or negative effect on a
given individual.

Forces of nourishment and forces of destruction exist within the contents of the unconscious. We may see a personification of this twin potential
within us projected in many myths. In India, for example, Kali, mistress
of a mother goddess cult, may bestrow grace or destroy as she sees fit.
She is a personification of the mothering nature of our collective stuff.
That kind of mothering disregards the individual, whom she may destroy
or nurture as benefits the cult (collective). In our culture, we tend to recognize the destructive side of nurturing forces only in a "step-mother"
image. Yet, in the earliest version of *Hansel and Gretel*[2] the children's own
mother suggested that the children be left to starve so that she and her husband might survive. Some experimental evidence for the nurturing aspect of
the unconscious may be found in research on dream deprivation and the
known negative effects it has on the state of the personality of one who is
artificially deprived of his dreams.

An important part of our task will be to examine the Rorschach experience against possible influences from archetypal sources. Some hypotheses
require massive samples to satisfy the nature of the questions asked, and
some do not. Just as it is we find one individual in a hundred who can
teach us something because no one else took the trouble, so we can sometimes learn more from a single Rorschach subject than from hundreds. If a
sample of 50 cases does not contain one who is open to unconscious processes, the data that the cases yield will tell us nothing about those processes.
We would be willing to wager that Rorschach's patients, his population for
selection of his blots, contained those open to unconscious processes in sufficient number to draw critical parallels about the power of his plates. Nevertheless, patient populations do not necessarily contain a high number of
the variety of the "great teaching records" we mean. If a student masters a
Rorschach record in which the mixture of the range of psychic variables
and variety of source springs are sufficiently rich, he is in much better shape
to move on than if he had ground out and scored 50 routine records. There
is no substitute for the excitement of discovery from an exceptional case.
We expect to include case materials because they show a considerable
range of psychic activation. These were culled from materials gathered
over almost a quarter of a century.

---

[2] A tale whose main theme pertains to nurture.

We would like to emphasize again that we are not attempting to "isolate archetypes." We are interested in *looking at what comes into consciousness when stimulus qualities which we will identify as archetype-potentiating activate psychic processes.* Usually, what we obtain is highly valid for the conditions that our patient lives in at the moment. We must take our responses as we find them. We must define how the patient seems to be living psychically at a given time, and so long as we can make an educated guess about the sources for the material at hand, it does not matter from what "level" it may have come. We will attempt to observe the processes that accompany the material *as they happen.* We then attempt to extract what we can about the intrinsic nature of the happening, store it for comparison with whatever else we find, and then move on.

Because life has proceeded far along the evolutionary way, it is rare for nature to have left things that are not now useful to us. The dream, an everyday experience common to all, must be an instrument of importance in nature's repertory. We spend a great deal of our time in it. Most cultures have provided a tradition with an attitude toward dreaming. It is usually within the matrix of the philosophy or mythology of that culture. This is as true for us as it was for the Sumerians or Egyptians. Our own culture's attitude has been so conditioned by psychoanalysis that it has left powerful marks on art, literature, and all of our forms of collective expression.

The dream is the window through which we look at qualities within us which seem strange to consciousness, and we do not infrequently disclaim them as unreal or nonsense. Yet, insofar as they emerge as *experience,* they are real. There is a reality for outer experience and a reality for inner experience. These realities may overlap, but they are not the same. The Rorschach provides conditions that pertain to aspects of both inner and outer realities. We must learn the language of the inner reality, if we wish to comprehend it. Symbols and images, carried through a natural form of projection, appear and thus make themselves available for interpretation. They are like ripened fruits. They must be picked and eaten to experience their taste and grasp their capacity to nourish us. We cannot fully understand the meanings of subjective data if we do not use the same natural form of projection and participate with the data ourselves. Projection from the observer must be done objectively, since imposition of one's own distortions or pathology onto the data simply muddies or contaminates them.

Many authors have written about the extent to which we have lost the art of understanding symbols. One reason for this lies in the belief that all subjective qualities of an observer must be excluded to achieve objectivity. This is true for a number of endeavors, but not insofar as grasping the meaning of inner reality is concerned. A symbol's meaning may be perceived through the *law of mutual projection.* Extracting the essence of meaning often requires the observer to participate with the host or symbol carrier. We must learn to look at symbols as the product of a mixture of important conditions that have to be grasped. Our own participation is required to illuminate meaning fully. Freud's libido theory gives us a set formula for interpretation which does not include the necessity for observer participation. While often useful, that approach is frequently not inclusive enough to enable us to comprehend symbols that do not apply to sexual matters.

In a poignant, uncomplicated way, Lydia, a figure in one of Somerset Maugham's (8) novels, tells us how to extract meanings from symbols. The story is of a young Englishman on holiday in Paris who stumbles upon the raw stuff of life for the first time. Thinking that Lydia, a prostitute, might serve as a kind of weekend Pygmalion, he takes her to the Louvre to explain to her the meanings in great art. He is filled with erudite information and expounds to her what he has been taught to think of the great pictures hanging there. After having listened patiently, she finally grasps his hand and leads him to a remote corner of the museum and shows him a tiny still life by Chardin. Through looking at the image and projecting her own substance in it, she extracts its universal meaning for the young man, who could not project anything of himself into what he saw.

We, too, as viewers of Rorschach art, must extract meanings through constant work and discovery. That is the reason that we have said it was a distinct advantage to move through Rorschach material without a specific theory for interpretation. It is an essential condition for acquiring objectivity in relation to subjective data, especially if one wishes to liberate his perspective and extract wider meanings. That way, the excitement of challenge sustains the task.

REFERENCES

1. Behn-Eschenburg, Hans. 1921. Psychological Research with the Form Interpretation Test. 67 p. St. Gallen: Zollikofer & Cie.
2. Bender, Lauretta. 1946. Instructions for the Use of the Visual Motor Gestalt Test. 7 p. New York: The American Orthopsychiatric Association.
3. Blum, Gerald. (1949) 1960. In: A. Rabin and M. Haworth (Eds.), Projective Techniques with Children. New York: Grune & Stratton.
4. Evans, Richard I. 1964. Conversations with Carl Jung. 173 p. Princeton: D. Van Nostrand Co.
5. Hens, Szymon. 1917. Phantasieprufung mit formlosen klecksen bei schulkindern, normalen erwachsenen und geisteskranken. Zurich: Speidel & Worzel.
6. Holtzman, W. H. (With co-workers). 1961. Inkblot Perception and Personality: Holtzman Inkblot Technique. 417 p. Austin: University of Texas Press.
7. Leroi-Gourhan, André. (1965) 1967. Treasures of Prehistoric Art. 543 p. New York: Harry N. Abrams, Inc.
8. Maugham, W. Somerset. 1939. Christmas Holiday. New York: Doubleday.

9. McCully, Robert S. 1969. Archetypal qualities underlying the Rorschach experience. Quadrant, V: 13–16. In: Friedemann, A., Phillipson, H., Scott, B., and Williams, C. (Eds.), 1970, Rorschachiana IX, Rorschach Proceedings. Bern: Hans Huber.
10. Miale, Florence R. 1959. An approach to projective materials. Doctoral dissertation, The New School for Social Research, New York.
11. Mindess, Harvey. 1955. Analytical psychology and the Rorschach test. J. Projective Techn., 19: 243–252.
12. Piotrowski, Zigmunt. 1957. Perceptanalysis. New York: Macmillan.
13. Rapaport, David. 1946. Diagnostic Psychological Testing (Vol. II). 516 p. Chicago: The Year Book Publishers.
14. Rorschach, Hermann. (1921) 1942. Psychodiagnostics. 263 p. Berne: Hans Huber.
15. Schachtel, Ernest. 1966. Experiential Foundations of Rorschach's Test. 342 p. New York: Basic Books.
16. Schafer, Roy. 1954. Psychoanalytic Interpretation in Rorschach Testing. 446 p. New York: Grune & Stratton.
17. Spiegelman, Marvin. 1955. Jungian theory and the analysis of thematic tests. J. Projective Techn., 19: 253–263.
18. Symonds, P. M. 1948. Symonds Picture Story Test. New York: Bureau of Publications, Teachers College, Columbia University.
19. Wertheimer, Max. 1923. Studies in the theory of Gestalt Psychology. Psychol. Forsch., 4: 300.
20. Zeigarnik, B. 1927. Memory for uncompleted tasks. Das berhalten erledigter und unerledigter handlungen. Psychol. Forsch., 9: 1–85.
21. Zulliger, Hans. 1941. Behn-Rorschach Versuch. Bern: Hans Huber.

FOUR

The Archaeology of Archetypes

Before we can fully appreciate an exploration into Rorschach's plates in in search of influences associated with archetypal activity, we must establish a well grounded frame of reference for what we are talking about. This is particularly useful since we have indicated that archetypes are forces or energies which can never be seen directly. As we trace the sources of this energy, we will also be illustrating our method for apprehending meaning in symbols.

We must pursue our course back in time and deal with simple instances. Comparative anthropology is a means by which we may glean information about ourselves. We are too close to our own complex culture with its obsession for ratiocination to discover what we need to widen our scope as we have defined it.

As we move into Paleolithic[1] times in our search for the source pots of the *form* of psychic structure, we will proceed from broad speculations. Recently, several significant works have appeared, drawing together a comprehensive account of what is known about Paleolithic artifacts. We will rely heavily on those sources. However, we will do this not as an archaeological anthropologist, but as a psychologist dealing with projective materials. We will keep to what we have been able to identify about the laws of subjective processes when they seem useful and as they pertain. Since in our view, the main scientific efforts to understand Paleolithic artifacts have yielded incomplete information, our efforts may show a means of extending method in paleoanthropology. Our aim is not to provide a scholarly account of the psychology associated with artifacts from the Paleolith, but to extract broad generalizations that may extend our grasp of sources, and to augment an embryology of consciousness. The approach we take may have useful implications for several disciplines other than psychology.

We have been conditioned to think that information received through media that are not immediately identifiable in all their components should

---

[1] The Old Stone Age or Paleolithic period of man's history lasted roughly one million years until the end of the Ice Age, about 10,000 years B.C. Neolithic sites date from around 7,000 years B.C. The cave art we refer to herein ranges from 26,000 B.C. into the Neolithic period.

be regarded with caution. When the information obtained from that kind of source is not wholly amenable to our particular, and sometimes circumscribed, way of apprehending and using data, our caution turns to fear. There are well known reasons for these attitudes. "Emotional" factors creep into our best efforts to be detached. Yet, as scientists we are sometimes not precise about what we include inside our term, "emotional," and we can be found excluding certain factors we may need if we wish to deal fully with our hypotheses. An investigator can be trained in how to use subjective material objectively. We cannot fully exclude ourselves if we wish to understand the psychology of subjective processes. Some components that we tend to exclude as "emotional" may include either information we are not ready to receive or qualities that we do not understand fully. When we look into those areas defined by the presence of semiunknowns, we may come to the threshold for discovery.

At the same time, we have to reach a stage in which we *can* extend our means of study. Our grasp of logic and the means of applying it toward understanding natural phenomena were acquired only yesterday. We have but to glance back and see the sloughs of superstition and states of cloudy misapprehension from whence we have just emerged. We do indeed need vigilance to keep from slipping back. We need to understand "causes" if we wish to order our grasp of things, though it is useful to remember that "cause" is not much more than a reliable statistic. Even though we have made great progress in understanding the laws that govern phenomena in the outer reaches of our milieu, we are not in much of a position to congratulate ourselves about what we have discovered about our inner environment. The laws that control our inner world still lie in penumbra.

It is necessary to take some risks if we wish to ferret out new or additional knowledge about subjective affairs. Our task is to accept those risks. With the advent of projective techniques, we have the means of understanding more about the inner world. Someone is yet to take hold of dream material and deal with its essential nature beyond interpretation. Just as with Rorschach material, we have been obsessed with meanings in dreams as they are related to pathology or personal development. A projective technique is an artificial way of setting off chain reactions. Some aspects of consciousness have to be diminished to accomplish this. The data we catch become the objectification of subjective happenings. We hope to push our knowledge of how this happens further.

As we undertake some first steps in our task, we will expect to fail to grasp or misapprehend what others may see as crucial parameters among those that merge to create our subjective world. It took an extravert like Alfred Adler to grasp the importance of social phenomena for theory. No one can do more than he is best equipped to do. For our task here, we do not

accept the proper risks if we limit ourselves in the freedom to hypothesize.
Since we do not expect to proceed along the lines of conventional modes,
whatever accrues, if anything, will be an easy mark for criticism. This should
not prevent us from taking a shovel in case we break new ground. As scientists, the *way* we approach data, insofar as conventional modes get wide
usage, may give us clues about where we are in the development of science.
We may get a projective estimate of ourselves. In psychology, we have not
infrequently considered wide subjects with an inappropriately narrow means.
We can become prisoners of our own "scientific" rigidity. One-dimensional
modes cannot be expected to be always sufficient when data are multidetermined. Our present means of dealing with subjective processes in research tend to discriminate against them through certain rigidities common
in design for research. The main reason for this lies in the extent to which
they are not well understood. We believe it is wholly unscientific to disregard forms of experience because their sources are elusive to us, especially
since we often misapply means that have relevance in other contexts. We
can, however, hold ourselves in account if we fail to grasp or admit that
some data contradict the habit of expectation we have relied on in our
thinking.

So that we may *apprehend* our data differently, as they are gathered by
projective methods, we will refer to archetypal influences in Rorschach
processes. Some features of our method cannot be fed to conventional
means of analysis, but this is only because we have not yet extended method
to include laws that control subjective processes. We will look at inkblot
stimuli with an eye toward law-containing data. If we isolate those data and
examine them, we or others may be guided toward discovery.

Both the dream and the Rorschach serve as kinds of nets that gather
symbols. The symbol is not the dream, nor is the image the Rorschach. The
structure on which dream or Rorschach symbols *form* is complex, certainly
extraordinary, and yet little considered. We have no knowledge whatever
about the stimulus properties in dream structure that further symbol formation. The *power* of consciousness is in some way changed so that a dream
appears; but it is not necessary that consciousness be wholly absent for
dream states can appear alongside it in some pathological and visionary
experiences. It is the *state of awareness* about the stimulus for a symbol that
has to change. This applies to some aspect of the law of symbol formation.
In the Rorschach experience, we know a great deal more about the stimulus
than we do regarding the dream, insofar as the outer half (or whatever proportion it takes) of the mediating process is concerned. The inkblots potentiate subjective responses, and a full state of consciousness (but not
aspects of awareness) still pertains. Any application to consciousness one
makes from dream material has to be inferred. By contrast, unconscious

processes in Rorschach happenings do not have to be inferred, since they determine the nature of much of what transpires. The subject remains *not* conscious about the nature of the stimulus material that sets unconscious activity going.

Since some Rorschach processes are allied with dream processes and some are allied with a functioning consciousness which responds, we are in possession of an instrument that provides us with information about both states.

We posit that the structure of *the psyche itself may be something like ink-blot structure.* Both the substance in Rorschach's inkblots and the substance of the psyche itself provide the conditions which allow images to form around *stimuli that are potent enough to precipitate them.* Inkblots are as potent as their stimulus power. Our task is to identify some of the ingredients in Rorschach's plates that have potentiating power. We are calling that power archetypal power.

An archetype, or image that represents it, takes its power from prototypal sources. This power has the capacity to *force* a visual form representing its existence or its archetypal nature. Archetypes are a form of communication about the conditions that they themselves may influence. An archetypal image contains the essence of a particular human experience that has been repeated enough and has been formative enough to make a permanent, but not necessarily inalterable imprint on neural structure. They are for the human animal what Lorenz (5) has called "innate fixed patterns" in lower animal life. However, it does not appear that archetypal patterns are necessarily fixed. Inherent capacities for flexibility may be a chief difference between neural structure in man and other animals. Nevertheless, some of our experiences are so fundamental in existence that one cannot expect the human condition without them. We would call those the *archetypes that are permanent for expectation.*

Form and function may be aspects of the same thing as regards psychological forces. Certain archetypal forces which men have repeatedly experienced in common since the dawn of consciousness are those forces which *formed* the psyche.

Archetypes include such prototypal experiences as food gathering, elimination, fertility, father, mother, authority, self, femininity, goddess, eternity, childhood, circle, square, devil (evil), god (good), maleness, and sleep. If we look at the core or essence of a symbol, according to laws pertaining to subjective processes, we will find evidence for archetypal influences.

Since all men have created some form of religion no matter where they sprang up, religion should provide us with residues of concrete deposits of archetypal action. Christ and The Buddha symbolize some essence of archetypal deposit for us, since they are the religious representatives of our era. They are carriers of archetypal energy. Many aspects of the development of religion in East and West were widely diverse and alien to each other in form and content. All religions function through symbols, and, since many of them are ancient indeed, they contain source data for our purposes. Not all religious symbols serve as carriers of archetypal power. Numerous religious symbols are not necessarily universal. They have a local power and may not qualify as having archetypal influence, except on a local level. A Westerner may look at a Tibetan religious object and not recognize its symbolic qualities as such. The Vajra, a stylized combination of a lotus blossom and a thunderbolt, may stir a Tibetan Buddhist powerfully, while its religious significance may be totally meaningless to someone from another tradition. The Menorah unquestionably stirs someone of the Jewish tradition in a way different from a non-Jew, even though the Jew may not be religious and the gentile may be aware of the meaning of the Menorah. When a religious tradition is long and has had powerful influences on shaping consciousness, one may expect some of the contents of the psyches of persons living in that tradition to carry qualities that are particularized for that tradition. This has important implications for the understanding of intra-cultural exchanges, since members may express aspects of their psychology differently because they *are* different. We all share the human condition and many archetypal potentials collectively, but our psyches also contain differences. Just because those differences are based on *local* archetypal power does not necessarily mean that they disappear easily. Education alone may not alter them. If influence from local archetypal power is destructive for interchange among people from radically different traditions, we must learn more about the *laws of archetypal extinction* if we wish to control them.

Our concern here is not about influences from local archetypal power. We are interested in those with the power to influence all men alike. The Buddha and Christ had this power. They have shared this with other mortals in history who changed from the human state to the divine. They became divine because they discarded human values. That change is a symbol of an altered state of consciousness. The universal quality in them having archetypal proportions was a capacity to sacrifice personal, ego-oriented values in favor of something beyond them. Early Christian saints sought that state as they rejected material values. Yet, a desire for sainthood alone may not transcend ego ideals and values. Divinity is a state that is invested through archetypal power. For example, a rejection of materialism may be no more than an effort to achieve immortality for the personal ego. A mortal who achieves a state of divinity has lost *all* connection with *all* the old values associated with the ego. Consciousness makes a *total* shift and takes up entirely new values.

Yet, the archetypal quality we speak of here is *not* associated with specifically religious values. It is no more than a symbol of the psychology that surrounds changing the dimensions in which one lives. Belief in religions has been *one* way all men alike could change those dimensions. Some kind of psychic substance has been laid down around this, since its symbol or archetype can potentiate psychic activity in us *despite* a conscious wish to exclude it. A man may be a disbeliever in any form of religion and still hear the voice of God in a dream, or in a waking state, if he becomes open to certain inner processes. From whence comes so ego-alien an experience? From the potentials that exist within subjective substance and through the laws that belong to it.

It appears reasonable to assume that prototypal images, along with other unknown agents capable of storing energy, played powerful roles in the development of consciousness in man. Just as evolution has developed within us a physiological isotonic seablood essential for life on dry land, the psyche contains the symbol projections and images that were necessary for the survival of consciousness and its development. The substance or contents in the collective currents in the unconscious may have been a substratum associated with the state that was *precursor* to consciousness. Archetypal power directed things prior to the emergence of a consciousness that got pitted against it. Consciousness as we know it does not define life. A substratum in the psyche is collective because it went *before* as we *became*. It is reasonable to assume that the collective repository contains archetypes once potent and now extinct. There seem to be *laws governing extinction of archetypal power* and *laws of constellation of archetypal power*. We do not know anything about them, but we expect to describe a clinical case in which one can assume that an extinct archetype became recharged with power. An archaic image took possession of consciousness in a modern youth.

Because archetypal power is ancient does not mean that it is necessarily archaic. Naturally, some experiences became archaic as man developed. Perhaps we may define "archaic" as a state of an archetype on the road to extinction. It still retains some power that may be potentiated. At any rate, some very ancient archetypes have remained very much alive. The Rorschach plates contain stimuli which can potentiate some hoary ones that are as potent now as they were in remote ages. As psychic currents in the unconscious become more remote to the shores of consciousness, collective contents in them tend to wash up only in our dreams. This does not necessarily mean they have lost all power. We do not know much about what they are up to in our dreams. We stare curiously, and mostly without comprehension, at them, like country cousins or objects from a psychological zoo. These generally remote contents may combine an infinite number of primordial counterparts which went into the wresting of consciousness as we know it today from its darker past or millenia of greater unconsciousness. Thus, we suggest that archetypal images have served as building blocks for consciousness.

If we look to the oldest records in our tradition,[2] the Bible, we should find a rich store of information about archetypal power and its relation to man's development. No matter what one's personal opinion about the Bible may be, it contains our *mythos*. It contains a developmental record of the most powerful influence we have had play around us, that is, the Judaic-Christian tradition.

While myth has come to mean "not factual" in our language, the ancient Greeks used the word *mythos* to mean a container for essentials of truth. They had a different word for "not factual" information. Essential truths in the sources within the Homeric epics inspired Schliemann to discover major Achaean sites like Troy and the palace of Agamemnon. He understood Homeric myths as *mythos* while archeologists had not only ignored, but had deliberately avoided those sources as "myth."

We will look to mythos for sources insofar as they may aid us in digging for artifacts of paleopsychology. We intend to proceed on the assumption that essences of truth have been preserved from remote times in certain media, and that some of these contain packages of archetypal significance. Like mirrored amber entombing an insect, our myths contain well preserved psychological images which arose from a confluence of formative conditions in remote times. As the most ancient, direct source in our tradition, the Bible contains a number of fundamental archetypal accounts or patterns. Analysis of some of those patterns around source-images may illuminate our understanding of some of the stages of transition and development in Western man's consciousness. In analyzing certain of those patterns, we illustrate how we approach symbols. Genesis[3] provides us with evidence for archetypal imprinting through the symbolic language of descriptive mythos. Examples from that source may augment understanding about the way we are using the term *archetype*.

Adam and Eve, as the prototypal ancestors, held significance for *all* men first; then the account in Genesis traces them to the specific tradition that has become our own. One of the earliest psychological tasks for man was to acquire freedom from bondage to the instinctual laws that applied to all animal forms of life. It was probably acquisition of that freedom that gave power or energy to it as an archetype (separation from instinctual laws),

[2] Excluding the *Gilgamesh Epics*, the recorded Assyrian legends that had some influence on the Judaic tradition.

[3] After dealing for a time with the origin of all men, Genesis takes us into the origins of our own tradition, which began after the Neolith, roughly after 5,000 B.C. The second millenium B.C. begins with the overthrow of Ur and produces people and events familiar to us. Akhenaten introduced monotheism in Egypt; Moses led the Exodus; the Shang Dynasty arose following the legendary Hsia period in China; Vedic hymns were sung in India; the Phoenician alphabet arose beside the Minoan civilization; Stonehenge was built; and Abraham, Moses, Saul, Samson, Agamemnon, and Theseus flourished.

as the first flickers of consciousness got imprinted into neural structure. Genesis begins with an account of that task. In the Paleolith, consciousness in man widened as he learned to grasp his *difference* as a collective assembly from other animals.

Adam and Eve lived in a garden, a symbol of their archetypal home, that of living *in* nature and not consciously apart from it. At first, their self-awareness had not developed to a point that allowed them any independence from *nature*. Their potentials for the human condition had not been realized. Separating from nature's dominance was similar to the task every child has in separating from his mother. It requires energy and risk, and it becomes archetypal insofar as all men go through the experience, though the degree of success in separating is an individual matter. Nature, then, was the archetypal *mother*. In the beginning, the separation had to be accomplished *if* Adam's and Eve's consciousness could be expected to develop. When they ate the fruit from the tree of the knowledge of good and evil, a change was evoked in them. It was a change in the state of their consciousness. An archetypal force imprinted itself and got into the position of energizing neural structure through the power of changed conditions. Eating that particular kind of fruit symbolized their becoming *aware* of themselves in a new way. So long as that energy or force kept its charge, there was no easy return to their previous state of unknowing or innocence. This shows us a *function* of archetypal power. It helps to *maintain* the conscious state through having helped build or create it. Apparently, a law governing the maintenance of consciousness involves *excluding* awareness about the particular archetypal force operating. In other words, one is not aware of those forces that keep him conscious.

As the meaning about good and evil burst upon Adam and Eve, they could no longer rely solely on those instincts associated with life in the natural state or garden. Paradise was a state of unconsciousness that Adam and Eve lived *in* along the banks of the Tigris and Euphrates. For better or worse, being possessed of awareness forced them to take responsibility for their behavior themselves.

God was the source in the unconscious who could not be apprehended except through a powerful form of symbol. Those are the conditions required for an archetypal presence, and man's development has always been furthered by God through archetypal power. Deities in the East were recognized as specific projections of the same inner source-power. A major difference between them and Western God archetypes was the split from its opposite. Evil was split from good into the archetypal power symbolized by Satan. The split was not so complete for the God of the Old Testament. Yaweh behaved at times as having a relationship with the power of evil. God in the New Testament appears to carry only archetypal power for good. Eastern deities often retained destructive forces along with constructive ones. Different archetypal conditions underlie monotheism than do polytheism. The same is true for male and female deities. The traditions in the East have included a different relationship to the state of consciousness than is found in the West. Because of their longer recorded tradition, as well as their somewhat different relationships to unconscious processes, a study of the paleontology of Eastern consciousness would be a fruitful undertaking.

As Adam and Eve undertook the first steps toward assuming their own responsibilities, their consciousness advanced. We see this repeated in every child that grows today. It is an archetype identical with the human condition. Like their other siblings-in-nature, the animals, Adam and Eve had cohabited automatically or unconsciously. They had not been *aware* of their differences as male and female, either physically or psychologically. The moment they apprehended their differences, an archetypal force began to influence their behavior. Previously, that force had existed as a potential only. Nothing had been powerful enough to energize it.

Their first task was to cover themselves. It symbolized their separateness from other animals. Even today, we view our sexual instincts as our closest link with animal nature. Covering the genitals meant awareness about responsibility associated with sexual expression. The power of that archetypal message reaches across the span of time to us as freshly as it influenced the first parents. They had become conscious of their differences; energy was constellated and imprinted in their grasp. There is more in this fragment of our prehistory. The power associated with the *difference* between the sexes packed enough energy to serve as a fundamental step in changing the structure of consciousness. That power has been retained as a part of the human condition since it arose.

As we look at ancient images, symbols, or accounts, through our method of paleopsychology, we may find preserved for us the impact of powerful primordial happenings. We infer that archetypal power was constellated through natural laws.

The Book of Genesis provides us with information about another basic archetypal pattern or condition. It was Eve and not Adam who had the relationship with the snake. She had a source of information not available to Adam. The snake was a symbol of the female's subtle way of *knowing,* information sprung up in her from instinctual sources. Eve's instincts told her about *how* knowledge could be acquired. Used in this way, the snake was a symbol of the archetype of the female form of logos, a sort of phallic knowing-power in the woman's psyche. That its nature is indeed archetypal is shown through its emergence in a similar fashion in the East. Kundalini is the Hindu concept of the serpent as a symbol of apperception through instinctual forces. In Kundalini Yoga, one meditates to look within in search of the source of the "serpent power" of instinctual knowledge. Hindu Yogins have developed a whole sequence about the development of stages of consciousness around this way of apprehending.

Eve's separate kind of relationship to her instincts existed in the beginning. We may see this state objectified in the artifacts that come to us from the Paleolith. Fertility goddesses were shown with the snake or the horn of a bull, symbolizing powers attributed to women *because* they had special relationships with animals.[4] Paleolithic fertility symbols were not specifically sexual. They were religious symbols associated with the magical qualities possessed by women in their capacity to give birth and, through this function, insure survival for a species that was constantly in danger of extinction.

The male's prototypal form of relationship with animals was different from that of the female's as early as Paleolithic times. We will show that the Paleolith is important psychologically in that, during that age, males were involved in the task of entrenching their awareness of themselves as being different from the animals around them, while females were not. That set the conditions for differences which allow us to designate masculine and feminine psyches. This difference is further based alongside chromosomal differences. It has grown up around different modes of apprehending and experiencing existence. Paleolithic woman remained attached to instincts *because* they provided her with a special status. How she apprehended some of the data she expressed was a mystery to men. Its range of accuracy probably exceeded that of the males, who were wrestling with how to apprehend via primitive logic. The woman was closer to nature's laws insofar as conscious awareness was concerned, and those instinctual qualities gave her power as goddess. Insofar as we can speak at all of the structure of consciousness, when it was being laid down in the Paleolith, prototypal experiences affected those elusive neural structures that support consciousness differently in males and females.

Eve saw *more* than Adam did through instinctual sources. It was her hunch, and then the action she took on it, that produced a change in their combined consciousness. Women have been at the door of liberation since the beginning. Yet, it is very important to note that Eve did not become conscious *alone* or simply because she heard what the snake said. Adam and Eve had to eat the fruit and assimilate it *together,* before its archetypal power could evoke change. There was nothing to prevent Eve from popping down a couple of apples or plums while Adam lay napping in the sun. If she had, we suggest no archetypal potency would have arisen. Neither one of them could have grasped the meaning of the powerful symbol of the fruit alone.

---

[4] Buddhist deities have a vahana, or particular animal, associated with a quality in common between the animal and the deity it accompanies. In the West, an instinctual connection between animal and deity would be that of Saint Francis of Assisi's connection with nature and birds.

Their state of consciousness was too frail and pale singly. Grasping the meaning of a symbol requires personal participation with the symbol, and it took all the resources of the male and the female of the species to break through the heavy crust of unknowing.

Eve may be viewed as a projection of the symbol of instinctual sources within masculine consciousness. The embryology of consciousness would not necessarily allow us to turn it around and view Adam as the logos principle in the consciousness of the woman. He does not symbolize that, at least not in our account in Genesis, which is our source of data. She may have been his symbolic feminine source, an inner element, projected into the objective world as a manifestation of his structure or rib-stuff.

However, it is more useful to separate them as prototypal members of the species, and take them at face value. Our view of them is that they perceived or apprehended the *means* that advanced their combined consciousness differently. The symbolic meaning in the information that Adam *preceded* or antedated Eve historically may have been that he separated from his instincts first. He became lonely because he had grown distant from his animal friends, so Eve came, and she, who knew the snake, connected him again with his old friends. After that, she became *more;* she became his partner in consciousness. At least part of her meaning to the man was her consciousness-potentiating power through her facility of instinctual *knowing.*

These are the means by which we look for archetypal imprints and tackle symbols. An application of Freud's libido theory to the mythos of Adam and Eve would provide us with different and, we believe, much more limited data. It is naive to consider sexual discovery as the disguised aspect of the allegory. Nothing whatever would have prevented prehistoric men from expressing preoccupations about or obsessions with his sexual impulses. If such was the case, no records of it have survived. The ingredients for an Oedipal setup were absent in those conditions associated with sexual expression in the late Paleolith. We would not find it surprising to discover that Adam and Eve were more advanced than we in the range of their sexual repertoires. There are other Biblical conditions and happenings which do provide conditions which the libido theory that Freud proposed may illuminate. We have to decide if it takes us far enough in a given instance. Through the means we have discussed, it is up to us to decipher archetypal messages. They appear inside the mythos of various traditions, in art forms, and in artifacts. It is possible to use them in apprehending the earliest or embryonic beginnings of consciousness, and to discover the developmental stages of its history through what comes to us from the dim past. We will tackle Rorschach symbols and inkblot art forms in much the same way. We will search for archetypal sources in the nature of inkplate structure, and we will work toward deciphering the symbols that emerge from and through their influences. The information we gain provides us with a frame against which we may extend our grasp of the nature of psychic processes.

We seek aid from archeology and anthropology in our efforts to trace sources of psychic substance. The appearance of complicated tooling and artifacts proves that early man's capacities to deal with abstract symbols appeared in the late Paleolithic and early Neolithic ages. Some estimates suggest that the late Paleolithic age may have lasted a hundred thousand years. Those were the eras in man's history when major strides took place in the development of consciousness. Patterns were laid down at that time which came to constitute the structural foundations that support psychic functions.

The parietal or mural art created by Paleolithic and Neolithic men on cave walls offers us some rich interpretative data or source material. Discovery of this ancient art in remote European spots began in the 1870's and continues today. Some of the paintings are masterful accomplishmens of esthetic beauty. Capacities for those skills must have predated complicated forms of consciousness.[5]

We will conceive of the walls of ancient caves as the frame on which early men penned or drew their psychology. The chief principle which operated for them is the same principle operating when we project visual forms into inkblot structure today.

In her book on the paintings and engravings in the Paleolithic cave at Lascaux, Annette Laming (2) noted that in some cases the actual surface of the rock "must often have suggested the silhouette of an animal to the Paleolithic artist." Laming compared the experience a cave artist may have had as being similar to Rorschach's test. She said, "the natural curves of the rocks, the bosses, the hollows, the stalactites, and the variations of color in the world underground conjure up an extraordinary variety of animal shapes—croups, legs, necks, shoulders etc. In the silence of the cave, the flickering light of a handlamp intensifies illusions; and if but a day is spent in the study of the Paleolithic paintings a whole world of fauna of infinite variety of form and movement will seem to come to life." Annette Laming has given us a wondrously accurate description of the Rorschach experience as she portrayed the visual and psychological response that comes from a visit to those particular caves that caught the psychology of our ancestors.

Ucko and Rosenfeld (8) have provided us with critiques of one of the recent, objective efforts to draw together the meager amount of work that has been done on extracting meanings from Paleolithic cave art. Until recently, it was assumed that most of the ancient pictures on cave walls were

---

[5] Recently, the paleobotanist Mme. Arlette Leroi-Gourhan established that Neanderthal men had an esthetic sensitivity. Working with Solecki (7) in examining contents of Shanidar Cave in Iraq, she identified pollen clusters from eight species of brightly colored flowers woven into branches of a pine-like shrub, which bereaved Neanderthal 1 en used as funerary offerings 60,000 years ago.

pictorial expressions of a means of magic to insure success in the hunt. Though both Paleolithic and Neolithic men lived in hunting cultures, Ucko and Rosenfeld (8) doubt their use or meaning as hunting magic. They pointed out that early men would have no practical reason to be concerned about either killing or increasing the numbers of *imaginary* beings, and they drew them rather frequently. Also, not an insignificant number of dangerous animals were drawn. They were often not representative of potential food. In addition, since most of the animals they used for food subsisted on vegetation, one might expect appropriate flora to appear among the magical means of insuring a food supply. No drawings of vegetation have been discovered in any of the cave paintings.

Even though Ucko and Rosenfeld (8) cautioned about interpretation of the content in Paleolithic art, they concluded that some order and intent appears to underlie meanings in cave art. Up to this time, none of the interpretative approaches has been fully satisfactory. This is especially true for us insofar as we are concerned with them as psychological data.

A monumental work on the analysis of cave art appeared just prior to that of Ucko and Rosenfeld (8). In 1965, André Leroi-Gourhan (4) was the first to approach Paleolithic art through extensive statistical analysis. He made inclusive photographic surveys in a systematic fashion. He applied statistical analysis to the frequency, placing, and content of a large number of samples of parietal art. Ucko and Rosenfeld (8) have made some valuable criticisms of certain of Leroi-Gourhan's assumptions, but they readily acknowledge the vast importance of Leroi-Gourhan's findings.

Leroi-Gourhan's statistics yielded the presence of pattern in placement and juxtapositioning of drawings, as well as a statistically significant malefemale complementarity in ordering. Several recent workers have identified, counted, and interpreted what they have called "male" or "female" symbols in parietal art. Annette Laming (3) has been one of the most creative of recent interpreters. In 1962, Laming reported having isolated what she called "the eternal fertility symbol" associated with female qualities she isolated in Paleolithic art forms. Both she and Leroi-Gourhan described what they called "masculine and feminine principles" in cave art. They arrived at those conclusions from a careful analysis of their data.

However, Ucko and Rosenfeld (8) noted that, while both Laming and Leroi-Gourhan sometimes reached certain conclusions that were either identical or similar, they came to them through entirely different, sometimes opposite assumptions about the nature of the symbols they isolated.

That point is a crucial one for us. It has precise and important relevance for Rorschach interpretation. It is incorrect to assume correspondence between fundamentally different theories because similar conclusions emerge in given instances. We must keep this clearly in mind if we would fully grasp how Rorschach processes take place. If it is strong enough, the power of the psychology that is present in some instances *forces itself* on almost any means used to identify it. This often underlies success in a clairvoyant's predictions. Through qualities associated with heightened awareness and intuition, a "medium" identifies the psychology that is present in given conditions, but usually attributes the manner it was channelled to her to some irrelevant vehicle. It is interesting to note that persons attributed to have clairvoyant powers tend to be female more often than male. Eve, of course, was the first clairvoyant in our tradition. Insofar as interpretation of symbolic materials is concerned, we must not be led astray through awarding validity to the incorrect means or vehicle. Leroi-Gourhan and Laming have made some important discoveries. They designated certain groupings they found in their data as masculine and others as feminine. The content of what they grouped was not identical, and sometimes reversed. Under our definition, attributing female qualities to the painting of certain animals, or male qualities to others, is not an *interpretation* of symbol. We have suggested that we cannot know precisely what the meaning is that a symbol may hold unless we apply the *law of mutual projection*. While it may seem a paradox (probably because of Freud's influence, who emphasized pathological projection), this *alone* enables us to introduce objectivity into the means of interpretation. Whenever they relied entirely on the presence of patterning in their data as a means to interpretation, they were subject to erroneous conclusions about a given instance inside the pattern. Thus, the horse came to be a male symbol in Leroi-Gourhan's analysis and a female one in Laming's. They worked with care and precision, but they did not usually take the means to objectify their interpretations. Laming came closer to using the *law of mutual projection* when she extracted meanings associated with the female as carrier of a fertility symbolism. Both Leroi-Gourhan and Laming were quick to note that inconsistencies arose in the way they designated particular qualities to the animal paintings they analyzed. They attributed this to a particular symbol's having different meanings in different contexts. While that is often true, there is some order in symbol formation, since part of it happens outside conscious intent. It is not likely that a creative artist, who is in touch with processes that create symbols, would use an inappropriate vehicle in giving the symbol visual form. Our definition precludes it.

Leroi-Gourhan (4) appears to be convinced that parietal art is arranged on a dualistic system through male and female vectors. There is no question about the intimate relationship between the female and the bison as her vehicle. At Pech Merle five drawings display every conceivable transition in form from bison to woman and back again. Laming (3) has noted that the combination between woman and bison occurred so often and so widely that some mythology had formed between them. A linking of three symbols at several spots has provided a suggestion of a key for interpretation. A vulva, a phallus, and a bear's head were linked, and in another cave, bison, woman, and a chevron and barbed sign appeared. We suggest that the fact of decapitation specifies alteration in symbolic meaning, deliberately placing the image in an *abstract* context; the same applies to unattached vulva and phallus. A decapitated bear is dead. The symbolism may have to do with metempsychosis or the passing of a soul at death into another body. Both triple symbols probably had meaning around the means of acquiring a position on life-after-death. A by-product may have been the males' finding something about themselves as separate from females who seemingly had the means to bring new life into being.

Laming (3) has noted that many male figures in parietal art are associated with tragedy. While they are few, whenever a scene appears to have a narrative content, the men play the part of the vanquished. We suggest that Paleolithic men experienced themselves as something of the underdog against the power of the matriarchal goddess. Their arts were a means of objectifying the psychology of separation and discovery of the roots for masculine power. Physical strength did not provide psychological independence for men. A patriarchal god would have to offer as much magical means as a matriarchal one, and perhaps more if he would replace her power psychologically. Cults form when something different is offered psychologically. A male god would have to provide a means for insuring continuity of life independently, a means for furthering fertility and survival, a vehicle for projecting beliefs about life after death, and instinctual acuity, *apart from the female means*. Such a god was conjured up, visualized, and drawn on the walls at Les Trois Frères. He does not fall into Leroi-Gourhan's dualistic system of classification. We will discuss him in detail later.

Leroi-Gourhan (4) noted a third variety of human representation, which because its qualities were indefinite, he classified as "ghosts." The term is a good description visually. We would see them psychologically as expressing the unformed or forming male separateness. They may represent vehicles for expressing beginning awareness and newly extended consciousness that were appearing at the time.

As he made his interpretation about male and female symbols, Leroi-Gourhan (4) admitted his perplexity about the absence of scenes showing copulation, as well as any other example of sexual or erotic expression in parietal art. He attributed this absence to "discretion" or "prudishness" in the artists. Sexual expression certainly preoccupies us, and not to find it in Paleolithic art does indeed leave us in wonder. Our position is that eroticism did not preoccupy those Paleolithic artists insofar as their *intent* for their cave art was concerned.

The general way meanings have been attributed to cave art has not furthered our understanding of the psychology of our remote Paleolithic ancestors. This provides us with an opportunity to look at them psychologically, and to apply our concepts as we have defined them to parietal artifacts. We do this to extend our search for psychic sources. They will function for us to augment knowledge about psychological processes in Rorschach.

Cave drawings, the nature and arrangement of bone and other objects included in burials, as well as artifacts carved in stone or ivory, provide us with glimmers about the experiences early men had as they projected what impressed them into their art. They objectified their experience through creation of visual forms. We suggest this paralleled and influenced the development of consciousness.

Early forms of archetypal experience were doubtless simple. Simplicity does not itself diminish either importance or power to influence. Traces of simple, but powerful archetypal influences that may have originated at the time consciousness was being formed still influence us today. We expect to show correlates of those experiences in the stimulus power of the Rorschach plates.

Some qualities inherent in man's stuff causes him to create visual objects around some kind of medium that preserves them. All art forms probably grew out of that archetypal energy. We are calling some of the images man has created archetypal ones. They hold and carry a universal significance. Images that are created to stand for them, if they are genuinely archetypal, contain a record of the energy that went into making them. These images are not neutral for us. However, our awareness function is not equipped to apprehend the potentials of power they hold.

The structure of the Rorschach plates contains visual forms that are much more meaningless to us than they would have been to Paleolithic men. For that reason, through bypassing awarenesses, the stimuli reach into our root substance.

Commonly repeated images created by Paleolithic and Neolithic men include *round circular openings* carefully carved by hollowing stone; stylized, fecund *female torsos;* male and female *sex organs* joined but not engaged; *human* figures juxtaposed *with animals* in painted scenes; and application of *red ochre* to burial objects.

One may observe configurations identical with the smooth circles in stone made by early men in the sculpture of Henry Moore. Figure 7 illustrates this. A sculptured circle in stone probably had to do with Paleolithic men's psychological attitude toward the matriarch or fertility goddess and was perhaps meant to illustrate the birth passage. It was associated with men's grasping meaning about the power to give birth held by women. The highly stylized female torsos, referred to as "venus figurines," were doubtless fertility objects. However, calling them that does not take us far enough in understanding their importance to early men. They were religious-magical talismen and they point to the *importance* attributed to the female torso as bearer of life. Carvings of unattached (separated from the body) male and female sexual organs were formed for purposes other than erotic ones. The organs were juxtaposed, not engaged. The technique was so skillful in some of those artifacts that, turned one way, one organ dominated, and when reversed the opposite dominated. These were bisexual symbols, and they had significance as basic principles for creation of life. As such, they were magical-religious objects. Bisexuality includes the potential for self-regeneration. We will suggest later that one of the human figures drawn in a cave had similar qualities. These organ artifacts had to do with the man's preoccupation with his inability to give birth independently and, thus, how he was different from the woman who could. Grasping this was a psychological task transcendent of physical differences. At a later time we will consider the importance of disembodied organs in detail. We will show that when body organs or parts are separated from their physical sources, they take on a different significance for symbolism. Archetypal energy is more readily associated with separated parts. There are analogies for this in the nature of Rorschach stimuli. On the walls at Lascaux one may see a disemboweled bison and a reclining male with erect phallus juxtapositioned to it. Nearby are a bird and rhinoceros. This may be a record for us of the significance of the removal of organs from their primary source so as to extract meanings about them and to get in touch with their archetypal significance.

Reproduction as a means of survival for the group had a paramount effect on early man's consciousness, since an individual's life expectancy was very short and his means of coping with dangers were crude. Red ochre painted on burial stones or other artifacts symbolized lifeblood and stood for a magical means of re-creation.

The ways men were mingled with animal life in their paintings reflected the importance of the nature of their relationship with animals. Some certainly pertained to success in the hunt. Yet, the search for food and clothing was only part of man's need to value his relationship with the animals around him. Their habits taught men a great deal about what they were themselves. Early men seemed to have *disciplined* their impulses through symbolic relationships with numinous or sacred animals. Animal siblings played a role in furthering man's consciousness. In Neolithic bear cults, one may see specific forms of self-discipline as their symbolic relationship to the bear was expressed. Brain and marrow were highly prized for food, but ritual animals' bones were left intact. Long bones and skull cases were not opened in sacral or symbolic burials. Since skulls were buried separately, we know that care and intent motivated this form of burial.

We would suggest that the psychological tasks we have outlined as of primary importance to early men had little to do with the development of *ego* values in an individual. We would guess that all of Paleolithic men's extra energies went into the major psychological tasks that preoccupied them. Some mysterious force from inside had gripped Paleolithic men, and they made first steps toward masculine self-awareness. Those steps we have called the means of energizing archetypal power. Much more work on the development of consciousness and many ages had to pass before the means were present for an individual's *ego* awareness to arise. Men had to discover their mysteries through group work. Women already had theirs. Male and female psychological tasks were different at the time consciousness was being laid down. Later, through chieftains, group leaders, or kings, someone *in particular* began to carry consciousness *forward* through having enough psychological leisure to do it. Ego values got started through the presence of extra bits of energy that could be reattached elsewhere.

The woman never *had* to differentiate herself from man; her difference, her status, and her power were clear enough. Male children have different psychological tasks from female ones as they differentiate and separate from the mother. In later ages, as men found their own psychological power through sharpened logos functioning, they began to share that power with their sexual opposite. As her power as matriarch diminished, the female has had to reshuffle values and her estimate of herself against her changed status. She is still caught up in that psychological task today.

Our thesis is that the majority of Paleolithic and Neolithic art that has come down to us was produced by means of the extra psychological energy available, apart from the energy needed for demands of existence and survival. Most of the energy required to maintain life was spent elsewhere. Their paintings and their artifacts were their treasures, since they enabled the creators to advance psychologically. For us it is a reservoir of the psychology of their nonmaterial existence. We maintain that many examples of their art were carriers of archetypal energy for them since they tell us how consciousness developed. For a hundred thousand years, they worked and reworked important themes, whose archetypal energy took them *beyond* where they were when they started.

We repeat that they were involved in certain tasks associated with the psychology of grasping their differences from animals and, through their knowledge about animals, grasping their differences from their sexual opposites. Both animals and women had certain powers men did *not* have. While their physical capacities were different, and they functioned differently in many ways, and certain advantages they had physically were obvious, who they were and what kind of power belonged to them may easily not have been clear to early men. Dealing with those tasks molded consciousness. Men were involved in their own fundamental liberation movement.

Insofar as animals were concerned, some Paleolithic drawings look as if men were expressing a *relationship* with animals. Certain scenes showed men hunting *with* the animals, not for them. Early men were seeking the "masculine mysteries," a search for what their own relationship with animal power was. The paintings sometimes show us the content of beginning consciousness, at a given stage of their grasp of themselves.

Differentiating himself from the bonds of instinctual laws, and then grasping his human condition against the condition of animals around him, must have preoccupied man from the beginning, as consciousness evolved. The task of finding out how he differed from his mate came later and may have been the primary task for him during the Paleolith. What were his own psychological qualities if he could not qualify as a goddess?

We suggest that one element of importance in understanding parietal art may have been early man's using animals as vehicles for elements of his own human psychology which needed objectification. Hence, animals may have not always been meant to portray the animals themselves. If we look at some of parietal art that way, one can see how designating an animal as representing a "male symbol" fails to take us far enough. We have exactly the same task in Rorschach images associated with animals. Animals have always served men as teachers. Perhaps early men drew them to objectify vague glimmerings about qualities in himself, and he selected some animals who had qualities like those he began to see existed in his own repertory. Since women extracted meanings from instincts, what could he be able to extract from similar sources in himself? Did he indeed have such sources at all?

While men had superior physical power, fertility goddesses held psychological power. The female began by being psychologically stronger than the male. Perhaps early men organized their forces in the dark of caves. One can imagine them huddled in the dark even while the goddess incanted for success in the hunt she may have sent them out on. As the rite proceeded, and because as males they were excluded, the men crawled on their bellies in the darkness and, by some rude flare, scrawled images in their secret search for meanings. The physical strength required suggests it was a man's task. To reach some of the chambers containing some of the most symbolically potent examples of cave art, one has to crawl on one's stomach through very narrow and low passages for considerable distances. Some of the spots are known not to have changed since the time the art was drawn. The artists crawled into dangerous and remote recesses and painted or molded art forms in tortured positions amidst swirls of smoke and fumes from pine torches. They created images which were vehicles expressing the conditions that drove them to the lengths to do it. The stuff was archetypal in importance.

Animal figures often serve as pegs on which projections are hung. Miale and Holsopple (1) made use of that knowledge in setting up the content of openings in their sentence completion technique. They found that sentence openings about animals and children were more potent in gathering richly personal material than openings about objects or adults.

We suggest that a key to understanding intent in early art forms, a kind of Rosetta stone, may be the application of laws associated with subjective experience. We know from Alexander Marshack's work (6) that Paleolithic men kept records incised in bone of the phases of the moon, and the menstrual cycle. Those early men were capable of systematic analysis 35,000 years ago. Insofar as we are the physical and psychological heirs of both Paleolithic and Neolithic men, we can apply what we know about our own psychology to the study of those prototypes that had similar, if not identical experiences. Further, from the study of what our prototypal ancestors did, we learn more about them as we learn what we are. At the very least, we may expand our views about how we became.

Paleolithic men were making hard-earned efforts to *grasp* and *extract* meanings. Their guides were those events in nature that recurred and the animals and plants that surrounded them. In order to discover themselves against their surroundings, much physical and psychological energy was spent, and this shaped consciousness. Paleolithic man's prime motive was his astonishingly consistent curiosity about himself. He had to find out the significance of his difference from his mate and his goddess. *The power of the tension between those sexual opposites helped to determine the nature of his consciousness.* Because there was a difference between the sexual opposites in power to influence behavior, each became archetypal in its own right and in significance. Men began to see themselves as something *besides* protector or gatherer of food. What happened in men as they became conscious of more in themselves influenced the state of consciousness in women. Yet, the task of seeing potential in herself beyond her other functions inside the fertility cults was yet to come for woman. In the meantime, she possessed psychological power as goddess. Figure 1 shows the nature of this power inside the roots of our own tradition.

Perhaps Paleolithic man dreamed he was possessed of the power only goddesses held. Upon waking, he may have wondered why he did not himself qualify as a goddess. Just what his sexual difference meant regarding the means to influence behavior perhaps began to concern him. There is rather direct evidence for this as a concern in the man of the Paleolith if we look at some of his animal figures as vehicles for projections of his psychology.

At Lascaux only stags and no does were shown on cave walls, while at

FIG. 1. The mother-earth goddess of the Creto-Aegean culture is shown at the moment of her manifestation, from the palace at Knossos, 2000 B.C. While her priests were women, here she is attended by male acolytes whose raised arms show reverence to her epiphany. Her goddess character as mother nature is revealed in the dress of the goddess, and in women's costume generally, which left the breasts exposed. Her cult dates back to the time of the Paleolith, as is indicated by the fur garments that were worn in her rituals. She holds double axes or labrys in both hands. The labrys, originally a flint knife, was held only by women, who used it to perform castration, first on humans, but later on animals as carriers of certain human qualities. This sacred sacrificial implement, together with bull horns, was a central symbol in Creto-Aegean shrines. In the Cretan fertility cult, the bull symbolized the son-lover, who existed to serve the goddess. Masculine servitude to matriarchal power was entwined inside the taproot of our own tradition. This shows something of the nature of matriarchal psychology against which masculine separateness developed.

Covalanas only does and no stags were represented. The single sex representations cannot be accidental. The matriarch had power as fertility goddess and she symbolized insurance for survival. Men needed to find a *grasp* of their own functions apart from the feminine in their consciousness. Male and female deer were drawn separately and grouped for purposes of *psychological* sorting.

Through objectifying their imagination in their art forms, early men showed us how they dealt with what concerned them. The cave at Pech Merle contains a mural of a series of *compound animals* derived from imagination. Some of them might have stepped right out of a Rorschach plate. The nature of the distribution of bison, human, and ibex in Paleolithic art did not correspond to their distribution in the environment. The figures drawn were seen through an inner eye, and they became psychological animals and people. So it is with animals and people that populate the Rorschach world, and they too carry highly personal projections.

The so-called "sorcerer" from Les Trois Frères (see Fig. 12) cave in France is a fantastic product of the imagination. This compound creature is part horse, human, bear, owl, and stag, while its penis and testicles are, as

Ucko and Rosenfeld (8) reported, "wrongly positioned for any animal or human." They hang reversely and turn back onto the figure itself. As depicted, self-copulation could occur. This is perhaps the earliest, and certainly the most complex projection of a particular archetypal power. This compound image reflects a unique concern in the psychology of early man. As a basis for hermaphroditic qualities in man's nature, it carries the archetypal energy associated with the image of his first *masculine* god. The visionary creature did not need the female of the species to acquire the power associated with creation and fertility. This was a masculine creation in man's effort to counter the power of the fertility goddess. If he combined the power of the instinctual qualities associated with the variety of animal parts in his makeup, and then fertilized himself, he would most certainly find himself in a position of supreme power. The goddess would have to slink into a cave, dream her dreams, and formulate her differences visually. The sorcerer figure had the eyes of an owl. Like the owl, man's task was to see in the darkness and find the light of his own consciousness through knowledge about his differences and powers. It was the objectification of a subjective idea.

As we have noted, not much about cave art suggests that the ancient artists were concerned enough about erotic pleasure to represent it. They left it for projections in graffiti of later times. Most of the female genitalia that appeared had to do with ritual associated with fecundity. The male organ appeared infrequently. When present, it was apparently connected with a particular ritual which was not related to erotic activity. Yet, the role of the phallus in creation was most certainly known to Paleolithic men. They observed its function through their great teachers, the animals around them. We would guess that *the mystery* in the act of generation caught the imagination of Paleolithic man far more than the sensual response. The reverse is true for us. Since our knowledge has destroyed all the magic and most of the mystery, we can do little else than overvalue the sensual side of sexual expression. We may have liberated ourselves into a prison.

If we are correct about the sorcerer of Les Trois Frères, it will have been through the means of mutual projection. If we viewed him as a misfit or pervert, we would have done no more than project the sexual psychology of our time onto an inappropriate vehicle. If we had data that showed us that sexual matters did indeed preoccupy Paleolithic men, then the symbol could have a different meaning, perhaps even that of trying sex a new way. We believe that grasping the psychological meaning of sexual differences and the nature of acquiring independent power underlay the intent in some of the content of parietal art.

Lively discussion has centered around the interpretation of hands having been drawn on the walls of some Paleolithic caves. The variety of meanings ascribed to them make up an interesting set of projective data. A favorite interpretation centers around the hand as symbolic of a magic "hold" over prey. One cave displays drawings of the left hand on the left side of the cave, and right ones on the right side. We would search for the meaning or the symbolism of the hands by looking for traces of a psychological task. When an organ is represented as separate from its body, it takes on a different meaning than it had when it was attached. We have noted before that early man had a propensity for creating images of separated members of the body. Rorschach stimulus plates provide potentials for either condition, organs connected or separated from a physical frame. We will indicate the importance of the difference of those conditions in their power to activate different sources. The physical context associated with an organ catches different forms of projection. Unattached organs tend to activate archetypal sources more, while attached ones tend to activate qualities associated with personal complexes. Detaching an organ enables the symbol that forms around it to move from concrete to abstract planes.

One of the two hands usually holds dominant power, even when the person is ambidextrous. That power may have defined the basic meaning of right and left for early men. We know for certain that left and right cave walls had different psychological meaning for parietal artists. The function of hands is more likely to take us into male than female psychology. While hands carry an archetypal meaning of power and control for the male, they do not carry those archetypal qualities for females. We would suggest that the hand drawings in Paleolithic caves had to do with a particular concern of those artists, and that it was associated with sorting some aspect of masculine power from feminine power. Something psychological associated with strength versus weakness on a plane that pertains to prototypal forces was involved. Hands are a tangible source of masculine power. Women even classify men according to their "handiness."

It has been suggested that the hand prints were the signatures of the artists. Hands are indeed highly individual. In a given instance, a viewer might observe "from that hand came the drawing." This would be a useful approach if we could suppose a differentiated ego consciousness in cave artists. There are data that argue against that. In the cave at Gargas, whole panels were devoted to hands alone. Also, since the majority of hand drawings were small, some have assumed they were female.[6] Leroi-Gourhan (4) has noted "male signs" associated with many of the relatively small hands. We cannot be sure that the signs he noted as male were meant to be that. However, perhaps we can assume that the drawings of hands were being used for something, since marks and workings accompanied them. Our

---

[6] In some instances it can be seen where a longer or larger finger had been traced originally, then altered, making it shorter or smaller through painting over the original tracing. This was done deliberately, showing that the artist's intent had nothing to do with the size of his own hand or his sex.

emphasis in interpretation would be an abstract one. It would have to do with one hand being more powerful than the other. Small hands are not themselves symbols for excessive power or strength. We suggest that the presence of hands was another manifestation of concern about the psychological difference between power associated with strength and weakness.[7]

It is possible to assume that these drawings were done by females who wished to acquire male strength inherent in hand power. Our thesis discourages that interpretation, since we do not see evidence that females had a need for the psychological tasks we have described for that age. We have provided a rationale as to why the "sorcerer" at Les Trois Frères was possessed of inverted sex organs. The psychology of male organs capable of self-fertilization would hardly be a matter that would further the psychology of a power-holding fertility goddess. Certainly not, if we keep to the notion of cave art as prototypal work associated with beginnings of consciousness. We must not apply the complexities of the time-layered consciousness we have acquired ourselves onto the work of men who were in a different developmental state.

Rather, we see the "sorcerer" as a manifestation of male psychology and having a function of helping shape the contents of consciousness. Through these images, early men grasped the significance of themselves. Portrayals of hands played specific roles in distinguishing aspects of masculine psychology.

In much the same way as painting female animals on one wall, and only male animals on another, hands may have been used by the artists in grasping more about the meaning of opposites, left and right,[8] male and female, strength and weakness, control and lack of it. Paleolithic men may have thought, one hand is less powerful, why is that? We do not see an analogy in animals. Does the power inherent in my hands distinguish me from the female? Is the weakness in my left hand a quality of mine that links something in me to the female? Both of her hands are weak when they are compared with the power in mine. It is possible to make my left hand as powerful as my right one? Will the gods endow me with equal strength? Perhaps those hypothetical questions can serve to amplify possible concerns that existed in the psychology of early men. The questions are consistent with our hypothesis that certain psychological tasks existed for Paleolithic men, and

[7] On the walls at Gargas, some 150 red and black hands were drawn, and 9 out of 10 of them are left hands.

[8] In 1957, Columbia University physicist Chien-Shiung Wu proved that nature can distinguish between her left hand and her right. Chien-Shiung Wu's experiments disproved what had been known as the law of conservation of parity, showing that if you perform an experiment and then do exactly the same experiment but reverse left and right, you do not get identical results. We would call the patterning of hand prints in parietal art evidence of man's first psychological experiment. Our suggestion is that it was based on the existence of natural laws that differentiate between opposites.

that one of them may have been a concern about balance of power, an archetypal quality associated with differences between hands.

Recently, Alexander Marshack (6) has begun to publish his work on microscopic analysis of parietal art, concentrating on the signs. His analysis shows that the engraved animals were not intended simply to be killed, but that they were designed for duration, to be reused or renewed. His work supports the presence of a body of mythology associated with the drawings and signs. He believes that the signs had a separate mythology and symbology, and his work shows that they were separately painted and decorated. He has concluded that parietal art was based on a complex use of symbol. Further, he has shown that simplification in symbolism is not a function of time and historical development, but a matter of contemporaneity in style in parietal art. For our purposes, this means that consciousness as we know it came into being inside an already complicated psychic apparatus, its archetypal substance.

The way we have taken in extracting meanings from artifacts of the remote past is similar to the way we will use to decipher symbols and images in Rorschach data. We will carry certain prototypal images and symbols back with us and search for their counterparts in some of the substance of inkblot plates. We do not do this because those images are "inherited" by us today. Their power exists against the effect repeated basic experience has had on neural structure, and particularly at the time consciousness was being shaped. The potential for response exists around images capable of igniting energies associated with those primary qualities that occur in all men alike. Since these images had a part in shaping consciousness, and because their power is basic to energizing aspects of the human condition, their virility has transcended great stretches of time.

Through having removed the means of analysis of symbols from some of the conventional frames which we have fallen into habits of using in psychological interpretation, we hope to have extended our view of the way subjective data may be handled. It goes without saying that there are many other ways of handling this form of data. Our position has been that some of them are limited in scope and that they leave important aspects of psychology dangling in the air.

REFERENCES

1. Holsopple, James, and Miale, F. R. 1954. Sentence Completion. 177 p. Springfield, Ill.: Charles C Thomas.
2. Laming, Annette. 1959. Lascaux, Paintings and Engravings. 208 p. Baltimore: Penguin Books.
3. Laming-Emperaire, Annette. 1962. La signification de l'art rupestre paléolithique. Quoted in: Leroi-Gourhan, A., Treasures of Prehistoric Art. 1967. 543 p. New York: Harry N. Abrams.

4. Leroi-Gourhan, André. (1965) 1967. Treasures of Prehistoric Art. 543 p. New York: Harry N. Abrams.
5. Lorenz, Konrad. 1965. Evolution and Modification of Behavior. Chicago: University of Chicago Press.
6. Marshack, Alexander. 1969. A re-examination of the engraved upper paleolithic materials of Italy by a new methodology. In: Rivista di scienze preistoriche, Bol. XXIV. Florence, Italy: Stamperia Editoriale F. lli Parenti Di G.
7. Solecki, Ralph S. 1971. Neanderthal is not an epithet but a worthy ancestor. Smithsonian, 2: 20–27.
8. Ucko, Peter, and Rosenfeld, Andrée. 1967. Palaeolithic Cave Art. 256 p. New York: McGraw-Hill Book Co.

FIVE

Archetypal Influences in the Stimulus Plates

In his novel, *Heart of Darkness,* Joseph Conrad (6) gave us a powerful view of the accessibility of our inner prehistory when it is activated by an appropriate experience. In the book, Captain Marlow (narrator of several of Conrad's novels, including *Lord Jim*) makes a precarious journey in a leaky boat up a river into the darkest reaches of the African interior. Conrad himself made such a trip in 1890. Marlow's goal is to discover the effect of isolation in primitive conditions on the values of a white man who had been known for his strict ethics and morality. Upon finding the man, Marlow discovers he has lost all vestiges of his former value system. Conrad showed us how thin our veneer of consciousness actually is, and about the great surround of darkness inside us all. Marlow describes for us his subjective reactions as he and Stone Age men look at each other from boat to shore and shore to boat again:

We were traveling in the night of the first ages, of those ages that are gone . . . [on shore] the black men were—no, they were not inhuman. Well, you know, that was the worst of it, the suspicion of their not being inhuman. They leaped and howled and spun and made horrid faces; but what thrilled you was the thought of their humanity—like yours—the thought of your remote kinship with this passionate uproar. Ugly. Yes it was ugly; but if you were man enough you would admit that there was in you just the faintest trace of a response to the terrible frankness of that noise, a dim suspicion of there being a meaning in it which you—you so remote from the night of the first ages—could comprehend. And why not? The mind of man is capable of anything, because everything is in it, all the past as well as all the future. What was there after all? Joy, fear, sorrow, devotion, valor, rage—truth, stripped of its cloak of time. Let the fool shudder, but the man knows and can look on without a wink. But he must be as much a man as those on shore. He must meet that truth with his own true stuff, with his own inborn strength. Principles won't do. Acquisitions, clothes, pretty rags— rags that would fly off at the first good shake . . . [is there] an appeal to me in this fiendish row? You wonder I didn't go ashore for a howl and a dance? I had to watch the steering.

In a lecture series some years ago at New York Hospital-Cornell, Louise Despert[1] described a case of an autistic child who had the motor ability to skin up the side of a wall, rather like a lizard. As the child improved, he lost that remarkable motor facility. Dr. Despert explained the phenomenon as having been due to an activation of a motoric archetype, which, though we have lost contact with it through evolution, may still exist in potential within us.

Joseph Campbell (5) has postulated that experiences which have grown out of late Paleolithic hunting cultures influence consciousness in Western man today. He has suggested that qualities associated with forms of experience in early men do not disappear because additional psychic substance has evolved in association with increased functional complexities. As this was being written, Gordon Bower (4) called for efforts to isolate and further features in us associated with simpler psychological states to improve our means of apperception. He noted the importance of visual images as a means of grasping the essential qualities of an abstraction. In emphasizing how language development inhibits imaginal processes in the young, he prescribed as follows for an adult embarked on new ways of apprehending: "he must become as a child again, to tap the wellsprings of his suppressed imaginative talents that have lain buried under years of linguistic development." In our search for meanings through imagery, we have had to displace the blankets of verbiage that blind us. Shorn of excess cerebral baggage, we must look at some of our Rorschach images with the eyes of a child, who, in the way his consciousness emerges, may experience some of his world not unlike the manner of early men.

Rhoda Kellogg (15) has called attention to the strong similarity between motifs which recur in children's drawings and motifs found in cave paintings. She provided us with some examples of those art forms done by children from widely disparate traditions. She postulated that a child's early pictorial abstractions derive from innate patterns.

Perhaps those patterns are innate. However, we do not necessarily need a notion of innateness for our thesis. Patterns may merely appear innate, an inference we make because they recur. Under our definition, archetypal energy may become extinct when the conditions that further it disappear. If children were incubated by artificial means, the archetypal energy associated with the psychology of childbearing would be altered in women.

We suggest that certain basic patterns in our psychic substance may have not changed or needed to, though man has changed around them as he grew into an organism with a capacity for more. We suggest that those stimuli which have the power to link us with our remote past do so only through activating clusters of energy that have remained viable. They exist in the

---

[1] Author of the Despert Fables and a pioneer in the study of autistic children.

foundation upon which the structure of consciousness has been built. Because foundation blocks cannot be seen does not alter their existence. There can be no superstructure without them. Remove them and the structure topples. The nature of the prototypal energy we refer to is similar for psychic structure, and those stimuli that have the power to activate our root stuff may be the *most potent* ones, not weak tracings. In short, they are not remote at all. They are among the cement all men share that bind up the human condition. Our tendency for excessive cerebration has made us remote from grasping these inner powers.

The Rorschach experience puts us into a condition of consciousness not unlike that of early man. Early men drew images so as to grasp how their meanings were linked to them. Picture formation was the mode he used for communicating with himself and with his gods. It is the recorded language of Paleolithic times. The Rorschach experience takes us to that same mode of communication. Language is no more than extensions from sets of pictures. Both the dream and certain Rorschach images are set in modes of pictography. Pictography *is* the means subjective consciousness requires for existence. Through providing similar conditions for a particular variety of communication, the Rorschach links us with the means of expression that dominated at the time of the dawn of consciousness.

A subject is put into a psychological state not unlike that of early man as he experiences the Rorschach. A subject cannot call on much of his storehouse of knowledge as he faces strange forms of projections from his inner substance. As was the case for men in the Paleolith, no rigid dictum from consciousness acts as an inhibitor for subjective happenings. Other than in experiences like the Rorschach, consciousness inhibits connections with parts of the unconscious in modern men. Psychic processes may be reconnected through symbols. Symbols conduct psychic current. Rorschach's plates have the power, at least in potential, to reconduct psychic energy through channels antagonistic to consciousness. Ignorance is the only source for mystery about subjective affairs. There is nothing mystic about how they operate. They follow definite laws and particular forms of order. Radio waves were not "mystic" before they were discovered in recent times.

It is possible to observe some general attributes of Rorschach's inkplates that we imagine were similar to the conditions of life for early men. The darkness and form of the first Rorschach plate might easily be associated with qualities of a cave. This occurs through sharp contrasts between the dark figure and white background. Men of prehistory penetrated into the deepest and often the most inaccessible part of cave darkness to deposit their subjective images in paint. Subjective experience seems to be furthered by a condition of darkness. The kinds of figures and elements evoked through the Rorschach experience would not be alien to Paleolithic men. Rorschach animals pop into view as if from nowhere. Subjects commonly apologize for reporting so many animals and even disclaim responsibility for their presence. A subject may be suddenly confronted with a member of an extinct species, or an ominous combination of several fearsome creatures. Paleolithic men pursued animals, lived among them, and painted them to express through animals something of their own subjective nature. Rorschach protocols tend to be populated with animals from our inner zoos, and they provide the opportunity for us to discover qualities associated with our subjective being through animal symbolism. As must have been the case for men living in a hunting culture, through Rorschach experiences, we may get surprised by creatures looming up before us, and we may even feel trapped by having been confronted with some creatures we were not prepared to meet. Individuals who have lost contact with the defenses of ego consciousness may experience genuine panic in front of a Rorschach bear or tiger. As in Paleolithic times, the Rorschach experience creates conditions in which animal and human worlds blend with ease. Elements that may stimulate facets of both animal and human worlds lie juxtaposed in our inkblot stimuli. Psychologically, modern man refaces some of the conditions that confronted his remote ancestors when he moves through the Rorschach experience.

Through empirical evidence, we have come to view Rorschach images of animal skins as symbols of adaptiveness. They are common Rorschach images, and qualities associated with their texture enable us to draw some conclusions about a subject's flexibility. The animal skin was a means of adapting to life in a very concrete sense for early men. Their appearance in Rorschach is commonplace, and skins were a commonplace object in the existence of our ancestors.

From our view, some of these qualities that Rorschach's plates provide which link them with counterparts in the Paleolithic world are not coincidences. We suggest that those links may be the central force of these plates as potent stimuli.

In a rough fashion, and primarily through the means of search, we will examine each Rorschach plate in an attempt to locate components that provide it with the power to evoke various types of psychic sources. However, we do not begin this task as either an artistic exercise or as a pawn of blind coincidence or chance. The foundations we rely on as we proceed are empirical data gathered through time about the differential stimulus qualities in each plate. Rorschach's inkblots vary in their capacity to stir different aspects of our inner worlds. Some blot areas are more potent than others for stimulating collective or personal sources. Our chief tool in this task will be certain common images that have come down to us from Paleolithic and Neolithic artifacts. Our efforts are bound to be incomplete ones, but they may be useful in classifying and understanding subjective data.

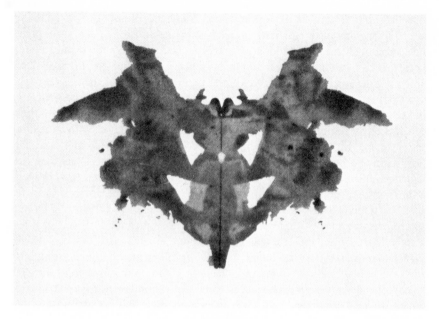

PLATE I

PLATE I

The stimulus power of this plate is complex, and it contains a capacity to activate archetypal sources. The large center detail (frequently reported as a woman's figure) is important in that regard. When that detail is experienced directly as a woman's figure, it does not generally trigger archetypal energy. This center detail has a startling resemblance to Paleolithic fertility figurines. Shaped in bone or stone, those figures had large hips and breasts, while arms, feet, and hands were often either completely absent or stylized. The significance of the figurines and sculptures centered around the fecundity of the female torso as fertility symbol. This may be seen in the low relief of Figure 2, which has been commonly called the "Venus of Laussel."

Some of the figurines had double neck stalks, and this represented the notion of two-in-one, the two-fold nature of the goddess (nurturing and destructive), as well as the unity between female generations, as goddess and priestess, or mother and daughter. A double-headed or -necked form exists for the central detail of Rorschach Plate I, along with single-handedness. Figure 3 shows a visual counterpart in a goddess from a Neolithic shrine.

These votive figurines were associated with psychic needs for abundant food supply and fertility, so as to insure survival. Archetypally, this takes us into the world of the matriarch. In Figure 4 we may see an example of how matriarchal power existed in the origins of Western culture.

FIG. 2. The goddess of Laussel (Dordogne, France), holding a bison horn, carved on a limestone block in low relief, around 22,000 B.C. The figure was heightened with red ochre. This goddess is said to impose an awesome presence as she is approached by an observer considerably below her on the ground. In side view the whole figure is carved to appear taut like a bow, and her feet and head melt into the rock as if she were hovering. Her right hand holds a bison horn. Its position gives the appearance of the crescent moon, while it serves as a container for blood. The horn filled with blood symbolized the highest fertility in Cretan bull cults. Her left hand sinks into her abdomen, the fecund zone of great significance in fertility ritual. Function of right and left is differentiated by the hands in this impressive Neolithic sculpture. (Leroi-Gourhan, André. *Prehistoire de l'Art Occidental.* Editions d'Art Lucien Mazenod, Paris. Photo Musée d'Aquitaine, Bordeaux, cliché Jean Vertut.)

79

FIG. 3. Front and rear views of a white marble mother-goddess figure from a shrine at Çatal Hüyük (22), a Neolithic town in Anatolia, 5880 B.C. The rear view of the figure is not dissimilar to the appearance of the central detail on Rorschach Plate I, which is also perceived as a rear view. The sculpture shows two heads, breasts, and one pair of arms, again like the detail on Plate I, which symbolized the two-fold nature of the goddess, and probably the interrelation between goddess and maiden, as well as between mother and daughter.

The central detail of Plate I may show us aspects of how a subject is related to the matriarchal psychological condition, when we can determine that archetypal activity was aroused. Matriarchal dominance was imposed through powers of nurture and insurance for survival through producing

FIG. 4. A bell-shaped earth-goddess in terra cotta from Boeotia, Archaic period. The bell shape represents the earth and its correspondence with the earth-goddess's womb, the lower territory of fertility. On the corpus of the bell one may see a complete ring of female worshippers in a dance. A Paleolithic rock painting at Cogul, Spain, portrays a similar round of black-pigmented female figures in an orgiastic ritual. Bell as a percept is a familiar Rorschach response for the central detail on Plate I. Structurally, there are blot counterparts for feet and an extended neck stalk like those fashioned in the terra cotta. The image of dancers moving around a central figure is not infrequent for the whole of Plate I. This terra cotta goddess comes from the times of the origin of our own tradition. It is of note to observe that the subject whose images are used to illustrate points in this chapter included a circular dance in her Rorschach experience. Her Rorschach sequence reflects the presence of a struggle with the matriarchal sources in herself.

FIG. 4.

young, who will become future hunters and providers. In fertility cults, the fecundity of the female was ritualistically associated with preserving a continuous food supply through an analogy with animal fecundity, and with acquiring success in the hunt. Our interest in this stimulus pertains to the nature of the subject's percept and to the form of instinctual energy that may or may not be released. When seen as a female form, the image may not be influenced by archetypal energy, but it may catch projections from a personal complex or persona problem. If the image is experienced as a masculine figure, there is a strong probability of archetypal influences which may combine with facets of a personal sexual complex. Whatever happens with it may catch projections of a subject's relationship with the effects of matriarchal power or association. This relationship may be positive or negative, whether the subject be male or female. Figure 5 shows the strength of the power of matriarchal energy on a modern person.

The frequency with which the large side details are seen as symbolic dancers, mythological figures, or witches suggests the power of Plate I to stir those forces in us that led to the creation of myths. It is extraordinary to observe a modern subject, who believes that the world is entirely rational, without batting an eyelash, report a string of supernatural creatures or figures from make-believe or myth in his Rorschach experience. Somehow, if an image comes from our imagination, we do not feel that we are called on to account for it rationally. The Rorschach experience takes us back to the myth-producing states in man's consciousness when imagination was freer from the tight bands of rationalism. Archetypal experiences fed myth-producing sources. "Witch" has always been a peg for the projection of those qualities in women that men either did not understand or refused to accept. For women, "witch" has been a reservoir for shadow projections. Satan, or the devil, has been the peg for the projection of those qualities in men that women either did not understand or could not accept. Plate I sets up myth-producing potentials in some subjects, and we must examine them for packages of projection. The most likely form of projection, when archetypal sources are activated, may be associated with the archetype of the matriarchal form of feminine functioning.

This plate has features that may be associated with the psychological climate of the Paleolith and with caves. Even the popular "bat" lives and moves in darkness, and several of the central white spaces have a distinct triangular appearance. The triangle is one of the oldest symbolic images men have used. Natural formations from stalagmite contours that formed triangles in certain caves were used for ritual experiences by early men. It represented the vulva, the female triangle, and its ritual use had to do with fertility rites.

It is both essential for our purposes and useful to distinguish between male

FIG. 5. Drawing by Mary Petty; copyright 1952. The New Yorker Magazine, Inc.

and female psychic structure, energy, and functioning. It enables us to grasp more about how certain plates vary in their potentials for particular forms of stimulation. We may see a predominantly feminine psychological *structure* in a woman who has little capacity to project herself as a *functioning* woman through absence of sufficient psychological energy. In another female, the structure may be more dominantly masculine with a recessive feminine component. Psychological impotence may pertain to female as well as male. Its source may be in structure, and that structure may be at odds with the form of identity one assumes consciously. The Rorschach plates are highly useful in delineating the inner state that pertains in association with structure. It is easier to effect changes through psychotherapy when complexes associated with energy predominate over structure. When enough assets are present, psychic structure may be modified also. It is a more difficult and longer task. Conditioning techniques are not likely to alter psychic structure.

In our view, Plate I appears to have a capacity to stir material associated with the *archetype of the functioning female* through its connections with matriarchal dominance as it functioned psychically. An example of the survival of matriarchal power today may be seen in the nature of our marriage ceremonies. Sometimes matriarchal power is revived when monies earned by a husband and its budgeting are turned over to his spouse. The traditional marriage ceremony is under fire today. Some young couples have worked out intricate ways to defy that aspect of matriarchal power. Manufacturers of bridal arrays might do well to diversify, if they have not done so already. However, defying does little more than call attention to discontent; it does not alter structure by itself. The distaff group is reshaping the way it expects to wield matriarchal power. The sweetheart of Sigma Chi is becoming extinct.[2] It is a time for males to be wary, not naive. All must find a means of adapting to the new wine, but it is reassuring to realize that the archetype of the bottle is old indeed. It is the Rorschach that can place these fundamentals into perspective for us. A comparison between Plates I and VII may be illuminating in that regard. Plate VII reflects another side of the feminine and pertains more to *structure* than functioning.

It may be useful to look at the images that occur from Plate I against a frame of the archetype of the functioning female, femininity as it is projected through its energy into life. This may include sexual energy, but the context is much larger and refers to modes of behavior psychologically associated with matriarchal power. A female subject may be in opposition to that power as much as a given male, or male and female alike may identify with that power in modern subjects. Some years ago a *New Yorker Magazine*[3] cover by the cartoonist Mary Petty depicted an Edwardian scene as follows. A

---

[2] An observation made by the author's wife.
[3] May 3, 1952.

silver haired mother with a black velvet ribbon about her neck was seated at the dining room table across from her meek, broken, balding son, each spooning soup. On the oak paneled wall above them was a painting of mother and son, each in youth, a little boy in a blue sailor suit nestled against the skirts of a beautiful mother. The artist has not shown us an Oedipus Complex, but a son in the power of matriarchal dominance. The son is lover against his will. How that son might experience the center detail on Plate I would give us some crucial insight into whether his destiny includes a potential enabling him to break the bonds of matriarchal power. We do not know until we see what happens. Our point is that the painting illustrates how our own psychology has roots that derive from the archetypal world of the functioning female of a certain variety, that of the matriarchal world as it functioned psychically. We cannot assume that a male subject would automatically oppose matriarchal power nor that a female subject would identify with it. A female subject, granddaughter of two world-famous musicians, who was suffering from a severe psychological complex, responded to the center detail of Plate I negatively because the power associated with the figure was experienced by her in a masculine mode.

The ritual masks, head of a primitive animal, figures whirling in a dance, and other fairly common images or associations for Plate I may or may not carry some relation to the individual's psychological relationship with the archetype we have described. "Wolf's head" may carry a clue as to the primitive instinctual mode the patient uses to escape matriarchal power, *if* we find evidence that that power has the proportions of a complex for the person. In order to remain objective, we must assume nothing that does not come to us through data. Each plate must be approached with an open-minded attitude and a sense of awe.

In singling out matriarchal energy as central to what may be potentiated by this plate, we recognize that we may see much or little of it in a given individual. This does not alter our thesis about it. We may find material associated with the persona, the shadow, or any conceivable source or combination. Linking and tying together material from different sources may be simple or complex. We would suggest that whirling side figures on this plate may be investigated around the possibility that there is a repetitive, compulsive quality associated with the subject's energy expenditure which may be connected with his relation to matriarchal power.

We would not wish to limit ourselves in interpreting Rorschach material to the suggestions we have made here. If we are circumspect, we must discover if they lead us to anything fruitful in a given case. *We rely on data, not theory, for precision.*

We will draw on the Rorschach material of a 22-year-old female subject to illustrate the points we wish to make regarding archetypal sources in each plate. This subject is open to inner processes, but, other than that, she is an ordinary patient such as one might meet in everyday practice. Her response was:

D
A two-headed conductor in a great Russian overcoat. I see a policeman's badge which would be the buckle of the belt of the great coat which comes out heavy; it has a fur fringe at the bottom. The lower trunk looks like the legs of a woman turned backwards and away from the light.

W̊
Two griffins, wings, heads, four feet; half bird, half lion.

Di
Two Picasso-like breasts.

(Here, the central large detail was experienced as a masculine figure, while the lower half was experienced as female, all of which was covered by a great coat. Side figures were griffins.)

Subjective experience in the subject was influenced by the center large detail, and it affected her logic. Since something unconscious interfered with conscious judgment, we suspect archetypal energy at work. She did not bring critical judgment to bear on the obvious fact that she reported a composite figure, part male, part female under one coat or covering. The image was contradictory. Masculine experience partially superceded an experience of the figure as feminine. In the beginning, we could assume an identification problem. What, though, does that mean for this individual? Does she have a mother complex or a father complex, or is it something else? Are her impulses associated with her own female functioning and its power in matriarchal life experiences contradictory? At the moment, all we can assume is that something has probably gone awry with her relation to her female core or feminine essence, as it functions and as it is connected with the matriarch. Even though she experienced two heads, both male, a two-fold impact from logos, something about her instinctual femaleness crops out in the end. As a conductor, the heavy logos (two male heads) quality about the figure is seeking harmony (conductor) as it might be psychologically related to the nature of feeling (music). There is certainly a positive feature within the complexity of this image. On the other hand, the instinctual side of the woman is fragmented, legs here, breasts there, and masculine top. We feel reasonably safe in assuming that Plate I did indeed activate something of the archetypal sources in this subject. Picasso, who paints archetypal images, is brought in. Quite as for the patient we describe in Chapter 6 on process analysis, the *subjective law of excluded awareness* has been at work. The conditions for symbol formation and archetypal activation are present. Consciously, she did not experience breasts on the upper torso of the central figure (which, as for Plate III, are objectively there), while separated breasts popped out on the Rorschach screen before she got through with the plate. What is there about this subject's capacity for nurturing or need for it that clashes with both her view of herself as a woman and her functioning authority? Something of nurture and fertility have gotten split off from psychological sources in this woman. What is the relation between that split and the form of instinctual energy that is released? What animals appear? Griffins, mythic beasts, who as forms of imagination are among our oldest images. They appear on cave walls and may be dated from the early Neolith. The subject is aware of their composite nature, calling them half-bird, half-lion. The griffin became associated with rituals of fertility goddesses in Neolithic times.[4] We do not know their exact meaning, but they appeared on cave and shrine walls among bulls and bison. They were connected with hunt and fertility cults. At any rate, for our subject, the griffin carries masculine values, and our task is to find out what they mean for her against her conflict about her feminine core. The lion has to do with power and authority, and the bird with the soaring spirit or mind's soaring ideas, both carriers of masculine energy. Someway, masculine values tend to run this subject's personal show. Her instinctual vehicle, insofar as this plate is concerned, is mythic, not real, and even the female body structure is experienced as fragmented. She has a strong shadow problem. Feelings, relatedness, emotions, and Eros, those qualities associated with defining the archetype of the female have become disharmonious in this woman, whose psyche projects a double-headed masculine conductor, who guides qualities associated with her inner state.

These images may be approached from a number of other standpoints. We have avoided all else as we looked at them in search of their sources and the strength of energy that is attached. In some instances, the source may be wholly archetypal. The author has the materials of a male psychotic patient who experienced this plate as his "physical and spiritual mother." The patient was totally under the power of the matriarchal archetype.

PLATE II

Our position has been that those men who existed at the time consciousness began to develop have left us clues in their artifacts and paintings which reflect their psychology. We have interpreted that psychology as reflecting developmental tasks that were needed so that the human condition could

---

[4] The griffin-vulture as symbol was used in shrines at Çatal Hüyük (Turkey), dating from the seventh millenium B.C. There are data to suggest it may have been related to the death aspect of the mother archetype. At Pech Merle (discovered in France in 1922) a painting of a dying lioness among stalactites resembling human breasts which were painted black may be the Paleolithic precursor for Çatal Hüyük art symbols that showed a connection between griffin, vulture, and breasts. In their combination with one another they had ritual meanings.

PLATE II

emerge. After the long stretch of time required to differentiate himself as a separate species of animal, man had to learn what defined his masculine substance. We suggest that they did this through grasping their differences against the frame of their opposite, the female of the species. Animals, ritual, and religious fervor probably served as vehicles assisting in objectifying psychological experience. In his discussion of the religion of Paleolithic man, Leroi-Gourhan (17) made some interesting parallels between paired sexual opposites among parietal art animals and the Chinese principles of *yin* and *yang,* yet he concluded that the reason for pairing may require an explanation that we cannot imagine. Plate II provides us with an excellent example of paired animals. This takes us into the archetypal world of opposing forces. Paired animals that face each other occur often in parietal art. At Lascaux, bulls and cows follow one another, and at La Pileta they are side by side. While sexual attributes are rarely defined, the secondary characteristics in profiles and through horns or antlers are often very explicit. For our purposes, this represents the psychology of differentiation from the opposite, male and/or female. We may expect that Plate II may lead us into the psychology of that form of psychological endeavor. Each gender of the species is closed off from certain experiences that define the existence of his opposite. Even when we can explain those differences with scientific precision, what we cannot experience remains veiled in mystery. The mysteries of the woman as fertility goddess were part of life for Paleolithic and Neo-lithic men. They led to power and a matriarchy. Men may have had to ex-aggerate matriarchal aspects of life in their artifacts so that they could grasp a means to separate from it. Their psychological task was to absorb mean-ings so as to define themselves as being separate.

Through its color contrasts, Plate II has certain qualities commonly found in parietal art. Black and bright red constitute the color medium. Alongside their paintings, cave artists applied a series of signs or symbols. These are consistent throughout all cave art. Leroi-Gourhan (17) has as-signed male and female designations for those signs. While his means of ar-riving at conclusions about what is male and what is female may not hold up (in fact, we doubt that it will), the importance of male and female vectors and a dualistic system of psychology corresponds with our view of psycho-logical tasks for the Paleolith. "Barbs" or chevron-like symbols were often black in color and dots or circles were frequently done in bright red color. At the same time, one may see red chevrons and black dots in some caves. We suggest that color was useful to Paleolithic men in noting differences and making contrasts. At Marsoulas, a bison is rendered exclusively (the figure has no outline) through a composition of red dots and a red barb exists be-neath. We would suggest this attributes an immortal quality, since red-painted stones accompanied bones in burials. The woman, through her birth-giving capacity, and perhaps through the mystery of her menstrual cycle, was connected with "red" and "bison" for cave artists. They had to differentiate themselves in relation to those qualities. Color was one means to do it, and Plate II carries us to those colors in a unique context.

Paleolithic artists experimented with visual images showing stages of transition between a bending female and stylization of that shape into the lines of, and then to, a full figure of a bison. This can mean nothing but a *psychological* connection. The bending woman has been interpreted as the position taken by a female as she received her mate. That may be so, but it would not seem reasonable to assume that the artist who drew the transi-tional images planned to mount a bison. It is not consistent with the absence of sexual psychology in parietal art. The data that we have tell us that the artists were serious and working on something psychological. When narra-tive scenes appeared, men were often shown fleeing before a charging bison. Men at grips with a bison had psychological significance for Paleolithic men. We suggest the concern was that of differentiating from the power of the wo-man. We know that fertility goddesses were closely connected with the bison. The famous fertility goddess found at Laussel shows the goddess holding a bison horn in her right hand, while her left is pressed tightly against her fecund belly. The mythology of her connection with bison may have been connected with the meaning his mortality had for man.

Plate II provides a fantastic combination in its lower red detail. Held up-right, a detached vulva is apparent, and it occurs in and is surrounded by bright red color. Archetypally, this area may take us to a transcendant plane having to do with mortality and survival. This may not occur, and one may respond to the sexual features alone, but no archetypal energy may have been involved. If one looks at the lower red detail reversed, there is an astonishingly complex series of animal figures associated with the vulva and with animals important to parietal artists. We move as if through magic into the world of the Paleolith. Centrally, there is an exquisite ibex with moulded horns, whose facial outlines are made up by horns of two more ibex or reindeer in apposition. Parietal artists often drew animals facing each other. Right side up, the commonly perceived animal figures, bears or elephants, are engaged in an appositional stance. As is true for Plate II through pro-jection, parietal artists used apposition to express sometimes play and some-times struggle. The carved animals of the Paleolithic spear thrower (Fig. 6) may have had heads that were detachable, animal or human. Either way, Rorschach Plate II is remarkably like the animals of the carved implement. Capturing animals required masculine skill, while psychologically the act may have been used to express acquiring control over the animal side of life and nature. Giedion (9) estimated that a zoomorphic age, when the animal world was supreme, lasted forty thousand years or more. He noted that we have lost the capacity to comprehend the tremendous strength of the ties that have bound man to animal. Probably through having made the animal sacred, early men attributed qualities to their animal gods that belonged to them. The process of externalization enables some form of differentiation to de-velop. As early men learned to discipline their instincts, those psychological aspects bonding them to an animal state, they were initiated into a new stage. Plate II may call up elements related to initiation, some roots of which may go back to dethronement of the animal gods. Our ancestors, as they began to carry consciousness, were apparently immersed in such a psychological task, alongside a more immediately pressing one, that of separation from matriarchal dominance. We suggest that Plate II has the potential to stir aspects of the psychological task of differentiation in a subject. That *task* (not something we inherit) relates us to the Paleolith, since all men recapitu-late aspects of those tasks in their development. Plate II has a potential for becoming the arena for the psychological qualities associated with *masculine mysteries*. Paleolithic men had to initiate themselves into masculinity. The meaning of Hercules's labors was that of overcoming various mythological animals (composite ones similar to those found in parietal art) so as to overpower the dominance of destructive instincts. Paleolithic men had to differentiate themselves psychologically, something beyond and not inferable from masculine behavior or masculine labor. The human condition requires

FIG. 6. Spear thrower, carved from reindeer horn, from Les Trois Frères, about 23,000 B.C. Carved from the part of the antler where the two tines come together, the animals may be identified as two ibexes playing or fighting. (Leroi-Gourhan, André. *Prehistoire de l'Art Occidental*. Editions d'Art Lucien Mazenod, Paris. Musée de l'Homme, Paris.)

that each man do this at some point for himself today. All men move from a state of helplessness to a state of relative independence. Men begin through the grace and nurture bestowed by matriarchal energy and care. When no psychological differentiation takes place, one remains a drone in the service of the mother. Psychologically, one slips into the place of the son in Figure 5.

One should be clear that initiation is not the same thing as identification. Identification pertains more to the persona or face one has selected to show the world, while initiation is a separate process which may lead to changing the persona but is not the same thing. The nature of a subject's identification may have several faces. It is a complex matter, requiring that we gather information from several Rorschach plates before we can get a full picture of what it means for the subject. Plate II provides structure for

Fig. 7. An artificial ring carved in a block of stone from the rock shelter of Labatut, (Dordogne, France), about 29,000 B.C. An artificial ring is connected with bison in some instances, linking them with matriarchal goddesses. The hourglass shape of the two cupules which meet to form the perforation was done with great care and precision. Giedion (9) noted that the shape of the opening as a double cupule announces its connection with fertility symbolism. (Giedion, S. *The Eternal Present.* Pantheon Books, 1962. Reprinted by permission of Princeton University Press. Photograph by Achille Weider.)

archetypal energy used in discovering the means for separation and definition. Sources of masculine and/or feminine traits in a subject may be found more precisely on other plates.

Figure 7 shows an example of carefully carved circles in stone among the artifacts Paleolithic men left us. Their specific use or meaning is unknown, but for us their presence means that something psychological became associated with the circle as prototype for the experience. The animal shapes in Figure 6 form a circle roughly similar to the circle on Plate II.[5] The large,

―――――――――

[5] Note that the subject whose material we are using to illustrate points about the plates caught something of the psychology of the circle when she saw bears dancing the *hora*. The hora is a Roumanian dance done in a circle, with participants locking arms.

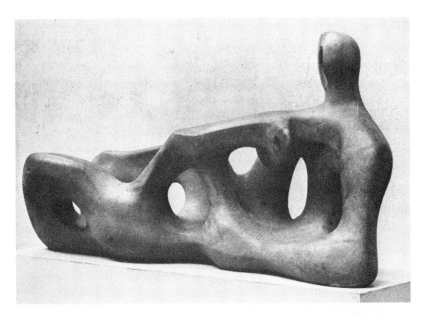

FIG. 8. "Reclining Figure," by Henry Moore. Carved from elmwood, 1939.

dark details of this blot surround a central, circular zone of white space. Some intrinsic quality gives it a sense of space, even depth, like the Paleolithic artifacts exemplified by Figure 7. Smooth circles perforate bone-carved artifacts like the double phallus. In Cornwall on the English open countryside, one may see huge circular stones with smoothly carved central openings among the Neolithic monoliths left there. Perhaps these were familiar to the British sculptor, Henry Moore, whose work abounds in the use of an open circle in its relation to the female torso. Figure 8 shows Moore's means of expressing the significance of the circle and its relation to matriarchal fecundity.

Some have suggested that the importance of experiences attached to the circle began through its use as a protective means. Early men slept inside circles of fire laid out to protect them from wild animals. An easy connection between darkness, fire, and wild beasts comes readily with Plate II's stimulus forms and colors. The bear, a frequent animal percept, was central in Neolithic cult life. One by-product of those cults was the means for disciplining instincts (as noted elsewhere, marrow and brains were not eaten in sacred burials of the bear as a psychological symbol).

While a precise meaning for Paleolithic circles in stone is obscured or lacking, it is consistent with what we know of their rituals (and hence, their psychology) to assume it pertains to the birth channel as a symbol of the source of emerging life. Figure 8 illustrates that connection in a clear fashion. Neumann (26) has analyzed Moore's work in a book on that subject and has shown how much Moore was at home in the matriarchal world as he created sculptural patterns using the archetype of mother-child relationships. Moore has noted the same feature in observing himself. For us, Moore's art shows the viability of an ancient archetype.

Subjects frequently experience Plate II through images of female pelvis, birth canal, and sometimes express its connection with ideas about giving birth.

Unlike Plate I, we are not assuming that this plate has a primary significance or potentiating power associated with the power of functioning of the female and her spheres of life. Our suggestion is that the psychological energy summoned up pertains to differentiation from the feminine and from the power of animal instincts. Correspondingly, we may see how a subject is related to the feminine and his instinctual energy. The problems are masculine in nature, insofar as we may speak of the archetypal significance of this plate. How a female subject responds pertains to whatever it is in her psychology that emerges around her personal experience (positive or negative) of those images as a woman. It is useful to compare this against what emerged for Plate I, and when contrary data emerge (as, what seemed negative on Plate I looks positive on Plate II), then our grasp of the psychological tasks before the subject is widened, possibly offering hints of the directions a subject must take. This kind of comparison often shows us the contrary streams inside one that need to flow together.

A potent stimulus force inherent in this plate centers around its bisexual structure. Female and male sexual organs are positioned opposite to one another. They are *not* attached to a body structure. Plate II, like some Paleolithic cave art, shows male-female complementarity. Thus, it provides qualities conducive to symbol formation and for activation of archetypal energy. The conditions present further the activation of the *law of excluded awareness*. As we have noted, the symbolic significance of bisexual artifacts and sculptured stones showing the birth canal was not erotic. Their function seems connected with ideas about sources, life and its meaning against death, nurture and fertility. These were the psychic substances that led to primitive religions. Paleolithic men lived in a theocracy.

We have suggested that Stone Age artifacts were used in rituals as a means of objectifying differences in power that existed between males and females. Through these means, men learned more about their own essential nature. Matriarchal power constellated a response in males that led to psychological discoveries, on the one hand, and the advancement of consciousness, on the other. The latter may have been an accidental by-product of the former.

When Plate II is held right side up, the smaller phallus is above, and the larger, more visually dominant vagina is below. We have proposed that, when organs are separated from the rest of physical structure, they take on special qualities which may have nothing to do specifically with erotic impulses. Within the laws of visual symbolism, a change in physical state influences the meaning of psychic awareness. In our tradition, the "cross" symbolizes immortality for us, while a bisexual image may have symbolized continuity and immortality for Paleolithic men. Our thesis is that Plate II provides conditions for symbols to be formed around detached organs. When a symbol forms, meaning is transferred from the erotic to an abstract plane. We have found that discoveries about an individual's uncompleted tasks emerge more clearly at an abstract level. Since all men experience them, those tasks are archetypal.

Plate II provides us with a masculine source, a separated phallus, which is more recessive visually than the more dominant female organs associated with giving birth. In the Paleoith, men were faced with a task of finding themselves against female power associated with her birth-giving capacity. Plate II may reinstate qualities of that task in a modern individual. One may ask how strong is this male subject against the power of the feminine. "Feminine" may be his own feminine component, but it will have been shaped by the women who influenced his development. A subject may function physically and sexually as a male and still be unconscious of his lack of differentiation from the power of the feminine. As provider of erotic pleasure, a woman may rule a man in much the same way as a fertility goddess. That kind of man has to differentiate himself from the power of eroticism to find out what he can be *apart* from it. It is a common psychological task of our time, but it links us with our remote ancestors.

For a male subject, what we find on Plate II sets the stage for the kind of masculine structure we may find on Plate IV. For a female subject, this plate may provide an opportunity to collect further data about her own relationship to matriarchal qualities. It elaborates more about how her instincts are connected to or disconnected from feelings. We may see a female subject who has a negative relationship with matriarchal power using masculine modes to defy that power. Psychologically, this has different implications for the female than the male. Thus, a female may find herself isolated from feminine roots, and, unlike a male use of masculine modes, remain undifferentiated from matriarchal power. On the other hand, a male has to take a route in opposition to female dominance, if he wants to differentiate and discover who he is.

Some of the structural qualities of this plate takes us to the sources of mystery in men. We may examine the structure of the phallic figure itself and find it composed of male-oriented elements. Symbol formation requires purity in structure, and exact conditions, or it does not appear. Symbols follow definite laws. They never appear haphazardly or by chance.

As an image divorced from its erotic values, the phallus may represent the means of insuring the continuity of life as much as do female regenerative organs. In a materialistic culture like ours, it is extremely hard for us to separate eroticism from transcendent qualities. We do not even recognize it when we see certain forms of art from other traditions. The content of parietal art is an example. Buddhist art includes a grasp of the nature of symbol formation which has never been achieved in Western art. Some of the subjective phenomena we have called laws, like excluded awareness and psychic correspondence, were known to painters of Buddhist art before the Romans brought Western culture to the shores of Britain. They knew the means of using physical vehicles for transcendent meanings. Through a technique called *arupa dhatu,* a Sanscrit term meaning "formless form," the physical was transferred visually to another plane. Cave paintings at Ajanta[6] in central India are the oldest surviving Buddhist art in the world. The murals there were rediscovered by the British in the last century, but their meanings have been misinterpreted by Western observers up to the present time. In a recent book on Indian art, a Western art expert interpreted the artist-monk's use of transcendent physical vehicles as "decadence." He assumed what he saw referred to carnal fantasies, when those artists painted scenes from the life of the Buddha as theological exercises. Females on the Ajanta murals are especially lovely, but their voluptuous qualities had to do with a symbolism associated with transcending instinctual pleasure. Unlike Western art, Buddhist art is not ornamental. It has the purpose of explaining theology. Monks were artists, and they painted psychological experiences associated with theological problems. They were able to grasp physical qualities on a transcendent plane. Quite like the men of Paleolithic times, they used their physical opposite, qualities of the eternal woman, to discover values in themselves. We believe that Buddhist art represents evidence for our position on Paleolithic and Neolithic art. It shows that men do use art to aid them in accomplishing psychological tasks. We have done little of this in the West, except in some forms of our religious art.

Nepalese and Tibetan art often appears lascivious to a casual observer, but the physical portrayals are transcendent symbols carrying theocratic meaning. Reproductive organs and acts have no erotic meaning in their art forms.

Leroi-Gourhan (17) was perplexed as he failed to find any traces of erotic meaning or sexual fantasies in the parietal art he examined. A Frenchman

---

[6] The author (18) has described the Ajanta murals elsewhere. Murals in four caves antedate the Christian era. Those that contain the finest paintings date from the Gupta period, roughly within the fifth and sixth centuries A.D.

simply could not believe it. We would suggest that *because* parietal art had a religious purpose, it put them in touch with certain technical qualities that we have lost through the material emphasis in Western art forms. Even though prehistoric cave artists lived culturally and psychologically simpler patterns than we, some of their paintings were as masterful as anything we can do today. They were in possession of some facilities we have lost. Following the beginning of the second millennium in the Christian era, we began to lose contact with sources associated with natural symbolism in art. Picasso, cubists, and surrealists have experimented with the sources of symbolism in their art, but for the most part symbols and meaning have been fractionated and not synthesized in their works. The Belgian artist, René Magritte, has made a fruitful effort to synthesize symbolism in his surrealism, but too much conscious intent with a view to effect separates the symbols in his work from the sources we have described. Perhaps the American Negro folk artist, Minnie Evans[7], comes closest to painting symbols that occur from spontaneous subjective sources like those we have described. Unable to read or write, she paints images that appear in front of her. She has said she does not think of them; they occur and she copies them. Almost no consciousness is associated with their emergence. The heavy layerings of consciousness in our Western development have built distance between us and the sources we have referred to in certain forms of art.

The phallic figure on Plate II has a startling resemblance to the so-called "key of life" symbol that is commonly found on ancient Egyptian monuments. As a symbol for life or immortality (an essential meaning for the phallus), it may be traced hieroglyphically to two pictographs.[8] One is T-shaped, and symbolized man, and the other an orb, which symbolized the sun. Ever since Prometheus, man has been associated with his function as bearer of light (fire) and identified with the sun. Man in contact with the sun defines essential maleness through man's function as an organizer of the means for enlightenment. The nature of the structure in this plate may be charged with elements of the "masculine mysteries" and his destiny. Man may pit himself against eternity through experiences with this plate, especially if he (or she) is a disturbed person in a depressed state, toying with suicide or intervention in his own destiny.

Plate II has qualities which may enable psychological experience to transfer spontaneously from physical to transcendent symbolism. This plate has well defined blot contours which look like the primary sexual organs of both sexes. When these organs are separated from body structure, their mediating

---

[7] A detailed account of her art forms has been described by Nina Howell Starr (30). *Newsweek*, August 4, 1969, carries a description of what they described as her "archetypal symbolism."

[8] An observation made by Dr. Edward C. Whitmont, of New York.

power becomes more potent as energizers for archetypal activity. Through this means, some component within our psychic substance separates, in a corresponding way, male and female psychological elements (whichever blot detail is involved) *apart from* sexual impulses. This occurs through the subjective *law of psychic correspondence*. In order to operate on different planes, the context for symbol formation must change. When organs are separated physically, a corresponding psychic change occurs, altering the significance for meaning inside a symbol. The ingredients necessary for a change of plane (and meaning) takes place outside of conscious awareness. Hence, meaning attached to a symbol by the subject who produced them may be entirely erroneous. He has not been conscious of what was happening, and, if he was conscious of it, in some hypothetical sense, it would not have happened. If a subject sees a sexual organ as such (which is often the case), then no symbol formed and the law of excluded awareness was *not* at work. When that is the case, the source for the image was probably in a shadow or persona problem as psychic sources. We may find amplification and meaning for them through appropriate aspects of Freud's libido theory. This may provide us with meaningful and pragmatic data for use with a patient. On the other hand, when we find that the sources for data are archetypal, we may have to move to another plane to decipher the meanings of symbols. On Plate II we may find this plane to include age-old energy at work, that associated with the means for differentiation and separation from the power of the opposite.

As a bisexual vehicle, Plate II does not correspond with those visual qualities found on Plate III, which may elicit comments in a subject about "hermaphroditic features" on the figures. Usually, Plate III's double sex characteristics merely stimulate comments about a subject's visual observations. If, however, Plate II takes us to the symbolism of the hermaphrodite, the plane is different, and the meaning has to be deciphered.

Kerényi and Jung (16) have observed how important it is for us to rediscover symbolic meanings associated with the myths of our heritage. The conscious focus which leads to ascribing meaning to an image may literally displace those qualities the same image carries as archetypal of particular human experiences. A conscious "set" restricts meaning to a single plane. Kérenyi and Jung (16) noted that Priapus carried a symbol for different, even opposed archetypes. It would be interesting to study the psychology of the changes that occur around a symbolic vehicle through its history. Early meanings and functions attributed to a deity often get shunted onto its opposite. When that happens, some subjective law is at work. Priapus, in Greek myth, was the masculine fertility god, and he was in charge of reproductive power. His earliest function was to protect gardens, shepherds, fishermen, and farmers. Yet, he was the son of the chief diety of lasciviousness and obscenity.

We must differentiate the qualities associated with an image or vehicle for energy on different planes, because they may have been experienced differently at different times in our psychology. We must recognize that so much more exists than our conscious attitudes. Consciousness can become much more itself, if we bring to it experiences from wider reaches inside ourselves.

A given individual's problem about differentiation may have to be fought out on two planes, that of the instinct, and that of the transcendent. We need to be circumspect about symbols themselves, since they inform us as to where a subject's battle rages and where solutions may be sought. Our psychological ears must be alert for *double entendre*. The nature of our psychic substance seems to demand it. In so doing, we must not rise too high or sink too low. It is essential to be guided wholly by the data that obtain.

In understanding archetypal forces associated with Plate II, it is useful to consider their range as being restricted. As we see it, its stimulus potentials focus around early stages of individual growth, taking us in a rough way to the level Paleolithic men faced as they differentiated themselves. We may see potentials for more advanced tasks, such as may be required in the process of individuation, as we examine Plate IX.

One of the extraordinary features associated with Rorschach's plates seems to be related to chronology. From the first plate to the last one, some order in sequence appears to correspond to progressive stages in man's psychological development. We, as modern individuals, may be fixed at a stage, anywhere along the course of psychological development.

The subject's imagery for this plate included:

W   Two dancing bears, they have slippers on their forepaws, dancing the hora, they are all bloody, and the butterfly is squashed in between them.

D   Down here I've found the Pietà, it doesn't look like human . . . the face and body lying over like that, the body is across her knees, in the red, the body of Christ is still bloody.

d   Two bookends, maybe of monkeys, with dunce caps on.

Our female subject responded to the phallic form on this plate as "bookends," and she attributed monkey and dunce qualities to that inanimate image. For the lower, large red detail (female area), she reported a highly complex image, "Pietà, Mary and the bloody body of Christ." The *laws of altered perception and psychic correspondence* must have been at work for the second image to have occurred. In simplest form, the patient experiences the feminine with an element of high sacrifice, and the masculine with books, the record of knowledge. We have have already seen how much differentiation between masculine and feminine elements is problematic for her. She attached a characteristically masculine value to the male area, but we do not view that image of hers as a symbol. More likely, ego values and energy associated with a personal complex served as sources for the image. We have seen that logos power is important to her. Perhaps "dunce" reflects how impotent she feels against logos power, and "monkey" reflects an instinctual aspect of coping with striving for logos power, on the one hand, and feeling impotent against it, on the other.

At any rate, this plate stirs up energy associated with pain, sacrifice, and pathos for this subject. Through a subjective means, she projected inside the lower red detail, an image of Mary, the archetypal vehicle of purity in feminine instincts, the mother of Christ. Mary was invested with powers of intercession through her purity by the Catholic Church. However, in her relationship with her son, she did not carry much archetypal energy as matriarch. She had no power over her son by the time he reached 13. He was totally identified with the archetype of God the Father. Mary was impotent to influence her son as he went about "his father's business." Yet, through her as a symbol of purity, she had the archetypal power to transcend instincts sexually as a means for reproduction. Some aspect of the psyche of our patient was caught up in that psychology as her perceptual process became altered and she experienced a transcendent symbol. Mary's behavior and her psychological abilities set the stage so that her son could accomplish the task of discarding human values. Yet, as "Pietà," Mary is her most human self, set among those forces in her that were in complete identity with human values. We refer to motherhood and the loss of her son. The "Pietà" does not pertain to the symbolism of the divine mission her son succeeded in accomplishing.

A struggle in our subject seems deeply rooted in archetypal energy. Through the *law of altered perception* and the *laws of excluded awareness* and *psychic correspondence* a powerful image was forced on the screen of subjective consciousness. She perceived a male form inside the confines of the blot's female sexual area, and a complex form of the symbol of sexual reversal ensued. We must discover what discarding instincts means for this subject. We must analyze if it is appropriate for her particular stage. Her ego may not be able to tolerate it. She may be in danger of totally sacrificing her feminine instincts for a chimera. This is the stuff of deification, and it requires long preparation (that is, to grasp its symbol). Psychologically, this subject is in full face with her destiny, and the pressures may be so strong that she may destroy herself. However, we see that she has a source within her that enables her to displace her problems from the instinctual plane. If she can make use of this, she may be able to get perspective about what this means for her as an individual. Much of her psychology (so far) suggests that a resolution of contrary forces within her may demand a high price. We need more data from her psychology to predict more at this point. It is not difficult to connect the complicated symbolism that emerged from this plate with its being a carrier of special energy associated with the archetypes of birth, rebirth, reproduction, sacrifice, and death.

In order to keep to our mission, we will not complicate interpretation of the subject's imagery beyond the specific purposes we have for it. Her material illustrates the concepts, terms, sources, and laws we have proposed. What we conclude about her images may not be either complete or fully illuminating insofar as her dynamics, defenses, and complexes are concerned.

PLATE III

Since this plate is dominated by two large details usually seen as human beings, one would expect this blot to stir up the more socialized, humanized, personal contents within the psyche. The complexes that are activated tend more to be associated with persona and shadow problems. Corresponding psychic sources come into play. It is important to note that each figure has well defined appendages that may be easily observable as sexual organs, which lead to a subject's identification of the gender of the figures. Designation of male or female or hermaphroditic qualities may be made through

PLATE III

objective perceptual evidence, and those sexual characteristics that are
present are appropriately placed on a body structure. The qualities we have
discussed about bisexual features in Plate II do not apply here. Other
psychological determinants are involved when a subject reports these figures
as "hermaphrodites." The *law of excluded awareness* is not at work nor
has a symbol formed. One would not be dealing with an archetypal source.
Such an image may reflect aspects of a personal sexual complex, but its
nature and degree cannot be determined from such an image taken alone.
Since sexual organs occur appropriately on Plate III, they tend to specify
perceptually an instinctual response associated with sexual impulses. Someone who refuses to make note of the gender of the figures is usually avoiding
doing so consciously.

As a hook for projections, this plate commonly supplies us with information about shadow problems (the figures are appropriately dark) and
qualities associated with what the subject has become as a result of his experiences with others. Extraversion is that mode of perception in which data
for judgments are gathered externally, through experience with others.
People are the major means of apperception. Introversion is that mode of
perception in which data for judgments are gathered inwardly, and values
are determined through subjective, not objective experiences. Inner experiences are the major means of apperception. While all people have
potentials to experience and perceive through either mode, developmental
processes in a child influence a dominant perceptual mode. Habits form
which get fixed. Experience suggests that children begin with a predilection
toward one mode or the other. When an opposite mode is furthered by
important figures in a child's development, problems may arise. On the
other hand, the ratio between degrees of introversion and extraversion in
a person is not fixed, but in flux. At the same time, preponderant patterns
exist and an absence of extraversive energy in an extremely introverted person may endanger the power of his conciousness to control his behavior.
Schizophrenia is a pathological form of introversion and manic states
represent pathological extraversion. Circumstantiality in an individual who
is in danger of a psychosis often reflects that person's maximal efforts to keep
hold of extraverted qualities.

Youth is the extraverted time of life, and it is rather common to observe
an extraverted youth become more contemplative and introverted in middle
life. Nature often balances us against an introversive-extraversive axis.
Plate III may give us valuable information about those modes of perception.
Both introversion and extraversion are archetypal; they are energized by experience that has been common to all men.

We must be careful to distinguish between ego attitudes and archetypal
sources when we consider the kind of movement the figures of this plate

FIG. 9. "Family Group," a bronze by Henry Moore, 1947. This sculpture ex-
presses the archetype of *interaction* in the family unit, and the figures on Plate III are
perpetually drawn into a form of interaction by the lower large detail that their hands
join, as in the Moore bronze. We have emphasized that a central meaning behind the
significance of human figures in movement in the Rorschach experience includes what
the subject has become himself through interaction with family figures and others in
early development. Moore's bronze provides us with a powerful experience of the
meaning of interaction which underlies later interpersonal behavior.

may show. If the figures are in extraverted activity, it is naive to assume similar qualities in the subject. They may be present in the subject, but that is not the route to confirm it. Further, the nature and depth of human relationships are not defined by the perceptual mode. An extravert may have no real friends, and an introvert may have many. *Balance* between introversion-extraversion is more closely related to the extent and quality of an individual's relationships. We may look for clues about these matters in Plate III.

The significance of human movement in Rorschach imagery has been a subject of much controversy. It has generated some of the best research design that has been applied to projective techniques. The author (20) studied a group of preadolescent boys with muscular dystrophy with a view toward how much they used fantasy and what sort of movement appeared in fantasy, since they were unable to move about independently. While the boys showed qualitative differences in their fantasies, the inability to move probably did not alter the amount of fantasy engaged in by an individual. Further, because they could not move about, we did not find that they turned more toward subjectivity or thinking because they needed substitutes. Some did fantasize about physical feats they were incapable of and some did not. However, we failed to establish a proper criterion for each boy studied. If we had obtained an index for each subject's *perceptual mode,* our findings would have held more general significance.

Hermann Rorschach's (29) most penetrating insights and grasp of human psychology centered around his view of the significance of human movement in inkblot experience. He connected its meaning with an ability to fantasize, and with introversive tendencies. It is consistent with our definition to assume that an introversive perceptual mode moves more easily inward. At the same time, we do not have any evidence that an individual with a predominantly extraverted mode uses fantasy less. Fantasy may be an outgrowth of whatever perceptions may be present, but it is not the *means* by which the percepts were gathered. We would assume that the content of fantasy tends to differ in relation to the perceptual mode that gathered it. While color in Rorschach is clearly related to the quality of feelings in human experience, it is not identical with an extraverted perceptual mode. Since Hermann Rorschach tended to rely on the manner color was used by the subject to define his view of extraversion, it should be clear that we are not using these terms in the same way that he did.

Because *Erlebnistypus* as conceived by Rorschach denotes a balance between ratios of extraversion and introversion (and it does not define the source for those qualities), we have used that concept of Rorschach's in much the same way as he did.

We cannot assume that a person with a dominant introverted mode tends to fantasize in an extraverted one. It may happen, but we cannot assume it. We would be inclined to expect the reverse; that is, a dominant mode tends to influence the content and perhaps extent. A multidimensioned personality may have the facility to move about in different modes owing to a more balanced state between introversion and extraversion. Patient populations do not commonly tend to show balance between modes.

In order to distinguish between archetypal sources and ego attitudes in relation to material associated with Plate III, we must be on the lookout for the conditions that further them. When the human figures are experienced as animal figures, we should be alerted for possible signs of the *law of excluded awareness*. This kind of experience may take us to a state in an individual in which a natural tendency for an opposite perceptual mode was tampered with in development. We suspect that a wide variety of disorders and symptoms may take origin from the manner in which parents' ambitions condition a child against his destiny or Karma or *Erlebnistypus*.

Experience has shown that the lower half of the human figures on Plate III can be a hook for powerful projections. These projections may be specifically sexual and they may not. When the lower half of the figures is perceptually split away from the upper (and there is objectively a separation of the blot), the conditions for symbol formation may pertain. The lower limbs of the figures are often seen as "fish" when they are reported separately. A Paleolithic artifact of fish-phallus may have a great correspondence to those large details. An appendage on the upper thigh of either figure may be seen as the figure's phallus. Images of phallus-as-fish come to us from the most ancient times. It had a fertility meaning. When this blot area (lower part of the human figure) has not been experienced as part of the figure, and the upper half of a human was seen, the nature of the image associated with this part of the blot may have archetypal sources.

Our subject experienced Plate III as follows:

W   Two blackamoors warming their hands over a fire. They are men, maybe they should be women because of the breasts, but they are men to me, they look like men.

D   I see the lower trunk (legs and skirt) of two women with high heels, but you can just see the lower part of their trunk. Skirts blowing in wind.

S   The blackamoors look like they have on high white collars and frilled front shirts and studs on the collars, and handkerchiefs inside pockets.

We have already seen that our subject is open to inner experiences. Does this mean that her perceptual mode is an introversive one? Perhaps, but her psychological disturbance may force her to attend to inner processes because the ego has lost some of its energy or power to direct psychic activity.

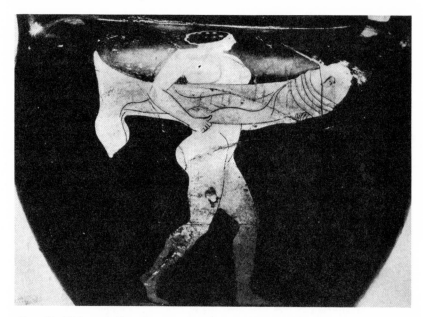

Fig. 10. Fish-as-phallus. From a Greek vase by the Pan Painter, sixth century, B.C. The painting celebrates the Haloa Festival, one of the mystery rites for women (only) at Eleusis, in which the fish-phallus was a regenerative symbol. Since certain Paleolithic bone carvings show fish (and feather) on one side and the phallus on the obverse, the roots for this Greek festival probably extend back to the fertility rites of the Stone Age. Connecting the phallus to particular symbols shows how this organ was subject to a two-fold psychological meaning from the beginning of our cultural origins. The rites were performed by women who were examining their own nature against male energy. Feather-as-phallus suggests the rising, or soaring aspect of masculine energy, while fish-as-phallus suggests the sinking, or downward plunging aspect of masculine energy. The latter may pertain to sexual pleasure or fecundity. The fish-like large detail under the torsos of the figure on Plate III also carries the phallic form for the figures. The detail is well known for its capacity to catch projections associated with phallic complexes. The winged phallic detail on Plate VI may carry the two-fold psychological meaning for phallus as the concrete reference for masculine energy. The way a subject experiences these details offers us clues about his level of psychological development.

We see that this patient shows clear signs that archetypal sources have been activated through Plate III.

Because of the way outer appearances and nuances about what she sees on figures are important to her (despite what we have seen to be an inner pull), we may tentatively assume that prior to a more disturbed state, the subject's dominant perceptual mode was extraverted. She is acutely aware of outer data, which influence her judgments. On the other hand, there is a major exception to that: her perceptual mode is wholly introverted when "breasts," outer data, are noted but ignored. "Breasts" tend to be a kind of *bête noir* for this subject. A subjective source determined the nature of her experience of the gender of the figures. Our guess would be that because the subject had too little introversive capacity (contact with inner sources) prior to her disturbance, when she came into a state associated with a lowered level of consciousness, the power of inner (introverted) experiences overwhelmed her. Because she had so little contact with inner resources, relationships were problematic for her. Extraversion does not guarantee good relationships. We do not view her designation of maleness for the figures here as having involved excluded awareness or symbol formation, or reversal. An introversive mode imposed itself and rendered the power of the ego impotent for that particular decision.

When the lower halves of the bodies of the figures were separated and seen as female, and the male appendages were perceived as "skirts" then the *law of excluded awareness* did influence her experience, and something akin to sexual reversal did take place.

No human movement was projected onto the figures. Her percepts of them tended to prevent natural movement. However, we are not able to say that therefore we see no evidence for the tendency to use fantasy. Her history did indeed show that she had had an extraversive manner, but she was plagued with an inability to sustain relationships. She had been "too busy" for reflection, and when she became disturbed, she fell headlong into the power of inner experiences.

She has a powerful complex associated with her female identity. However, it was not her facility to produce human movement against Rorschach stimuli that shows us that her fantasy world is rich. Ascribing a "capacity for fantasy" as the primary meaning for human movement in Rorschach material is too narrow a use of the meaning movement may have. Introverted fantasy uses a variety of vehicles (other than M) as it becomes experience.

We suggest that human movement associated with Rorschach images carries information about what one has become through experiences *with* others. Insofar as a subject is introverted or extraverted, the content of its meaning may differ. When we frame the meaning for human movement against what we can discover about the dominant perceptual mode, interpretation may be enriched. Techniques other than the Rorschach provide us with information about characteristics of a person's perceptual mode. It is highly useful to compare data from other sources with data from the Rorschach in that regard.

After one has established what has transpired naturally as a subject experiences Plate III, images that occur may be used to push the subject for more data. This may be more useful for data obtained from this plate than for data from several others. Subjects are in a good position to use memory and the contents of consciousness about their personal experiences. Human figures may take us immediately to complexes, and the subject may be relatively aware about them. On the other hand, even an original image may have no meaning to the subject who produced it. When the sources that spawned it (frequently archetypal) and the *laws of altered perception* or *excluded awareness* participated, a subject's free associations about the image may never take him to deciphering its meaning. In fact, we must always be on guard against a subject's own guess about the meaning of Rorschach material. His state of openness to inner processes tends to influence what he may apprehend. However, conscious associations are an inappropriate means for deciphering material from archetypal sources. We interpret the image against a need to bring back some form of excluded awareness. Consciousnesss may not contain any data at all about the matter: hence, the necessity for the skill of grasping meaning for subjective experiences through an objective observer. We must apprehend subjective data through the means that are appropriate for them. When contaminations from personal material for the observer are absent, awareness in an observer (interpreter) is the only objective means we have for examining subjective data.

PLATE IV

Usually, archetypal energy is at work when the qualities aroused by a stimulus are consistent, though those features which account for stimulus reliability remain elusive. Most clinicians agree that Plate IV consistently produces material associated with masculinity. It is often referred to as the "father card." Quite unlike the Thematic Apperception Test (T.A.T.) picture associated with images of father and son, it is hard to explain directly Plate IV's relation to masculinity. This is because conscious connections about masculinity are by-passed through Plate IV, and not with the T.A.T.'s picture which portrays fatherhood or masculine authority directly. This plate takes us into the *patriarchal* world, including fatherhood, as it is related to the family, clan, or tribe. Psychologically, its substance has accrued through the work of the Paleolith, but its form comes more from Neolithic times when men had acquired a degree of separation from matriarchal power. Definition for malenesss had taken form, and aspects of a separate masculine psyche had emerged. "Bull's head" is a not infrequent association for this blot and that image has considerable correlation in appearance with bull heads and horns in Neolithic religious cults.

Various means have been used to account for Plate IV's masculine qualities. These have included the plate's impact of power and strength, the common image of "giant," images of a giant ape, and the power evoked by the qualities of its shading. Boots, animal skin as trophy (prowess), horns, a

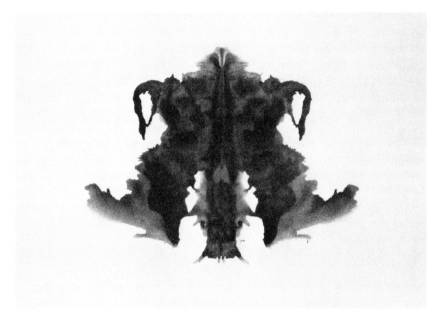

PLATE IV

large phallic form between two huge legs, easily seen dogs, dog's head, and other features do pertain to the masculine side of life.

As we look at Plate IV in the context of paleopsychology, archetypally we may be taken back to the roots in us associated with the hunting culture from whence we came. Sometimes, a Stone Age implement is reported for the upper central portion of the blot, as an arrowhead or spear. With the recent disappearance of the American frontier, the hunt has been diluted to a sport. In his book on hunters of the northern ice, Richard Nelson (25) has described how hunting skills disappear rapidly in youngest Eskimo generations as the American way is brought into an arctic village. When he hunts, modern man in the West is impelled by something with archetypal power. While fantasies about an African safari may still capture the imagination of an adolescent boy, the hunt as a means to masculine initiation is on the wane. Plate IV may best be understood as an *encounter*. Its structure links Captain Marlow and Stone Age men as they glance at each other for the first time. John Milton (23), writing in *Natural History* magazine, described an encounter he had with a grizzly bear in an arctic wilderness. Man encounters his own brute force if archetypal energy is activated through Plate IV. That is different from prowess as hunter or skill in the chase. Those aspects of the male archetype may be on the road to extinction. Its energy may be taking shape through a new vehicle, that of conservation and protection of the environment. Our concern with the state of our environment is becoming so charged with energy, this decade may see the birth of a new archetype. It is a collective and not an individual affair. Recently, the author spoke with a small boy who was startlingly concerned about pollution.

Plate IV may provide us with information about the *archetype of masculine structure* as a basis for the *masculine psyche*. Something of its essence includes components related to what Paleolithic men had to grasp about themselves to discover their nature and find the masculine source of psychological *power*.

Masculine power requires energy. This plate enables us to observe qualities about a subject's personal masculine structure against the archetypal one, and how his personal structure is energized. Whatever the conditions are for an individual that lead him in adulthood tend to bring him to a conscious appraisal of himself as a man. That part of him is his "identification." We do not see anything about identification *directly* from this plate. A subject who sees the plate as a "caterpillar" (and this is not rare) shows an extremely weak energy source in his masculine structure. This may lead to a negative identification with his masculine substance and problems associated with sexual behavior and adaptation.

Some of the psychological structure of Plate IV allies all men, linking us with the Paleolith and all that went before it: the male inheritance. It enables us to define what we mean by *collective*. It is chromosomal. The essence here is not identical with the many-layered cerebral folds that support the complicated psyche of modern man, but the understructure that has supported man's ability to become. It does not have to do specifically with thinking or logos power in masculine structure; it is the nature in man having to do with his brute force. This does not mean that we may not catch a male subject's ego complexes or psychological correlates with problems about "identification." Any Rorschach plate may catch them, but human figures and certain animals are better vehicles to catch those forms of projection than this plate, *per se*. We must be rigidly circumspect about the route for a psychological interpretation. So long as we examine sources and the nature of image ingredients, we have a basis for objectivity. The patient who saw a "caterpillar" for this plate did indeed have what is commonly called an "identification" problem, but knowledge of that alone does not really provide us with more data than if we had simply asked the patient to describe his level of esteem of himself as a male. Chances are high he would say it is low.

Commonly, Plate IV carries us to a mythic figure, that of "giant." As an image, giant carries psychological importance as a container for *aspiration*. It is outside the psychology of a little girl to aspire to be a male giant or, if she does, the quality of her development is in question. This is not the same

FIG. 11. Bison from the nave at Lascaux, 13,000 B.C. These bison with horns curled back onto the head, like the horns on Plate IV, provide us with an idea of the meaning of *encounter* with brute force, an archetypal aspect of the structure of the masculine psyche. This encounter may elicit a sense of weak helplessness in a male subject who is in a negative relationship with masculine power, or fear and panic in a female subject. Like the impersonal quality existing at the roots of the feminine psyche, brute force in masculine structure can be destructive in the experience with the sexual opposite. The sexually obsessed female, who usually is in a negative relationship with her matriarchal energy, throws all her means into an attempt to subjugate this aspect of the male and to put his energy into her service, as Ishtar or Hecate may have done of old. The difference lies in the obsessive nature of the complex, since the matriarchal goddesses were free to nurture and further the cause of the male, because part of their function was to preserve the species. (Leroi-Gourhan, André. *Prehistoire de l'Art Occidental.* Editions d'Art Lucien Mazenod, Paris. Photograph by Jean Vertut.)

thing as aspiration for phallic power, which is a wholly different issue. In the beginning, a son is small and his father looms large indeed, and he aspires to be *big like* his father. He may not even like his father and still have that aspiration. The son sees that size brings power. In fairy tales, where we find psychological authenticity about the child's nature, giants usually display a *negative relationship* with power. Giants, through an abundance of power supplied by sheer superiority in strength, usually subordinate humans and keep them at bay. *Jack and the Beanstalk* shows us about the importance of power in a boy's fantasy. Jack became "somebody" through his own efforts. In the earliest version, Jack's father was dead. Even in those versions in which the tale was tampered with and a father was included, the father was made an invalid. Nowhere does Jack's real father play any role in the story. Since Jack lived with his mother, and he certainly became the family provider, if it was an Oedipal complex that had bothered him, there was nothing to prevent him and his mother from living happily ever after (if on slender means). No story would have emerged. His mother, if anything, hindered Jack's endeavors, though she applauded him when those endeavors raised her standard of living. Jack's fantasy was not to be big and strong like his father, who, if he had any at all, was very weak, but to make discoveries and kill someone with great strength and power. We could say that Jack's mother had no relation to the power of masculine energy, and that, because the giant's wife did, she enabled Jack to overcome the brute strength of her husband. She was a fantasy mother for Jack, who was different from his own mother, whose views were limited on every matter that emerged. Through a new kind of relationship with a protective female helper, he dealt in fantasy with the vacuum that existed for him about the meaning of masculine power. The story includes other psychological symbols such as the bag of gold, a hen that laid golden eggs, and a magic harp. It is, though, Jack's relation to the negative use of masculine power that pertains primarily to our understanding of the psychology of Plate IV.

The God of the Old Testament, Yahweh, tested Abraham's relation to his masculine power when he ordered the sacrifice of his own son on an altar. Yahweh was interested in Abraham's faith, but he observed its strength on a male power plane. The power Yahweh held could be positive or negative for the children of Israel. Plate IV may potentiate qualities associated with the *archetype of God-the-Father*. Modern man comes into contact with the archetype of this experience when he hears God's voice speak to him in a dream, or in a psychologically disturbed state. One may have no conscious involvement with religion and still experience powerful Yahweh qualities in himself through this plate. A son may be in a negative relationship with the power held by his father. One sees this in situations where a father forces his son into the family business against his son's wishes. The negative relationship is not based on competition for the mother's affection but on sheer power imposed through the masculine line. A son may be in a negative relationship and not be aware of it consciously. We can see how an identification with the father may be a negative one. A son who acts according to masculine modes, yet jumps through hoops set up by the power of his father through material control and the family business, may never have found his own sense of independence from patriarchal power. *Jack and the Beanstalk* has to do with that realm of psychology.

We do *not* suggest that each time a male subject reports "a giant" for Plate IV that the subject is in a negative relationship with his father's power. Only if we can show that archetypal energy was included in the source for the image may that be the case. The figure central to this plate is balanced around power. His upper half has qualities suggesting an impact much weaker than the lower half. This differential (above and below) may set going an archetypal reaction through a symbolism contrasting weakness versus strength, as it pertains to a subject's masculine structure and the way it is energized. Plate IV seen as "a caterpillar" by a male subject probably emerged through the laws of symbol formation. Psychologically, the strong was rendered weak via psychological experience through the *law of excluded awareness*. The subject experienced a power problem, and, while it may find expression through sexual energy too, it is basically an aspect of how one is related to masculine power similar to Jack's tasks as he climbed into his fantasy through his beanstalk.

Plate IV has to do with the natural man, not the good man or the bad man or the ideal man, but man as he is related to his personal source of masculine energy. We need specific data to substantiate it, if the subject's power problem gets fixed to a sexual mode.

A female subject is more likely to connect sex and the function of power psychologically than a male subject through this plate. Plate IV is not related archetypally to the sources of female power. A given female may have a power problem, and she may have a high index of masculine traits, and both may be projected onto this plate, but Plate IV is not associated structurally with psychic power in women. We have no *Jill and the Beanstalk,* because it is outside the psychology of the girl. The giant's wife may have relevance for her development as a woman against the male (as husband and son), but the fantasy is not a girl's fantasy. She has *Cinderella* instead. That has relevance to matriarchal power, and its psychology is appropriate to Plate I for a female.

Yet, a daughter comes into relationship with the power of her father's authority (or lack of it), and she may develop a complex as a consequence. Some aspect of that psychology may emerge in connection with Plate IV. A woman's relationship with masculine power is not necessarily negative.

When it is negative, her psychological task in coping with it is different from a male's. A woman's power problem is usually associated with the matriarch and how she energizes her power. There is no corresponding matriarchal substance in the structure of Plate IV. It remains that any subject, male or female, may have such a pervasive power problem, or sexual complex, that it is projected on every plate. That indeed occurs. However, it does not aid us in our search about the stimulus qualities that are individual for a particular plate.

The authenticity of the structure of Plate IV as a prototype for the masculine psyche is shown through an additional arrangement and presence of recessive feminine qualities. The genital features which may be perceived are appropriately placed for psychological impact. The large lower detail positioned between two well defined legs is often seen as a penis. It is large enough to match other physical features when an image of "giant" is reported. It is, in fact, too out-sized, and it is not so much its form quality, but its position and the generalized masculine power of the plate that tends to bring penis to mind in an observer. Most importantly, it is positioned properly, being attached to a physical frame. On the other hand, the female

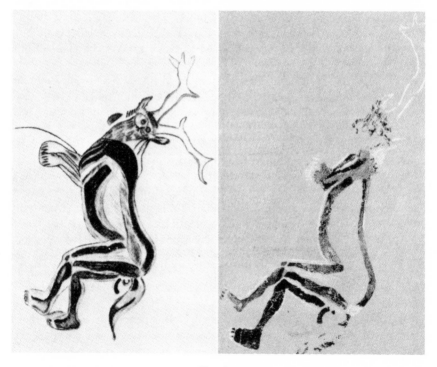

Fig. 12.

organ at the top of the plate is not positioned on a proper body, it is displaced, and it is much less easily perceived than the penis. There are size differences between them, though the form quality for an image of a vulva is more accurate than the form quality of an image of penis for the areas involved.

Plate IV has a structure which provides for an expression of masculine qualities as dominant, and feminine qualities as recessive. The large lower detail may be seen as the head of a cow, doe, and even a snail (less frequently). The plate's bold masculinity does not exclude stimuli appropriate for passive experience, which is part of a differentiated masculine structure. Paleolithic men, in their search for psychological definition, used palettes and brushes, a passive, introverted means, as they expressed themselves psychologically. Masculine endeavors for them were not simply hunting or the means for requiting physical appetites. Some of them were consummate artists. So, even though stimuli for male functions of power, strength, and virility tend to be dominant vehicles, recessive traits of a more feminine mode must be present for authentic masculinity. Because those traits are

FIG. 12. The "sorcerer," engraved and painted in a recess in the sanctuary chamber of Les Trois Frères cave in France, 10,000–12,000 B.C. This drawing may be as much as 3,000 years later than Figure 11. The left drawing was done years ago by Abbé Breuil, the right one from recent photographs, both taken from Ucko and Rosenfeld (31). This figure occurs at the highest and innermost point of a chamber that is decorated with hundreds of figures, displaying perhaps the richest symbolism in parietal art. The legs and thighs are human, the tail is that of a horse or wild ass, the paws and upper torso and head of a bear, the eyes of an owl, and the horns of a reindeer. Other horned, dancing male figures have been found in the remotest, deepest aspect of other caves, but none so complex as this. Similar to Plate IV, the feet and legs provide the dominant cue that the figure is a human one, while certain animal qualities are superimposed for symbolic purposes. We suggest the "sorcerer" was a composite, imaginary masculine god for the Paleolithic artist, who served as a means of offering to the male a psychological sense of independence from matriarchal rule which dominated his life. The hermaphroditic quality of self-fertilization leaves out the female as necessary for the life cycle (taken from the position of the sex organs). Further, the figure's composite nature includes those qualities the male needed to discipline his various instincts. Thus, the "sorcerer" may represent the prototype of man's effort to differentiate his masculine structure and extend its meaning beyond brute force and undirected instinctual expression. We take this as evidence that parietal artists were working psychologically to extend self-definition in the Paleolith. This was the means of the formation of the structure of the masculine psyche. One may note a correspondence between the sexual parts of the "sorcerer" turned back toward the body against the frame of a large tail and the large detail between the leg portions on Plate IV. The visual connections between forms in ancient art and a modern subject's perception of Rorschach contours are not a matter of some vague, inherited "memory." The correspondence exists in the nature of the psychological experience which may be triggered, and these experiences are universal inside the human condition.

generally recessive in men, and because an individual's conscious estimate of himself as a man may exclude awareness of his own feminine traits, the primary female vehicle, vulva, appears on Plate IV in a displaced fashion. Symbolism associated with recessive traits requires archetypal power to be energized. What happens in a given person, whether a subject is male or female, tells us something about how masculine energy is experienced. For a man, we see something about how he projects himself in relation to his masculine structure. For a woman, we may find a persona problem or a complex, or we may find information about how she experiences the masculine side of life. A male subject with a powerful complex about his feminine traits may experience recessive feminine qualities in Plate IV as the dominant ones. It is then necessary to identify sources for that subject's imagery, if one wishes to remain objective. This enables us to learn whether there is a structural defect or an energy problem. The prognosis for development is different in each case. Structural problems are much more difficult to overcome. A male subject who reports a female sexual organ for the appropriate area of this plate may or may not have a structural defect or sexual complex. We need other images and a context, and a judgment about the source of the image before we can establish an accurate evaluation.

The perceptually recessive female area is rather uniquely juxtapositioned to the head of Plate IV's figure. The head is the seat of consciousness and the organ that enables us to govern our impulses. The art forms that come down to us from the Paleolith show us that those men had developed *controls* as pertained to their sexual impulses. They had separated the sacred from the profane insofar as their view of women was concerned. Archetypal experience grew around that relationship. When this aspect of existence is ignored, trouble may develop psychologically. We can see that brute force is only an aspect of masculine structure. Stanley Kowalski, in Tennessee Williams' *Streetcar Named Desire* is an example of a male undifferentiated from his brute force. He was not, though, psychologically a "cave man," since we know early men expressed the collective experience of separating spiritual from carnal qualities. An image of "a giant with sex on his mind" would be an example of a subject who has lost the power to differentiate himself as male. Taking responsibility for his actions is an essential aspect of the archetype of masculinity. Early men learned this through comparing themselves psychologically with the female of the species. The female had different psychological tasks.

At times, the contents caught around a specific detail may carry crucial information, while the rest of the images for a given plate may be relatively sterile of psychological information. Surprise, the unexpected, a sudden sense of awe, and an unlimited arrangement and rearrangement of patterns make the human psyche the most exciting and complicated product of nature.

Through experience, one finds that the side projections that extend out and down from the upper half of the plate often serve as hooks for the projection of the state of male sexual energy. Goose or swan necks are not infrequent images for the detail. These projections make up the horns of a bison or bull, when the head of either is experienced for the whole of the blot. The horn of a powerful animal has carried meanings about fertility since men left off dreaming and became conscious of themselves. They take us to the psychological world of the mother goddess, and not to the more obvious power, strength, and aggression we associate with a bull and his horns today. Archetypal meaning is seldom, if ever, connected with external appearances and outer qualities. From the fertility goddess of Laussel, holding a bison horn, directly down through Crete to Greece, the bull and his horns have been connected with the rule of the dominant female, for purposes of fertility. That was the meaning of the giant bull horns at the palace at Knossos. Neumann (27) has traced for us how the bull, as the male instrument of fertility, symbolized the son-lover of the cult goddess. He was in her service and she sacrificed him at will for purposes of the fertility cult. The mother-goddess of the Creto-Mycenaean religion was worshipped in caves and her priests were women. Plate IV's horns may catch archetypal energy from those sources in us. A subject's relationship to his fertility and sexual potency may appear without traveling through an archetypal source. However, when this area is involved, sexual complexes may be a function of the male's being psychologically in the service of matriarchal power. A male subject, who had a sexual complex and then made considerable progress, reported two different images for this blot detail (including the connection from neck detail to body of the plate) a year apart. First, he saw "A primitive cross-bow, a weapon from olden times," and later, "An Irish harp." Potency was one aspect of his problem. It became clear that it was based in part on his inability to feel. As he became able to feel more with others, his hostility level diminished, and he learned to express his own brand of masculine energy. A magic harp was one of the giant's possessions which Jack gained in the beanstalk saga. Music is a form of feeling-expression, and it is usually hard to come by when one is in a negative relationship with power and force.

One might say that a subject who sees "limp penises" for the horn details probably has a potency problem, and one can grasp this without recourse to mythology. That may be perfectly true. While the expression may be simple and direct, ostensibly no symbolism was involved. Nevertheless, the complex behind diminished potency may be complicated. This particular vehicle may provide us with a particular kind of clue to an individual's problem, when we are alerted for it. Being in service to matriarchal power is only one avenue to impotence, and it does not lead inevitably to impotence.

Our female subject's imagery for Plate IV included:

1. There's the old sea monster again, and two shoes on front legs.
2. There are two hooks to hang it up with.
3. The wolf in *Brer Rabbit*, Walt Disney's version.
4. It looks like men's genitals up at the top.

When the inner masculine is so powerful for a woman, she may be unable to tolerate whatever is essentially feminine in her. It appears that this may be the case for our subject. Through the *laws of symbol formation* and *excluded awareness,* the female area was reversed into its opposite, male genitals. The subject has a sexual complex, but it was not the presence of the complex that produced a symbolism of her sexual opposite. Her relationship to herself as a woman is at stake and her consciousness may not be equal to its task of remaining in control. Sex is one avenue through which her pervasive problem is shown. Masculine sources represent the monster from the deep for her as she apprehends masculine substance and comes into an encounter with it. One gets power over it when it can be hung up by two hooks; it is deanimated and rendered impotent. She probably misuses her feminine power, her natural fecundity, for her own gain and feeds her sexual complex at the expense of males she needs to exploit. She even mixes predation with cunning. *Brer Rabbit* was in constant interplay with a fox and not a wolf. At any rate, through a folk tale, she shows us how something in her is in constant interplay with masculine forces, a power struggle in which each side tries to outsmart the other. In *Brer Rabbit,* the underdog wins out through guile and deception. The weak triumphs over the strong. It contains the psychology of the oppressed black man who, through a passive vehicle, the rabbit, outsmarts the much larger, better equipped, and more aggressive fox (white man). Children, as underdogs, easily grasp the nature of this power struggle. For our patient, the struggle is between masculine and feminine forces in her, and we have already seen the vulnerability she has about sacrificing her femininity. This struggle is played out on two planes. One is inside and archetypal; the other is external and is expressed in her relationships through a sexual complex. The Rorschach enables us to look behind the scenes and make estimates about the odds.

PLATE V

Like Plate III, a forceful design tends to impose itself on perception through the specificity of the contours of the blot. This leads the subject more to a conscious choice than do some of the other plates. However, more than

PLATE V

for Plate III, when a subject does not respond to the obvious shape of butter-fly or bat, rather powerful material from either a personal complex or arche-typal sources emerges. This is one reason why prolonged blocking in a subject for Plate V has been associated with schizophrenia. The subjective experience behind "blocking" may be the astonishment and confusion the ego experiences when it is confronted with images from two worlds simul-taneously. One is the obvious, the reasonable and the logical, and the other may be something fantastic, unreal, and even frightening. Plate V may chal-lenge the ego's authority to rule consciousness, under certain conditions. Something archetypal about the separation between consciousness and the unconscious may get stirred up by Plate V's center line. Subjects respond to a belief that "something is hidden," or one thing is behind another, for this plate. We do not believe this is mainly due to "blocking associated with a sex-ual complex." There are patients who have so powerful a sexual complex that they project that complex indiscriminately and everywhere. That may happen on Plate V. Yet, this plate has the stimulus capacity to split sexual energy from an instinctual base to an archetypal plane. There are recessive perceptual sexual organs that are not attached to physical frames. Among them are the double-pronged phallic forms at the top center, a central line which may stand for the vulva, and large edge details that might find perceptual form as breasts. If a subject is open to archetypal sources, this plate may stir archetypal energy associated with bisexual ingredients in the human psyche. We refer again to the hermaphroditic plane, which we have associated with the "sorcerer" from the cave at Les Trois Frères. It pertains psychologically to the question, if males and females are different, then how are they the same. Confusion in gender differentiation occurs in disturbed patients, and it is powerful enough to overwhelm them. Its expression through sexual energy is frequently out of the question for them; they are struggling against two forces that wish to dominate consciousness, the ego and negative power from archetypal sources. The ego of an examiner is much more comfortable when it lets the matter rest by diagnosing a sexual complex. However, when the proportions of struggle in a subject include something so much more profound, we have not gotten to the heart of the matter through a partial description about a concrete fact. A modern patient who is facing the sort of power struggle we have described is put into the conditions inside consciousness that are like those that pertained in Paleolithic men as they sought order, definition, and a means for differentiation.

Plate V has the potential to take a subject into mythology. There are two perceptually recessive, but well defined figures leaning back or lying back to back with qualities sometimes associated with Pan. Pan had a goat's legs and qualities like woodland creatures. The goat was Satan's animal vehicle, and Pan's influence got pitted against that of Christ's in the early part of the Christian era. Some patients even experience a cruciform shape from this plate's substance, taking them to ideas about Christ on the cross. We suggest that some of the stimulus qualities of this plate have the potential to set going archetypal processes that pertain to the difference between good and evil. This form of psychological energy often lies behind a paranoid person's projection of guilt.

Plate V has some remarkable parallels with the Paleolith and Neolith. There are giant horns which crown the plate, worthy of a mural at Knossos. When that area takes perceptual form through "rabbit ears," and the central figure becomes a human dressed in a rabbit's costume, usually attributed to the ballet, we may have traces of masculine energy in the service of matriarchal power in a male subject. The two large side details are not infrequently seen as heads of "cave men" or "giants." Archetypally, this may take us to a complex associated with a negative relation with masculine power.

Perhaps the most interesting quality about Plate V is its resemblance to a deltoid sign used by Paleolithic artists. The signs they painted tended to be geometric in character. Ucko and Rosenfeld (31) referred to this form of design as a "bracket." Paleolithic men used boomerangs in their hunting. At Altamira, there is a drawing of a boomerang with a startling resemblance to Plate V. A bracket design from Le Portel looks much the same. Leroi-Gourhan (17) has connected the bracket with Paleolithic stylization of the bending woman. A female figurine from Peterfels resembles the pattern of Plate V. The bending women have been said to be in position, on all fours

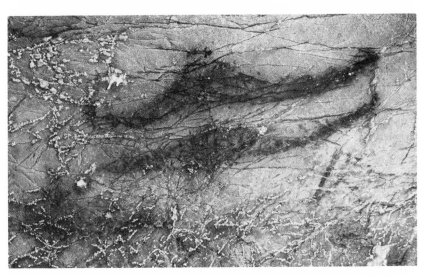

FIG. 13. Brace-shaped or early claviform signs from Gallery B at La Pasiega in Spain, about 15,000 B.C. Under these signs on the right are the schematized forequarters of a quadruped. Plate V has a remarkable correspondence with the form of these shapes as well as do certain Bender Gestalt designs. (Leroi-Gourhan, André. *Préhistoire de l'Art Occidental*. Editions d'Art Lucien Mazenod, Paris. Photograph by Jean Vertut.)

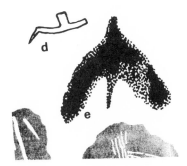

FIG. 14. A red painted bracket sign from Le Portel, about 11,000 B.C., carries the same deltoid shape as that of Plate V. The psychological meaning of the Paleolithic signs are unknown, though scientific evidence shows them to have an independent mythology. The deltoid figure and the boomerang which the hunters of the Paleolith used connect the signs with an aggressive means of overcoming instincts.

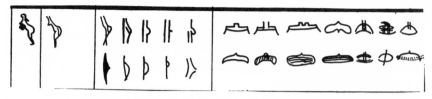

FIG. 15. Shows the varieties of claviform signs and their relation to the female form from Leroi-Gourhan (17). Plate V has a general correspondence to a number of those as well as to the highly stylized form of a bending female. We suggest that the mythology of the signs in parietal art had to do with male separateness and relation to his sexual opposite on an abstract level (rather than concretely through animal symbolism). The experience of clashing opposites on Plate V may be connected with an activation of the condition between inner opposites of several varieties. (Leroi-Gourhan, André. *Prehistoire de d'Art Occidental*. Editions d'Art Lucien Mazenod, Paris.)

with raised buttocks, to receive the male sexually. Bender Gestalt designs 5 and 6 have a remarkable correspondence with the Paleolithic signs, and there may be an archetypal connection between them and Plate V's stimulus value. We have seen how Paleolithic artists illustrated the way they stylized the female in a particular shape through stages into a full bison. Boomerang, a woman bent in a fertility rite, and bison may have all had a religious connection for Paleolithic men. Men threw boomerangs to capture prey. The woman's rites insured the supply of prey. Psychologically, Paleolithic men may have been comparing male and female power, or showing that their combined efforts made the stuff of survival possible. As we have noted, they may also have coveted full power apart from women altogether. The means to that end furthered the development of consciousness.

Plate V may bring a patient to imagery associated with power struggles on different planes. When the struggle is instinctual, it may be connected with a specific sexual complex. However, because of the way consciousness can displace the door to archetypal activity (through the definite form of the blot), when complex material appears here, it is more likely to have archetypal sources. There is a similar quality for experience with certain T.A.T. cards. Following the definite form of the previous card, T.A.T. card eleven throws a subject askew perceptually. There are few forms in it definite enough to recognize. Subjects tend to respond to it with either a rich crop of fantasy or little or nothing. Almost the reverse holds for the structure of Plate V, though it brings similar results.

In some subjects, the two sides of Plate V, each having a peripheral animal-like leg and tail, are experienced as animals clashing head-on. This repeats the archetypal theme of powerful instinctual struggle, but between opposite halves with identical qualities. Someone has remarked that images like "two rams with horns locked in battle" constitutes the most aggressive kind of image the Rorschach elicits. We do not suggest that this form of image necessarily means an impending externalization of aggression. More likely there is an inner power struggle in which archetypal energy has been activated. One must look to other instinctual images in the entire Rorschach sequence to discover a pattern from which to predict behavior. Externalized violence ensues when a particular kind of power resolution occurs. When two opposites are suddenly split off from a connection with each other through the ego (whether the connection is neurotic or adaptive), violence, self-violence, or withdrawal may ensue.

Our subject tended to be closed to archetypal sources for Plate V. Since we know she is open to unconscious influences, this must be explained. Her responses were:

1. Looks like a butterfly.
2. The hind leg of something, I don't know what.
3. The forepaws of a cougar.
4. A laughing alligator or crocodile.
5. Two gorillas jabbering, just their faces.

We see that ego consciousness exerted full control on this plate, and insofar as she is endangered by negative relationship with archetypal energy; this is data in favor of the ego's power. Aggressive instinctual energy and features

FIG. 16. Two old, battering male ibexes, from Le Roc de Sers, about 16,000 B.C. One of several sculptured blocks in low relief from the only known sculptured rock-sheltered sanctuary found at the foot of a cliff. Very similar figures with locked horns are sometimes perceived by subjects viewing Plate V. This is the prototype for Aries in the zodiac. (Leroi-Gourhan, André. *Prehistoire de l'Art Occidental*. Editions d'Art Lucien Mazenod, Paris. Photograph by Jean Vertut.)

about the defense mechanisms of the ego world predominated for her here. It raises the question, will aggressive instincts be strong enough or useful as vehicles to support the ego's power? If not, what other means, if any, does she have to help sustain that power?

PLATE VI

While Plate IV has to do with the structure and energy associated with the masculine psyche, Plate VI has to do with masculine functioning. Maleness has to function against structure, so this plate may add to the information one may have obtained with Plate IV. We may see qualities emerge that pertain to the way energy is spent in life. Through this we may see something of a subject's mode of adaptation. The quality of textured shading provides us with a scale along which we may measure a subject's degree of sensitivity. When large forms are easily identifiable in a plate, we may see how much power the ego has to discriminate perceptually. A given plate has qualities to push the ego aside or pull the subject toward it. This plate stands somewhere between IV and V in that regard. A subject may give little more than "animal skin" or "totem pole" here. Yet, through the powerful means of displaced sexual features (dominant male and recessive female), processes may appear through the laws of subjective consciousness.

PLATE VI

If a subject is male, some features of psychological initiation into masculinity must have been accomplished if he may be expected to *function* as a man. Hence, we have a reverse of Plate II, where the female organ was dominant, and the male more recessive. Here, the phallic form dominates, and the center line or other aspects of the lower part of the plate may be perceived as the female genitals. Displaced organs provide an opportunity to split subjective experience from instinctual sexuality. When a male subject has become independent from female authority (which rules more over Plate II), he is freed to form a different relationship with females and the feminine side of life. He is no longer frightened of anything feminine. The psychology behind weak masculinity or sissiness in a boy is wholly a matter of a son against matriarchal power. An effeminate male remains so because he has never been freed from matriarchal power. Men who show a great fear of being associated with any female qualities may do so with good reason. Even though they may have made a good outer male adaptation, matriarchal power is so fearsome, they run away from anything that stands for it. Usually, in such instances, differentiation from that power is only partial. We are never really free from anything until we can approach it without fear.

If a male subject has moved along the path of differentiation, the bisexual qualities of Plate VI may take him into a different sort of experience on an hermaphroditic plane. When that happens, we may see how a differentiated male functions and adapts in relation to his dominant masculinity *and* his recessive femininity. Most disturbed patients have not differentiated and are caught up in some form of maladaptation. Nevertheless, we may see clues through Plate VI that show both what has happened to the patient and what he has to do to change. When a subject is in better relationship to the opposites within him, his relationships with men and women are enriched.

A female subject responds to this plate rather in the same way for Plate IV. It does not contain structural qualities that pertain directly to her adaptation as a woman (against her female structure and its energy). Either she would tend to project some form of personal complex, or material related to her response and capacities against the quality of adaptation in those males who have been important to her. Archetypally, it may trigger symbolism or archetypal energy associated with the strength of her own recessive masculine qualities. It is not, though, a plate having to do with feminine tasks, female structure, or woman's mysteries as such. This does not mean that a female subject may not be in the power of phallic worship and project related material. A woman who is in the power of phallic worship may experience it entirely inside a sexual or instinctual plane, through forms of sexual obsessions. On an archetypal level, she may face her phallic aspirations apart from eroticism. She must come to grips with her desires for logos power, which also may energize obsessive behavior. The notion of "penis envy" is as complicated as "identification," though we tend to over-simplify it through applying it as a diagnostic conclusion. Longing for sexual union in a female may have nothing to do with the wish to possess a male organ. Apart from transsexualites, relatively few women lose much sleep over not being equipped with a penis. Likewise, few men long to have physi-

FIG. 17.

cal organs that belong to their opposites. Envy about qualities belonging to the opposite cannot be sexual in nature, since no man knows what a woman feels during the sexual act, nor does any woman know what a man feels. One may fantasize about these matters, and the fantasy may stimulate erotic feelings, but it remains nothing but fantasy. In fact, fantasy about how one's opposite experiences erotic feelings or orgasm is an important means of developing sensitivity about the other and may lead to psychological growth. Yet, it often leads to a repetition compulsion because the pleasure associated with eroticism grabs as much energy as it can when psychological development is arrested or neurosis occurs. Yet, there are female qualities which are appropriate to masculine structure, and, when they are absent in consciousness or are only partly assimilated, envy or longing may lurk in secret corners or even take possession of a male's conscious world. The opposite may take place in a female. The structure of the female psyche includes counterparts of her opposite. The psychology of each individual makes these matters complicated or simple according to what is present in a subject's psyche. Archetypes function to split an image or symbol from a

FIG. 17. Gilgamesh, relief, palace of Assurnasirpal II, Nimrud, Assyria, 885–860 B.C. This Assyrian hero's myth, carved along the face of massive stone hillsides, is the oldest in our tradition. Reversed, Plate VI provides easily for images of two bearded figures with arms horizontal. When seen, they usually appear to subjects as kings or priests purveying authority. The beards themselves, which touch the arms in three-quarter profile, produce this effect, and they are much like the elaborately plaited one Gilgamesh sports or the false ones worn by Egyptian royalty. Gilgamesh's mythology contains the essential elements which we may ascribe to the archetypal potentials of Plate VI. As a carrier for the archetype of masculine functioning or the way masculine energy is projected into life, it is necessary for a male to have enough independence so as to function. It is the opposite to the energy of the male in Figure 5. Gilgamesh went out into all the corners of life looking for immortality. In her role as enchantress, the Babylonian mother-goddess Ishtar made elaborate efforts to lure Gilgamesh through eroticism into her power. In a passionate eulogy, Gilgamesh rejected her advances and named dozens of her previous lovers she had wrecked or destroyed. He called her "a waterskin which soaks through its bearer." Through his detachment from the power of the matriarchal goddess, Gilgamesh demonstrates his capacity to function independently. His powerfully developed masculinity qualifies him as the first genuine hero. As portrayed here, Gilgamesh shows his capacity to function in different directions. His wings allow him to soar upward and explore the sky. He holds the magic herb which he gathered from plummeting to the bottom of the sea. His independence gives him a great range and flexibility of function. The magic herb greatly resembles poppy seed pods, which may symbolize the correspondence between his undersea explorations and grasp of the strange, unfamiliar world of dreams. Symbolically, Gilgamesh represents the prototype of the independent masculine ego, which connects conscious aspirations and the contents of inner depths. Plate VI may potentiate aspects of this psychology. It may provide material associated with a subject's differentiated masculine functioning or signs of complexes that interfere with it. (The Metropolitan Museum of Art. Gift of John D. Rockefeller, Jr., 1931.)

specifically sexual plane to an hermaphroditic one. Men have been at the task of differentiation from their opposite longer than the female of the species. When she held power as matriarch, the male was the underdog. The male, including his penis, was in her service. She could sacrifice him or further him through the power allotted to her by the collective or cult. If we had any data that supported erotic *intent* in parietal art, the psychology of the sexual underdog might be applied to understanding the meaning of the figure of the bending woman. The position that she assumes so that she can be mounted is an abject one, putting her on the same plane as all other female animals. It could have been an expression of derogation so as to define male superiority. Males had to get back in charge of themselves and their sexual energy if they would become independent. However, nothing about Paleolithic art supports eroticism, while much does pertain to its function as spiritual and psychological media. Plate VI tells us something about how liberated a male subject may be, though its structure is not appropriate to the nature of a woman's liberation (though Plate I may be). When a collective idea, such as the "women's liberation movement," gathers energy, the psychology of it should be sound. The need for the movement shows that the female of the species has not fully differentiated herself from the masculine. When she does, there must be an archetypal structure to support it. The female's tasks for differentiation and individuation must not be defined *inside* masculine values. Liberation for women may at times be nothing more than a fantasy. Collective energy may be bound together by psychological needs other than those which go with the conscious caption applied to it. A danger lies in its being bound to a negative relationship to masculine power. So it is with the civil rights movement and liberation of the black man. The struggle is for power, while the captions read otherwise. A chief task for the woman of today is that of adding to her archetypal structure, so that sufficient support exists psychologically for individuation. It should be a truly feminine one defined in female terms. It may be a long span of time before some of the ingredients of that task are known.

Like the phallic form on Plate II, the structure of the phallus that dominates Plate VI is composed of authentically male substance. "Totem pole" is almost a popular image for the phallic detail. For the primitive, a totem was an identification, a vehicle that designated exactly where you belonged. Hence, it has to do with how one functions and who one chooses in marriage. Archetypally, this is the stuff of definition and differences. Plate VI has qualities enabling the side features of the phallic form to be associated with images of feathers. A feather has been associated with the phallus since Paleolithic times, and it could stand for it in art forms. A carved bone from Paleolithic times shows one side as a feather and the other as phallus. From the wings of a bird, feather symbolizes the soaring male principle that aspires high. The winged phallus from Pompeii is a late version of archetypal energy associated with the liberating quality logos functioning has over instinctual demands. The cruciform qualities present in this detail sometimes takes a subject (who is open to inner processes) to symbolism associated with the sacrifice of logos power, or sacrifice of instinctual sexual power (counterpart with the subject's image about crucifixion and the woman on Plate II).

Plate VI may be associated with authority as it is derived from masculine power. Reversed, the plate often stirs up images of power carriers, like kings or some form of ruler. The figures are not opposed, face to face, but back to back, arms out and faces in three-quarter profile. Appropriately, power is extended outwardly. This plate's power may be illustrated by a response the author once obtained from a Jewish boy, who saw it as "the Torah." Archetypally, through providing laws and enforcing them, a king was given his power from the collective. It is interesting to note that the beards on "the kings" are perceptually authentic for the times when kings first began to carry power in the precursors to the Judaic-Christian culture. The beards are structurally identical with those false beards worn by Egyptian pharaohs and Assyrian kings. Hair differentiates the sexes, and its importance as an archetype of power and virility goes back in our tradition to Samson and Delilah. Samson represented the archetype of strength and power, and he was rendered impotent when Delilah snipped his locks. Then, his eyes were put out (his genitals, which got him in trouble, were left intact), rendering him dependent. The timeless archetype of power is recharged when our youths leave their hair uncut and oppose patriarchal authority. A need to escape authority and expand one's own strength may be energized at an archetypal level with this plate. Both male and female subjects may show elements of the same negative relationship with masculine power.

The animal skin (itself hair), considered a popular image for this blot, was acquired through the prowess of male hunters in Paleolithic times. In hunting cultures, females cured and fashioned skins into coverings.[9] We know that fertility goddesses adorned themselves with animal parts symbolically. As a symbol, the skin could represent cooperation and combined efforts of the work and energy of males and females. The texture of this plate takes a male subject to his intuitive mode, his recessive feminine form of apperception. When it functions for him, his inner masculine and feminine principles aid him in adaptation by working *together*. Individual differences about the way an animal skin is perceived may pertain to the inner state of a subject in that regard.

---

[9] In Egypt around 1300 B.C., only a high priest was allowed to wear a leopard skin, the symbol of his office.

Our female subject reported the following images for Plate VI:

1. Looks like some type of a skin laid out on a rug, but it's terribly moth-eaten. It's the furry side, all raggy-tarry.
2. The pincers of a spider.
3. The top looks like an oboe or cello, the tuning and all that of a stringed instrument.

We have already seen how inroads have been made into the quality of the subject's adaptation. It has holes in it, eaten away by bits of negative energy (insects), because precautions had not been taken to protect it. The phallic form as part of a musical instrument follows a psychological theme played before (conductor in Plate I). Phallic power was experienced against part of an instrument which can produce harmony. We suspect the *law of excluded awareness* was at work. It was promiscuity that had gotten this subject into hot water. Archetypally, the meaning of this image shows her the way to move out of her sexual obsession. An inner harmony is needed between inner opposites. The image suggests she has some potentials within which may take her to psychological growth. Her feelings (music) have been split off in her relationships with others, and particularly men, whom she related to as sex objects. She was not differentiated from the power of the matriarch. Some parts of her used men for her purposes, though she has qualities that may take her beyond that and free her from a repetition compulsion.

PLATE VII

The qualities of this plate that stir aspects of the feminine side of life are well known. Through its reliability as a stimulus source, subjects may be taken into the world of the distaff side. While matriarchal authority and its influence are not difficult to define, other aspects of the feminine psyche are. Beyond its essential ingredients, masculine qualities and functions may be isolated and defined with relative ease. We have assumed, rightly or wrongly, that prototypes for masculine psychology existed in Paleolithic artifacts. Paleolithic art provides us with corresponding female psychological structure only vicariously. The psychology of the feminine is much more elusive and fluid. For that reason, a thread around the feminine side has been pulled through all the plates, even when the focus was on masculine components. The masculine psyche can be comprehended, while the feminine can only be apprehended. This is because female psychological structure depends in part on *interplay* with the masculine.

Our task is to clarify further aspects of Plate VII that pertain to feminine experiences. In order to do that effectively through our point of view, we will need to look at an overview of aspects of paleopsychology which seem to pertain to structure and functioning in womanhood.

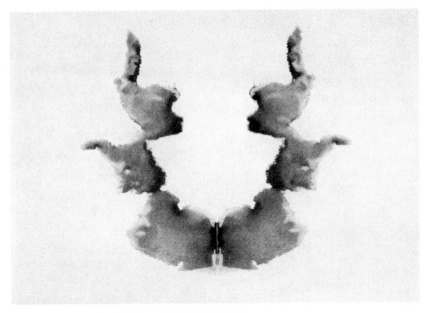

PLATE VII

The works of M. Esther Harding have aided us in this task. It is necessary that the means of apprehending feminine structure be done through masculine *and* feminine experience. Harding (11) and Toni Wolff (33), both students of Jung, have greatly enlarged our knowledge about the scope of female psychology. The Swiss social philosopher, Johann Jakob Bachofen (2), who died in 1887, developed the theory of matriarchal societies. Bachofen grasped that legends preserved collective memory. Hermann Rorschach was known to have been familiar with Bachofen's works. Jakob Burckhardt admired Bachofen's writings, and Burckhardt influenced Neitzsche's thought. Freud obtained some of his inspiration from Neitzsche and applied it to mental patients. Bachofen's works did not appear in English until 1967. Jung was considerably influenced by Bachofen, particularly the way Bachofen approached grasping symbolism, through Bachofen's study of Roman tomb paintings and ancient mortuary symbolism. Bachofen proposed that matriarchal cults made up the first societies and that patriarchal cultures developed out from them. Most sociologists and anthropologists disagree with Bachofen's theories about societal development. That aspect is of no concern to us here. We are developing a theory about the nature of psychological experience through looking at beginnings. Our notion of archetypal experience does *not* include pre-uterine memories. We use it in the sense of the impact on neural structure made by the *same* kind of psychic life in humans,

Fig. 18.

and we believe that the most powerful ones aided the development of consciousness. Our inkplates take us back to them perceptually. As George Boas (3) has said in his introduction to the Bollingen Foundation's publication of Bachofen's *Myth, Religion, and Mother Right,* no one has yet explained so common an event as personal loyalty, our fear of gods, our hopes for the future, or our desire for order. Those are archetypes that join us together. Bachofen recognized the synthetic power that lies in symbols, and Jung extended and enriched the scope of symbolism, in psychological subjective experience. Boas (3) remarked that "the beauty of myth and symbol lies in their synthetic power; they can combine in one presentation disparate elements which would be self-contradictory if put into a declarative sentence." These sources have been guides to us as we have approached our form of apprehending the feminine psyche, both inside the matriarchal world and beyond it.

In his novel about archetypal experience, *She,* H. Rider Haggard (10) portrayed the side of womanhood that pertains to matriarchal authority alongside a recessive pattern of mortal love between a male and a female caught inside the penumbra of matriarchal presence and power. The substance of his novel combined the psychological female qualities associated with Plate I and Plate VII, with the former being dominant. As his novel takes us into the dim prehistory of the matriarchal world of *She-Who-Must-Be-Obeyed,* Haggard gives us an idea of the frailty of a woman carrying the Eros principle against matriarchal power. Since earliest times, females who need to separate from matriarchal power and live through Eros have re-

---

FIG. 18. "Draped Reclining Figure," bronze by Henry Moore, 1952. Moore's bronze was struck in two editions, one for the Time-Life Building in London and the other for the city of Cologne, Germany. While most of Moore's women are mother figures, this one is an outstanding exception, expressing a maiden separated from bondage to the matriarchal substance, the personification of Eros and timeless relatedness. A profile of the entire figure (18a) creates the substance of a container, as the eyes pass down the lines from the raised knee into the dip of the abdomen and on up across the breast, neck, and face. Moore has created the essence of the archetype of the woman-as-container, functioning inside the Eros principle. It is the archetypal image of the capacity to contain the male and relate him to himself, her, and others through his feelings. Plate VII, if smoothed in the imagination, follows the angles and curves of the body of the Moore sculpture, itself forming a container. The moon itself takes on this shape as it emerges into the second stage, becoming at once like bison or bull horns, and a container roughly shaped like this plate. Taken separately, the lower, large detail has considerable correspondence to a view of the bronze taken from a three-quarter front across the pose of her knees and legs (18b). Seen this way, the maiden is an erotic invitation in timeless exposure, rather in the way Plate VII's detail presents itself. Both this plate and Moore's bronze include the essentials of the Eros principle, through the female as container and as an instinctual partner. Various facets of a subject's relationship or lack of it to this archetypal principle emerge through experience with this blot.

quired masculine support to do it. What a woman is, who lives in a genuine relationship with a man, is partly defined by that man.

Plate VII has to do with that side in woman that *contains* what a man is in relation to her, and what she energizes through that in him. Males do not have a similar psychological counterpart of containment for their opposites. This is because archetypal sources differ in male and female psyches. Plate VII may energize qualities associated with the sides of the woman that further companionship and develop spousehood. For a female subject, Plate VII may take an adult Alice through the looking glass, and allow her to see behind the veil of her ego and discover what she is against herself.

Ishtar was the Babylonian goddess of love and war, she was associated with the moon and Venus, and her power centered around giving and taking life. Members of her cult, which included the whole culture of Assyria, had to placate her; they never sought her love. Giving and taking life was literal for her. Archaeologists have uncovered numerous bones of infants sacrificed in cult shrines. She was not related to individuals; her function was to maintain rites that kept the species going. Psychological experiences in females were patterned against this kind of cult power in the Neolith and down into the times that antedated the beginnings of our cultural tradition. An impersonal quality is at the roots of the female psyche. While an individual mother may be altruistic, mother love has its destructive as well as its nurturing side. There are classes of mothers who feel themselves empty if they are not among broods of children, while they relate to none of them as individuals. This quality may have been necessary for survival. The archetype of this kind of multioriented mother appears in the nursery rhyme of the *Old Woman Who Lived in a Shoe*. When this sort of mother is not in a mother-child interplay, she ceases to function. The black mother in America has been able to survive without a means to birth control through this archetypal quality. The coldly impersonal side in womanhood is easily recognized in the characterization of the passively aloof Irene, in Galsworthy's *Forsyte Saga*. Esther Harding (11) has noted that there are classes of women who are as cold as icebergs even while living erotically, and as calculating as stockbrokers.

Plate VII extends feminine values beyond those qualities insofar as a feminine psyche is differentiated from matriarchal power. She becomes individuated when she discovers her own values apart from those of her mother. They may even be the same for the daughter, but she should win them for herself. Long cultural traditions have shaped the feminine psyche differently regarding patterns used by women as they relate to men and function with each other. Aspects of the feminine psyche belong more to a tradition rather than being shared among women in general. Local archetypal power has influenced their psychology more than it has that of men. Logos power tends to link all men, and it has widened consciousness for men in a fashion all men understand. How they relate to men depends on a particular tradition, but women are linked together by the facility for intuitive insights and the silent feelings of superiority they feel over men. As Harding (11) has observed, consciousness in a female is generally more comprehensive than that of a male, but less defined.

Apart from matriarchal links, feminine psychological development has been radically different in different cultures and different times and places. If our theory is a valid one, this means that flexibility for change in archetypal experience may be more fluid in women than in men. This baffles men, who simply cannot tolerate absence of order and consistency. Harding (11) has noted that the entire culture of Islam has ordered itself around the fear of fickleness in women. Islam placed a taboo on women as a means of controlling the demoralizing effect caprice in women has on men. The birth control pill may arouse this masculine archetype in Western men. Islam literally imprisoned women and still does to some extent. Certain Islamic writers have portrayed women as untrustworthy, venal, and highly lustful. Western men look on their women in an opposite fashion. Sheikh Nefzaoui (24), in his fourteenth century manual on eroticism, told us that as long as you have a woman in bed, you have her love. Medieval writers in Islam seem to have not grasped love as being a function of "I love *and* I am loved." [10]

Novels like the *Tale of Genjii, The Dream of the Red Chamber,* and *The Golden Lotus* tell us about womanhood inside the everyday life of the East. There was a considerable range of psychological development for women, especially if wealth was available. Oriental women were free to develop arts of inspiration and companionship in relation to men much beyond women in the West. A female might find considerable psychological development inside the Orders of the Church in the West, but not outside that. Oriental women, as well as men, developed against a rigid ritual system that held their culture together until recent times. Adolescent love and premarital experiences have never preoccupied the East as they have the West. Love *after* marriage is the principle theme in Chinese and Japanese poetry. This is because male and female psychology developed around different forces in the East.

While we like to blame the Victorians for those aspects of our psychology that we do not like, women in the West have taken their psychological image from qualities associated with the Virgin Mary. The ideal woman was the pure one. Most of the psychological energy of the Middle Ages was spent by men in protecting that purity. Chivalry was an archetypal attitude that was

---

[10] An outstanding exception to this in Islam may be found in Sufism, the mystic Mohammedan sect. Higher forms of love and a means to individuation may be found in Sufist teachings.

charged with collective energy. Pockets of it still exist today, though it is clearly extinguishing.

Through Homer, we can see archetypal aspects of Western woman's psyche which were clearly defined in the *Odyssey*. In *Penelope,* we may see the archetype of faithfulness in women. She remained by the hearth until Odysseus and his men returned. This is opposite to Islamic attitude about a woman's capacity to remain stable. This quality in female psychology furthers trust in men. It is the institution that holds the home together and is opposed to a what-is-good-for-the-gander-is-good-for-the-goose philosophy. Penelope had her chances, but she could say no for a cause she felt was higher. We must place no value judgment on what she did or did not do. The effects of a male's philandering on the psychology of the home is different archetypally from that of a female. Odysseus and his men did not find things all hay. Often, like babes in the woods, they fell from one trap laid for them into another, all designed by women. While life may not have been dull for them, the cost for their fun was high. *Circe* turned them on through their animal nature, leaving Odysseus's men wallowing like swine. Odysseus escaped himself through his source of masculine wiles. A modern Circe may ensnare a man (usually late middle-aged, and successful, since it costs) from his religion, wife, home, family, and even his profession (probably in that order). When the spell she cast wears off, or the money runs out, he may go home again, hoping Penelope is there waiting. The Homeric heros were especially taken in by the *Sirens.* They lured not for love, but to conquer. They were entirely loveless and cold-blooded women who could not get beyond desire. There are modern women, daughters of Ishtar, who systematically feed on conquests. They run into trouble when they get a little age on them, but they either stick to their job through artifice or "wear brave faces out of memory." We may also see this psychology in the woman who remains faithful but lives in the fantasy of her premarital courtship. It is not the romance *in* marriage, but preceding it. Psychologically, she is still at the dance at the country club. These are a few of the varieties of archetypal power that energize the feminine psyche.

Toni Wolff (33) has described four types of women in our tradition. These include spouse, mother, companion, and Amazon. She has defined female types against the psychology of men. This may be a sound means in obtaining definition, but the female will have to define herself against female values when she is ready for it. It may be a psychological task not possible today. Her values inside the matriarchal psychology are much clearer than what she may become outside it. Mother-child relationships are in a state of change. Women may have to redefine themselves against that relationship. In matriarchal times, men worshiped women and did their bidding. In medieval times, men glorified women. Matriarchal power was transferred to the Mother of Christ, who was pure and good enough to intercede for bad children. Today, men compete with women. The experience of competition may be a negative one for an individual male, but its general impact may be an invigorating one, pushing men toward psychological growth. Women are involved in redefining themselves. No one knows what will happen, but we may be sure that archetypal energy will dominate. Chaos may ensue if Western women form collectively a *negative* relationship to the *nurturing* aspect of their matriarchal substance. Logos desire could replace nurture. While she did not do it out of logos desire, Medea destroyed her children. In the West, women, like black men, must find their own values apart from dominant whites and males. Harding (11) has observed that the modern woman must define herself around her freedom to choose her profession and knowledge of birth control. Psychological change is never in a straight line but tends to move gradually forward as it meanders back on itself.

Plate VII has easily identifiable female contours. Rightside up, two female forms are easily perceived, and the lower large detail has a clear shape of a vulva. Reversed, two dancing female figures may be seen without a great deal of difficulty. The plate's open center has been likened to a safe place, like a harbor or a cove, a shelter from a storm. Motherhood provides such a refuge for her children, and sometimes her husband. As such, it would be inside the nurturing function of the mother. It is not unusual for a subject to perceive food in this plate, which may carry information about the subject's relationship to the nurturing side of his mother.

At an archetypal level, the whole structure of the plate may pertain to the female's relational side with men first, then herself, and through herself to her sisters. Held one way, the female figures oppose each other (perceptually suggesting anger); reversed, the figures dance. Traditionally, women are said to be competitive with each other and prone to jealousy. This gives the woman a feline quality, aloof, snuggling up to be rubbed, fickle because it does not matter who rubs her, and easy to get in a scrap. It is no accident that witches and cats get along well together. Often, these qualities are a function of a subject being in a negative relationship with matriarchal power. Cats are "feminine" and dogs are "masculine" because men project a different psychology onto them. Cat women have trouble relating to males and females, but often the primary problem rests on her lack of relation to her sisters. Plate VII may include energy in a female subject associated with her unrelatedness to her own feminine core. This takes us to the psychology inside the archetypal world of *Cinderella.* Cinderella represents the *puella eterna,* the eternal, flowerlike beautiful girl in possession of something excluded to her stepmother and stepsisters. It was the power to charm men, not through having done anything, but because she was as she was. She became the Sweetheart of Sigma Chi. She was in a positive relationship with matriarchal energy, and so she had a fairy godmother. That furthered her cause to a happy end, living as a natural woman, with a prince who would inherit the kingdom. Great responsibilities lay ahead for him. The prince "saw" that Cinderella had the capacity to *contain* his masculine energy through his response to her. This is the side of woman that becomes a companion and inspiration for men, while she herself usually does not venture far into the world of logos power. The tale provides us with clues about archetypal structure in the feminine psyche. Plate VII, with its opposed females, takes us to feline complexes, aspects of the psychology of woman-to-woman. When war takes American men to remote cultures, they often find natural women, undifferentiated around logos, who are fascinating because they are able to contain the man and his life's energy *and* further him, exclusive of competition. Many an almond-eyed Cinderella looms up before soldiers in Viet Nam. This does not necessarily mean that the male wants to dominate the woman. It may be true in an individual case. The whole meaning of falling in love centers around a man finding a container for his psychology. If he is still in the power of a matriarch psychologically he may welcome leadership from a woman. If he is in a negative relationship with patriarchal power, he may want a woman he can dominate. On the other hand, marriage through a genuine Eros principle is becoming hard to come by in our culture. That, even more than the breakdown of religious values, is basic in our divorce statistics. We are moving into an age in which the natural woman is competing with logos types of women for masculine approval. Collective values are changing for men as they relate to women. No one knows where this will take us.

Held rightside up, Plate VII is a vessel, a container. If it was smoothed out, it would make a crescent, giving it an essential moon quality. Likewise, when smoothed only a little, we find a perceptual form not unlike the bending woman in Paleolithic art and the sign of the boomerang or bracket. We have noted similarities between these percepts and Bender Gestalt designs 5 and 6 (each of which is frequently associated with breast forms and affect or feelings). Plate VII has a cyclic quality because of its segmented sections. Physical and psychological cyclic changes in women have connected them with the moon since earliest times. The moon comes and goes, and with it a female's capacity for fertility approaches and recedes. Bison horns form a crescent, and this may be part of the meaning of the Laussel fertility figurine, holding a bison horn in the position of a crescent moon (see Fig. 2). Two crescents crown the female heads on Plate VII. Interestingly enough, modern subjects frequently ascribe "pony tail" to that detail, inadvertently bringing in an animal quality. The crescent moon is a container. Through the *Eros principle*, the female functions *in relation to men* (apart from the nurturing mother, or from her relationships with women) to provide him with feeling-values and the social values of relatedness. She becomes a psychological container for his substance, including his sexual needs, but on many more planes. This defines Eros as the archetype of psychic relationship. It enables love to become a matter of *union* and not the pursuit of narcissistic appetite. In the recently popular folk ballad, *Honey,* we see something of man longing for psychic relationship and permanence against the present vogue of male-female encounters and some of the predatory eroticism found in the vagabond women seeking freedom in hippie cults. Suffering from an illusion that he was making sexual conquests, a patient of the author's lived in the East Village in New York in a manner that left him completely in the power of predatory, negative Amazon types who used him for their erotic needs. There was no possible means for the Eros principle to develop. In many instances, sexual "freedom" prevents relationships from forming. Archetypal substance and energy serve as unseen, natural psychological laws, and probably no psychological substance exists to support sexual license as a collective value. What Margaret Mead found in Samoa or New Guinea, where sexual freedom was permitted adolescents, pertained to the local archetypal structure.

We do not mean to suggest that an image of some form of "container" is required for archetypal qualities that are related to the female as a containing principle to emerge in a subject. Such an occurrence would tend to preclude archetypal involvement under the laws of subjective consciousness. Images that appear, if one identifies archetypal sources for them, may pertain to a female subject's relational qualities. While Plate III may take any subject to qualities about how he or she "relates," it does not take us through the direct root of a female's Eros principle. Plate III stirs up relational qualities based on the impact of experience with others prior to maturity, when the Eros principle begins to affect behavior. Insofar as a man's relations with women are concerned, the female constellates his relating capacities. If a man is in the power of the matriarch, a contemporary female cannot reach him through Eros, but only through her power side. In such instances, there is no possibility of Eros appearing. When one is able to remark that a couple appears to have an "ideal marriage," it usually means psychologically that the female contains her spouse's life energies, and that she and he are free from negative power struggles. Whatever they have together fills the container she provides for the relationship. Plate VII's containing form is appropriately vague. All males go on a *quest* for a personal woman who is able to contain him.

Since a great deal of psychological energy was spent in the Middle Ages around men's relations to an Eros principle, the notion of the Holy Grail has a psychological relationship to the elusive nature of the feminine as a container for the male. A religious quest requires a sufficient amount of psychological energy for it to occur. While the Grail had a religious meaning as "holy," psychologically, males were working out a new relationship with their opposites. Instead of being merely sexual objects or chattel, women were exalted. The holy wars were fought against Islam, who indeed did hold women as chattel. In part, the quest for the Holy Grail was psychologically the search for containment, through exalted union.

Stimuli with perceptual pushes toward male and female organs appear on Plate VII, and they are positioned provocatively. This, as usual, provides a means to archetypal sources and the unconscious aspect in female psychological structure. A recessive phallic figure tops the heads of the female figures, and the lower large detail provides for a dominant vulva. Through application to the opposite, all we have said about placement of sexual organs and their means to set archetypal laws into activity pertains here. The female organs are positioned in a roughly appropriate way, and there are female bodies to carry them. The male organ is displaced. As for Plate IV, in which the female organ is perceptually in contact with a head, so the male organ is positioned on the heads of the female figures. To function as a more complete person, a male must be conscious of, and in control of his generally more recessive feminine qualities. Quite the same holds for the female. Because the *Sirens* were unconscious of their responsibilities as females, they lived outside the principle of Eros, and relationships with men occurred only through their efforts to overpower and conquer them.

Even though a female subject may report two sets of perceptually clear female figures on the plate, we cannot assume that her adaptation as a woman is a complete one. Her problems against Eros may be projected entirely on Plates IV and VI, or somewhere else. We need to discover what her relationship between adaptation to her feminine core and maladaptation to the male is composed of for her. Qualities about adaptation vary and they depend on the nature of life experience at a given time.

There are contours here which often lead to the perception of "heads of dogs" and "dogs in contact, rubbing noses or kissing." It is psychically sound for this plate to provide a perceptual pull more to the instinctual symbolism or imagery of "dog" than "cat." It is interesting that cats, a common domestic animal, are relatively rare as Rorschach percepts. While a dog usually forms a genuine relationship with people and may mourn a dead master or mistress, cats tend to have a parasitic connection with humans. Cats are dependent and impartial (heresy to cat lovers, and there are many exceptions to these points), but unlike dogs, they not become *something else* through their relationship with men. Men have often been dependent on dogs for protection, food, and guidance. Dogs have become entirely faithful, and, while it is hard to get rid of a cat if you do not want it, they return primarily to be cared for. Dogs, as instinctual vehicles, may tell us something about the relation a female subject has to her Eros principle which cats would not. A disturbed patient is reported to have said "bitch in heat" for the lower parts of this blot. As image, it is replete with information pertaining to the subject's counterplay between Eros and lust.

Plate VII has other qualities that take us into the psychology of the Age of Chivalry. It has a capacity to energize aspects of the archetype of Good versus Evil as they may pertain to chastity. The middle large detail seems to carry a perceptual value of ugly disapproval. When the lower large detail is experienced directly as sexual, as "vagina, hips, and thighs," we may find a psychological response around inhibition or guilt. Archetypally, this detail may take a female subject into contact with her own sense of purity in herself, what she has become through how she has used herself (or allowed herself to be used) sexually. "Cherubs" are a not uncommon image for this plate in males. While Eros is symbolized by a cherub, perceiving one does not mean that the male subject is therefore in a positive relationship with the Eros principle in women. It usually pertains to a longing for its absence, and this may be due to his own infantilism.

Reversed, the white-containing portion of the blot may be seen as "George Washington." For a female subject, one needs to learn if the authority of her father has furthered or inhibited her relationships through Eros. For a male, one would need to examine how his power functions against Eros.

This plate provides us with yet another archetypal quality or ingredient indigenous to the female psyche. It is the archetype of temptation. Its psychological roots go back to Eve. Woman-as-the-temptress has tended to define a man's capacity to control his impulses. We see this in archetypal women from Jezebel to Eve. It is an aspect of female power.

The female area that dominates the lower part of this plate may be "tempting" perceptually. That quality gives it power to activate various *laws of subjective consciousness*. The psychology of the temptress side in feminine nature may come up when the plate is reversed. "Dance hall girls" and "can-can dancers" are common associations for the figures. In a female subject, this may reflect how a woman feels about herself along a good-evil, sacred-profane plane. A female subject may have a complex around oppositional feelings about how males have viewed her historically. Recently, the author was working with two female patients, each of whom had complexes associated with how they were viewed by males. In each case, their Eros principle did not function for them. One thought she was physically unattractive to men for cosmetic reasons (which was not the case), while the other thought she could not go into a restaurant because men looked at her differently than she actually was in her own eyes. Insofar as psychic structure is concerned, how men have *defined* women has a primary archetypal power inside the feminine psyche. All cultures, through time, have defined women against the two opposites of the sacred and the profane. She is, of course, something of both, but that is irrelevant insofar as archetypal structure is concerned. *How* she is experienced by men is part of her substance; she has been stuck with it. As a force, it may have ensured survival. While mother-world is badly battered today, a female moves in it on sacred ground. Men have deified it. As bearer and tender of future generations, she has archetypal inhibitions imposed around her sexual instincts. This has nothing to do with modern religion or the Victorians, or The Establishment. As an unseen "establishment," archetypal power continues until the structure that supports it loses its energy. It is a rare woman who can separate herself psychologically from the power of sacred and profane opposites within her. Further, because a woman's virginity has been important to men, archetypal energy exists around the state of virginity inside the female psyche. Analysis of dreams and other material show that *how* a female leaves her state of virginity remains powerful emotionally, quite apart from social standards and religious attitudes. Something in the female *self* may always have to be defined around the meaning of virginity. It is a female quality and its energy charge is archetypal. When a woman is experienced by men as "profane," she has to move through life with a different psychology than does a woman who is perceived as not that way. What she actually *is* may or may not correspond with how she is experienced. Freedom may be a difficult task for her, and she is unlikely to find it simply through behaving in a free fashion.

Masculine psychology includes different values from women around good and evil. Man has needed the female to define them for him. He is yet to define them in himself. The way a man "allures" a woman seldom provides a a base for a complex in him. Deception to gain a conquest does not get charged with much concern about good versus evil in men. In fact, if a woman suspects a man is up to some excitingly evil design, she is secretly pleased. Satan, as a personification of evil in men, is probably a projection from the feminine psyche. Since the female is required to act as if nothing profane were in her (as in the Middle Ages), projections of that inner state emerge. Hence, Satan became sexually enticing in a specific sense as *Incubus* to medieval nuns. Nuns had to define themselves against the archetype of the sexually dangerous male.

It may not be accidental that Plate VII has stimulus qualities that have psychological roots in the Middle Ages. The female psychology we have been discussing was probably not appropriate in Neolithic or Paleolithic times. In the Western tradition, the feminine psyche got extended in the Middle Ages through men's changed relation to it. Damsels were in continual distress, and this was often kept going by a fierce dragon. Since there were in fact no dragons, it was a world of psychological dragons and maidens, experienced *through* men. Dragons were the primitive, cold-blooded instincts men displayed when they took woman sexually and held women in their power. Her "distress" lay in having to endure it all in silence. As men were changing their attitudes toward their own feminine substance, changes took place in their opposites. This was probably true for women in Paleolithic and Neolithic times. This is another reason why the female is defined through the male's experience. Metaphorically speaking, the curved horn form on the female figures of Plate VII are Adam's rib. Women experienced males differently after changes took place in them. Earlier, men took the lead in major psychological tasks, and the female changed only passively around those male forces. We may be moving into opposite psychological tensions today.

Held rightside up, the center large detail or segment is sometimes seen as "a court jester," another symbol of the Middle Ages. This detail may stir up archetypal energy associated with the woman's role as an underdog intellectually. Drunk with his own logos power, man has a long history of making the woman feel inferior intellectually. Through archetypal energies, different females react to this differently. An inspirational woman tends to further a man's intellectual estimate of himself. Another woman may be competitive with his logos power or possess more than he does. "Instinctual mothers" tend to be indifferent to logos affairs. The difference between the sexes around sheer intellectual power has been due in part to differences between the sexes in what they were curious about. Women have been curious about people, while men have been curious about things. As Harding (11) noted, man's intellectual power is more defined than woman's. This may not be true in any given case, but it has a general relevance. The jester was the wise fool, and while he made an ass of himself to make others laugh, he played life back to those who watched him, giving those who grasped it a comprehensive view of paradox and social inequalities. Far less energy has been applied to widening the broad range of consciousness in women than has been the case for men. Man's estimate of himself is built on how much he thinks he knows. It has been male territory. Female psychic energy is being directed much more toward widening the range of awareness in the feminine psyche. Education, emancipation, and the Beatles have seen to that. Males are beginning to be less covert in how they display themeslves physically to attract females. Females are tending to be less concerned with how their appearance attracts men as they become involved in extending their intellectual power. Rubens might have to go on a safari to find a voluptuous model, if he were painting women today. Effects from the interplay of these forces may be projected on the hooks appropriate for them on Plate VII. Blurring roles does not alter fundamental aspects of archetypal substance. The changing psychology of our youths will have to come up against the Eros principle. Different modes of living do not in themselves solve problems about life and relationships. Power struggles may develop between the sexes in which Eros *and* logos may have to be defended by men, that is, if enough collective female energy charges against Eros negatively. A new form of damsel in distress may emerge in this Age of Competiton. The female of the species may turn out to be coldly indifferent to the male's loss of territory in the land of logos. For women, vanity may get attached to logos power, and this may displace woman's image of herself as the goddess of beauty. When this danger appears for an individual, the Cinderella archetype in her may get activated and restore psychological order. Yet, she may require a young prince who is psychologically more developed than the old-fashioned one.

Our female subject's images for this plate included:

1. Two little girls ready to fly off at each other, pony tails in the air, arms back ready to hit.
2. I see they've got jelly all over their mouths; they've got their feet together, the bottom of each, touching the other, they are in long dresses, and bodices.
3. This looks like faces Goya painted, half men, half animals.

Initially, these images look reasonably adapted, and to have derived from the world of ego perception, with possible ramifications from some complex. Dark areas about the face of the figures took her perceptually into childhood and to sweets. Thus, we wonder not so much whether her mother was strict about eating habits, but how she is related to her own nurturing instincts. We do not doubt that some emotional need around nurture is associated with feminine experience at its roots for this subject. Hostility is in some way tied in with her nurture needs. This influences her relations with other females. The vulva contour of the lower large detail was perceived as the feet of each figure pushed together. This may have come about through the *law of excluded awareness*. Yet, the image does not separate her perceptually from what she was experiencing, that of interplay between girls. It seems to be an image of opposition toward a childish aspect in herself that has extended into womanhood. She may have to deal with this in herself first, and then progressively, with it in relation to other women before she can function effectively through an Eros principle. The image "bottoms of feet" is unusual for the vulva area. As symbols, feet orient us, they take us places, and they have a relationship with what is being stood on. Here, they have an aggressive function, directing force toward an aspect of the feminine. Through this action the figures could topple. As feet, the image remains on a physical plane, and so conscious perception, rather than the subjective law we suggested, may have determined the image. The main point appears to be something directly antagonistic toward the feminine.

Interestingly enough, bits of the culture of the Middle Ages slipped into the perceptual range stirred by this plate. The bodice was a prominent quality in women's clothing in the Middle Ages. It was almost symbolic of something feminine. Goya painted life in the late Middle Ages. He often portrayed the seamy side of everyday life. Because her human-animal image was half and half *on this plate,* we may find it has psychological roots in a complex about instinct versus control, sacred versus profane, and good versus evil for this subject. What we know about her life supports this.

PLATE VIII

Up to this point, we have noted how there may be a perceptual correspondence between psychic structure and perceptual structure in Rorschach's plates. We have had to neglect the complexities of an individual's perceptual style in favor of archetypal similarities. We have differentiated between perceptual styles in male and female subjects and suggested that the four modes Jung described (thinking, feeling, sensation, and intuition) blend in a variegated mixture in particular indviduals. An investigation about these means of style in perception is essential in advancing Rorschach theory. We have been suggesting that there is some kind of psychological progression connected with the succession of the Rorschach plates. In order to give our hypotheses a structure, we have suggested that they may correspond in a rough way to the stages Jung described as individuation. Plate VIII takes us

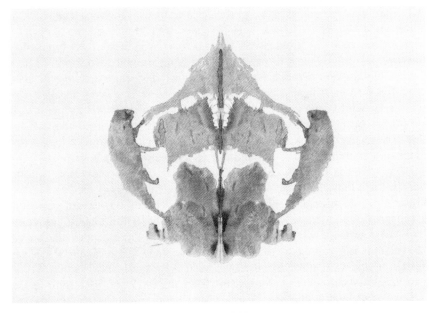

PLATE VIII

beyond structure and into functioning. Perceptual styles become more central as one compares psychological progression against psychological structure. We would conceive of Plate VIII's pertaining archetypally to a subject's manner of functioning through the combined forces of masculine-feminine interchanges on all planes of living. It is the stuff of what one becomes through marriage or an important depth relationship with another. We have called this central aspect of life functioning through Eros. A male, married or not, who lives with a spouse primarily through a relationship to matriarchal power is not developed enough psychologically to function through Eros. Figure 5 shows such a male. A female subject whose life is dominated by a negative relationship to masculine power wears a different shoe but is in the same boat. In order to be consistent, we will approach Plates VIII, IX, and X as higher levels of psychological differentiation. This keeps us to the task of dealing with archetypal influences in the stimulus plates, but we are quite aware that the level of differentiation we may refer to may not apply to a particular subject at hand. The last three plates may offer no more than a summary, or additional information about the psychology of the subject which has already been suggested, or new facets associated with the same may appear. We have attempted to illustrate the last three plates around psychological correspondence to what we assume to be the appropriate stage, and not so much to visual correspondence. In some subjects we may see evidence of the effect of not completing certain tasks that would fit one to move to the stage at hand. The plates have a way of reflecting what life is like, and each or any of them may open a subject to facets of regression or progression. Our task has been to identify sources for varieties of responses and to provide a theory to account for properties in a plate. Individuation through stages never precludes regression to a former state. Keeping hard-won psychological development at a given level is precarious at best. Usually, if one falls back, he does it differently, and with knowledge of the means to move forward again. Our major point has been that Rorschach's plates virilize experience through their potentials for a range of activity as wide as life and as real as the laws that govern us.

Plate VIII has primary perceptual qualities of bright colors and definite shapes. Like Plate II, these stimulus features bring feelings (color) and instincts (animals) into juxtaposition. Feelings experienced around basic instincts provide the essential ingredients of *initiation*. Traditionally, initiation serves to determine whether an initiate or postulant has a proper amount of *control* that is required to move into a new stage. Endurance is a usual means of testing control for a male. Seclusion, since she is a relational creature, has been an initiation means for females. Plate VIII follows the material associated with the structure of the Eros principle (how both sexes are, or are not related through it), so we are taken to a higher psychological task on Plate VIII than one of role definition (which was the initiation task associated with Plate II). Harding (11) has noted that in ordinary personal relationships, neither a man nor a woman gives himself up completely to emotional experience. A woman must not arouse a man's instincts beyond the place where she can remain mistress of the situation, for her human concern, as potential mother, is directed toward marriage and the establishment of a home. The man fears getting caught in the emotions of her possessiveness, and he wants to stay close to the ego so he can "manage" things. With its powerful qualities associated with feelings and instincts, Plate VIII takes us into the world of male and female initiation as they begin life *together* through the Eros principle. Qualities in an individual life associated with that task may get stirred here. It tends to stimulate aspirations about life and goals, where one goes, and what one builds. Figure 19 was selected to illustrate the psychology of Eros *functioning*. Usually, the animals of Plate VIII are seen as earth ones, three- or four-legged, and separated from each other. Between them the planes of the blot move the eye up and down rather than from left to right. Our illustration for this plate shows birds, integrated inside a pattern, separated by a vertical image pointing above and below. This is a fourteenth century detail from a tapestry, with definite Eastern influences, probably Persian. The Persian philosophers and poets were centrally aware of stages in psychological development and used the bird, which climbs or soars upward, as a symbol of development. Interestingly enough, some subjects actually perceive the animals on Plate VIII as birds. Birds symbolize aspects of some need associated with mating and its functioning. Avicenna in the eleventh century and Attar in the twelfth described lofty psychological development through birds as symbols. When Eros functions, the sort of unity expressed by the birds happens psychologically. This sets the stage for trans-material unity within the psychology possible for Plate IX.

The whole blot, supported by side animals, makes an easy perceptual push toward an image of "coat-of-arms" or "escutcheon." Those images were the badge of the family and what its behavior stood for. It is a "civilized" totem. The coat-of-arms is a Western counterpart using an animal means to symbolize certain human qualities. They are the vahanas of Eastern religion for the West. When escutcheons represent snobbish motives in modern living, it is useful to remember that, as images, they link us with instincts that made the family "noble" psychologically. That energy has usually run out when the image is meant to show a superior heritage. It was conferred when something was *earned*. Usually, the source for a coat-of-arms comes from the Middle Ages, the times in which men and women lived against a developing Eros principle. Psychologically, it was a task which had to be won, so that it could be sustained collectively through archetypal

FIG. 19. "Tapestries with Birds." Detail. Germany, first half of the fourteenth century. This motif of climbing birds was inspired by Byzantine silken fabrics, showing brilliant Persian colorings. The detail symbolizes goal-directed unity in functioning. Persian scholars used birds to express important psychological problems in personal development. Between the birds are two tulip-like flowers; one lifts the eye above and the other carries it below. This signifies that unity emerges when inner and outer experiences are connected. The pattern underlies the psychology of the Eros principle. (Augustiner Museum, Freiburg. Photograph by H. Weber.)

proportions. Plate VIII provides qualities that lie behind the archetypal power that energizes male-female interpersonal bonds. Plate III pertains to the personal or individual qualities acquired by the particular subject carrying that energy into life. Plate III carries the personal side, VIII, the substance or structure that enables a subject to act or be energized in a nonspecific way.

In comparing Plates II and VIII, aspects of their structure pertain to our thesis. Ostensibly, the central, rounded white space on II has disappeared on VIII. Perceptual stimuli for displaced sexual organs (male and female) are recessive on VIII, while one dominated over the other on II. Plate VIII has an evolving impact ("one thing growing out of another" is often reported in subjects open to inner processes), the action moves vertically, while on II, the action is horizontal, where two sides appear engaged with each other. Plate VIII's animals are separated from each other, while on II the animals are in direct contact. Linkings with the psychology of the mother-world and the tasks of the Paleolith or Neolith tend to be recessive or remote. The psychological roots of the plate extend more to archetypal sources from the Middle Ages. Matriarch has been replaced by Eros, as we perceive the psychological processes that underlie Rorschach experience. If a subject has a powerful complex associated with matriarchal power, he may project it here as intensely as on Plate I, because the psychology of the archetypal power of Plate VIII is closed to him. Instead of interacting between each other playfully or clashingly, the animals on VIII are more purposeful and engaged outwardly. Engagement dominates the creatures on Plate II. Plate VIII's animal figures give us clues about the quality and nature of the instinctual energy that supports Eros, when a subject is living through Eros. If there is no genuine relationship energized through Eros for the subject, the animal figures take on a different significance for interpretation. When a subject, who otherwise shows signs of being ready for or involved in Eros stage initiation, suddenly forms symbols, one must examine them carefully to see how well the postulant is qualified. Information obtained through subjective laws is impersonal; the data may be positive or negative. The animal figures here are subject to subtle perceptual alterations or preoccupations (concern over the number of legs and the presence or absence of a tail). These are among the most difficult animal figures to perceive as humans, but it happens in some subjects. Parrots, or mice, carry clues about the subject's instinctual resources.

The white spaces on Plate VIII have considerable power as organizers of perception, though it is a recessive power. The same holds for areas which tend to carry male or female sexual organ content. If Eros functions and partners are in harmony, the sheer power of sexual energy recedes. That is the significance of the absence of a dominant organ here, and of the separated animals. When the necessary control is gathered to dominate instincts, those instincts are freed from clashing. Then, they carry out their functions naturally. By running one's eye around the segmented white spaces contained by the animals, one may grasp a larger circle than one on Plate II, a smoother one, and one that is integrated by virtue of having separate segments. The symbol for matriarchal power is still there, but recessive and in relation to the whole unit of the blot. In the very center of the blot, the white space carries the lines of the delta form we have described in parietal art. The upper central, smaller white spaces have contours appropriate to a bison. Then there are vertebrae or animal bones, including splendid animal horns. Significant symbols and images from parietal art are still here, but they are perceptually recessive and greatly diminished in size, made up of ground (white), rather than field. White space images have been associated with oppositional tendencies and paranoid qualities. Experimental evidence generally supports that empirical observation. To understand *what* the opposition is toward in a more specific and meaningful fashion, one may use the structure of archetypal potentials inherent in a given plate to define the probable target for opposition. For Plate VIII, we suggest it is some aspect of the Eros principle as it fails to function or does so in a peculiar fashion for the subject. The same would be generally true for perception of sexual images here. The nature of a subject's image for those phallic or vulva contours that exist on the plate must be examined around the nature of the perceptual source.

Our female subject reported the following images for this plate:

1. Two wild beasts. Lions, going forward to the top.
2. Two bison, fighting over a carcass. The bison have bloody faces. They are like a cave drawing with blood on them.
3. A big skin thrown down in the road, like a rug, it's pretty in a weird way.
4. Two tiny feet, of a little old lady.

The subject's responses to this plate were the determining factors that led to selecting her as an illustrative case. This young adult female was a married woman, and she was also a mother of one child, a daughter. She felt that her daughter drained her or held her back, and, alongside her extra-marital promiscuity, she nurtured fantasies about being raped. We have not provided any details about her life until now, so as to keep the material separate from her life style. She had a problem about motherhood and she was living unsatisfactorily against the demands of an Eros principle, if indeed she lived in it at all.

The outer, usual animals were lions, carriers of masculine instinctual authority. Their behavior was purposeful. This may mean that she has a capacity to further instinctual aspirations in men. It may also mean that she feels weak against masculine instinctual power. Since we know a good deal about her psychologically, it seems more probable that she is psychologically confused about what side in her holds instinctual power over her behavior. Because of her negative relationship with matriarchal power, she tends to exploit men in search of definition and resolution in herself.

The images of bison were original ones. They each make up half of the central blue detail, they are paired, and the outer red detail in the blue is blood. This is a remarkably accurate parietal art image, with red signs or markings. The lower detail (butterfly) became an animal skin to her, a most unusual way to perceive a rug, and an impossible place to find it (road). Perceptually, the subject has pulled qualities from previous blots, particularly Paleolithically familiar ones, back into Plate VIII. Her primary problem rests inside her relation to matriarchal power, and this interferes with both her image of herself and her capacity to live through an Eros principle. Her power struggle with men stems from an inner one between opposites in herself. The matriarchal principle in this modern woman got related perceptually to a bison in a fashion linking her psychologically with the Paleolith.

PLATE IX

From the standpoint of psychological growth and what an individual expects to attain in life, Plate IX provides us with information about arche-

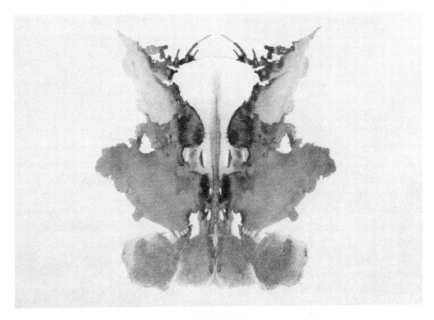

PLATE IX

typal energy associated with *goals*. It is the plate that may show us something about the way a subject's consciousness has brushed against his
Erlebnistypus or *Karma,* and whether he has taken an active or passive role
against it. By goals, we mean psychological ones surrounding development
as a subject passes or does not pass along a path of individuation. Inside
the viewpoint of archetypal psychology, that is one reason fundamental to
Plate IX's being frequently rejected, and its being judged to be the most
difficult plate of the series. Various theories have been put forth to explain
why Plate IX gives subjects so much trouble. The nature of the color, blocking because of sexual thoughts, too much blending of color in the central
portions, and a general perceptual poverty have all been put forth as reasons.
From our view, Plate IX *ought* to give the most difficulty since its archetypal power seems to pertain to goals and growth. This is not the same thing
as holding up a mirror to a subject, who then experiences the mystique of
catching a glimpse of his stage in life. The reality of subjective affairs does
not work that way. A subject who has not moved into life through the Eros
principle, or is not engaged in genuine relational behavior of an order that
is open enough for growth, may be quite realistically perplexed by Plate IX.
While patient populations need to be concerned about psychological growth,
it does not follow that other populations necessarily share that need. We
must take a general look at what we are suggesting about the stimulus qualities of Plate IX so that our meaning may become specific.

In Hindu thought, men have been classified into three groupings. One is
the naive segment, in which men are dominated by the search for self-
gratification. The second group includes ordinary development. In it, a man
has some control over his instincts, and he disciplines them, but he wants to
control his outer environment for purposes of personal satisfaction. The
third, and by far the smallest group, is the segment in which men seek beyond physical needs and look for inner values. No matter what one's view
about a particular religion may be, all religions have had as their functions
providing the means for serving the nonmaterial side in man. This need is
powered by archetypal energy. That a particular religion became corrupt, or
another did not fit in with the knowledge available in the time it flowered,
becomes irrelevant. If for no other reason in nature, the nonmaterial must
exist to define the material. For the Hindu, the struggle inside the third
group is one in search of *true perceptions,* not contaminated or false ones.
We would define a symbol as a means toward grasping true perceptions.
Usually, our grasps of ourselves and those close to us are clouded by illusions. We are applying this term, true perception, to everyday life, not to
some mystic vision into tomorrow. In a search for *self,* false ideas about
what one is tend to recede. Percepts are distorted in those men who have
never distinguished their percepts apart from their desires. One of the higher

stages of spiritual development in Buddhist thought is the *Prajna Parimita,* in which a postulant finds a means to true perceptions. If he achieves his goal, he acquires *Sila,* the fragrance of clear thinking.

If, in life, one has come into a broader relationship between ego needs and the kind of archetypal energy that tends to manifest influences in him, the values in consciousness change. Plate IX may give us clues about the psychology of that state. If one has none of it available, none will emerge. On the other hand, because a given patient is usually badly troubled, through that experience, he may be forced to face qualities in himself that he might not otherwise deal with in the outer affairs of men. Patients who contemplate suicide come into contact with experience that was closed to them before. The meaning of life and its relation to nonbeing is weighed, sometimes impulsively, sometimes with the care given to it by a saint or Christian martyr. Contemplating the difference between Wall Street and one paved with gold may take an ordinary stockbroker for the first time into a relationship with the archetypal energy that pertains to nonmaterial goals and meanings in life. How an individual stacks up against these experiences may have an effect on what happens to him in treatment.

As we have noted for Plate VIII, color tends to organize perception on a vertical plane on Plate IX as well. In a general way, color organizes percepts differently on the other colored plates. Plates II and III have two colors which sharply oppose each other and the black forms are large enough to stand in opposition to red color *per se.* Plate X's color does not tend to move percepts along either plane, though its form may. For Plate IX, color groups the blot into three segments and this takes place on a vertical plane. The idea of something evolving or a relationship between segments often occurs on Plate IX for subjects who are open to a corresponding inner state. If a subject is in a borderline state, he is indeed inside a process that moves him back and forth in stages. When this occurs through archetypal sources or through abstract symbolism (symbolism about form, not content), too often we stop at noting what has happened, and proceed to make a diagnosis. Through attending and listening, and interpreting the symbolism, we may get taken much further through the data at hand. This puts us in a better position to predict and to find clues about a subject's dilemma, if he has one. Often, what we traditionally call "failing repression" in Rorschach is actually *emerging symbolism.* Repression may have indeed failed, and it is important in its own right, but the process is not the gestalt. Our task is to discover the pattern associated with emerging symbolism, when we are sure, from the source, about the presence of symbolism in the material at hand.

Certain empirical consistencies have led us to describe particular and complex archetypal qualities about Plate IX. It is rather startling when a subject reports "a death's head" for the center arrangement in this blot.

Color is associated with feeling and life. This plate provides plenty of color for a subject's affirmation of life. There is the sun color of orange-red, verdant green for vegetation on our planet, and red for the feelings that require life for existence. Yet, subjects who are faced with ideas of destroying themselves are able to displace the bright color and zero in on a kind of skull-and-bones affair, usually because life for them has become like poison. If there is any archetypal experience, it is the archetype of the will to live. What happens then, inside archetypal powers, when a person elects to die, and indeed does so? The author's (19) study on boys with muscular dystrophy, all of whom knew they would die within a few years, showed that the fantasy of these boys affirmed life in the midst of attending to matters about their own fate. An individual psyche is determined by its beginning and its end. An archetype of death exists, and it joins all men in the same way that birth does. Death defines life for us. A person who kills himself would gain nothing by the act if he believed that life after death might continue the same pattern. The values in one's consciousness may change when the power of archetypal energy gets into a negative relationship with the ego. For a wide variety of different reasons, life's values may recede, and the energy associated with the archetype of death may pull one toward it. Paradoxically, we cannot judge, for this may involve a survival value for the species. For example, it may be that without a death-oriented form of archetypal power, more highly disturbed patients would turn their destructive forces onto others. Nature herself may have no prejudices about euthanasia. We are not advocating that useful people who are suicidal ought not to be helped to regain their sources for the energy of life. On the other hand, the mind of man is puny beside natural laws. It is conceivable that some individuals will never be able to cope with the proportions of whatever overwhelms them. When we chain people to life, and the archetypal sources that sustained life have become closed, we usually find that they move toward death aside from our best efforts to prevent them.

As the master explorer of ego psychology and its ways, it is not surprising to find that Freud's (8) most poignant writing was associated with his thoughts about extinction. Freud (8) noted that primitive man's realization of the death of a loved one may have instigated the spirit of inquiry in man. Yet, Freud (8) noted that "no instinct that man possesses is ready for a belief in death." Jersild (13) has pointed out that the theories and philosophies about death that men have suggested may not correspond at all to what exists as inner reality in someone grappling with death. Leonardo da Vinci (32) once wrote, "While I thought I was learning how to live, I have been learning how to die."

Since facing mortality must have taken roots or left imprints on consciousness in Paleolithic times, it is not surprising to find powerful Paleolithic

Fig. 20. Sensitive rendering of an open left hand, on a low ceiling at El Castillo in Spain, 20,000 B.C. The shape of this hand is not a simple imprint, but a product of refinement with the brush. Delicately formed fingers splay out over the rock, and the curve between thumb and forefinger is beautifully drawn. Giedion (9) indicated that the custom of reproducing negative or positive handprints tended to drop out of parietal art around 18,000 B.C., but that its profusion coincided with the period renowned as that one producing the female fertility figures. Left hands predominate, and in some instances they are associated with fertility symbols like pregnant mares. In some caves like Gargas, clouds of hands swarm about the walls. (Giedion, S. *The Eternal Present.* Pantheon Books, 1962. Reprinted by permission of Princeton University Press. Photograph by Hugo Herdeg.)

155

images present in Plate IX. Perhaps the clearest one perceptually, and the most startling correlate, is the somewhat stylized "hand print" between the green and red segments of the blot. Subjects sometimes report a "thumb" in the red in addition to the "fingers" or "hand" in the green. It may also be seen as a "bear's claw." We spoke earlier of a possible meaning for the hand prints in parietal art. We suggested that it was a means men used to distinguish themselves from their opposites. When that is accomplished (then and now), men become *conscious* of themselves in a new way. It is through the hands that a child becomes conscious of more in himself than his gastrointestinal tract. For a notion of the *self* to form in his life's development, a man must be *conscious* of more in him. The imprint of the hand on Plate IX seems related to extending awareness. Plate IX requires widened awareness to grasp.

Almost as if it were the purpose of the surround, the upper central portion of the blot carries us to a familiar Paleolithic image. Subjects tend to perceive it as "a violin" or "a cup or container of some kind." This area combines qualities of the stylized female torso in Paleolithic sculpture, which represented fertility as goddess, and a cup or medieval chalice, representing the way females relate to men, containing their energy. When the area is seen as a glass or cup, the subject usually attributes special qualities to it, though he finds it hard to say just what they are. The nature of a woman's containing capacities are elusive also. So is the psychology of highly developed human experience. The plate provides us with stimulus qualities of not only contours appropriate for displaced male and female sexual organs, but also, and for the first time in the series, perceptual appropriateness for those organs in union. There is a central phallic form, sometimes seen as a candle or a Bunsen burner with a bluish-green light, or some other form of light-giving object. It is elongated and extended, most of it being inside the violin-shaped detail. The central portion (referred to before as a death's head) is often associated perceptually with a pelvis. In rare instances, the two central segments inside the lower red detail may be perceived as testicles. At any rate, the human reproductive organs appear here in a displaced fashion, and against amply supportable perceptual contours, none of which impose themselves. We have subtle stimulus qualities that may activate archetypal energy. Through laws of subjective consciousness, that energy may split symbolism from instinctual sexuality to a different psychological plane. Opposite principles are contained in one. At a nonsexual level, the union of opposites embodies that stage in psychological development which may occur only *after* differentiation from the opposite has taken place. The recessive half that was split off so that an appropriate separateness could occur is joined again to itself. This is the meaning of the symbol of the hermaphrodite at this stage. As a symbol, its purpose may be to define self-

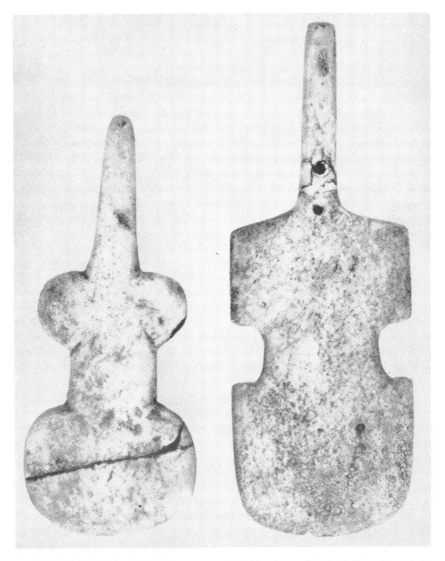

FIG. 21. Primordial fertility goddesses. Marble from the Cyclades, about 2500 B.C. (Photograph by Alison Frantz.)

containment. We suggested that Paleolithic men may have used it as a means to define masculine power apart from matriarchal power. Now it becomes the nonfemale (or beyond Eros) container, psychologically. It is *both,* neither is dominant, neither is recessive. Through the experience it symbolizes, illusions or distorted perceptions diminish. A male is no longer

under a compulsion to perceive *only* as men do, and the same holds true for
his opposite. Perceptions take on *Sila,* the psychological fragrance that pertains when thoughts are clear or not clouded or kept narrow through fear
of an opposite, outside and within.

We have defined this in detail because it may have specific relevance to
disturbed populations. We do not mean that Plate IX may have meaning at
the level we described only for a chosen few. Our task is to evaluate the
stimulus qualities in the inkblots as they pertain to life's psychologies. Some
patients are patients because they are caught between the archetypal power
of opposites within *to such an extent* that the rest of the world recedes. The
struggle of what that condition means to a subject may be so powerful that
he may destroy himself and/or others. Subjects who are not prepared may
suddenly apprehend the qualities of the split-off opposite in themselves, and
its impact may cause a paranoid break. Awareness of an opposite is thrust
aside through violent projection. An illustration of this will be shown in
the case materials.

All of these features may or may not pertain to a given subject. A rejection of the plate does not mean the subject is at an abyss due to archetypal
powers. The plate may take a subject nowhere perceptually for different
reasons. Our position is that, when it is rejected, through observations about
what other plates yielded, one may judge, for that subject, the reasons for
rejection. It may be due simply to arrested psychological development. It
is noteworthy to observe that while testing-the-limits usually yields further
data for most plates, it seldom does for Plate IX. It tends to set much or little
going.

The mystique of a spiritual "union of opposites" need not be removed
from ordinary life. Awareness about it shows us more about patients who, in
spite of their conscious wishes, come face to face with their destinies. This
brings nonmaterial values, if one has any, to the fore *in experience.* Even
the most blasé one of us gives pause, when our material existence is in
question. By this we mean, man and his fate, and what his fate may be like
because of grasping powers of the opposites within. Those powers may be
negative or positive for a given person.

The poet often notes a psychology about experience that a scientist may
exclude by his method. Shakespeare showed us the import of a union of
psychological opposites in his poem, *The Phoenix and Turtle.* The author
(21) has written elsewhere about the meanings possible in the poem, and
several observations in that may be useful for us here, as we attempt to
understand archetypal sources in Plate IX. It is necessary that we remember
that a symbol pulls together aspects of experience that a declarative sentence
cannot. Our job is to apply it to life and patients, to bring it to earth from
the abstruse. Any notion about a union of opposites may be offensive to

some. It may have no earthly meaning for individuals who do not grasp the importance of law and order in nature apart from the conscious world of logic. To aid us, we draw on literature to show parallels from the same sources carried through wholly different media. Shakespeare has shown us some of his clear grasp of the union of opposites in his poem. In the poem, the phoenix is unquestionably a feminine principle, and the turtle, a masculine one. It deals with the nature of their marriage prior to their death. All birds (turtle means dove here) admired their love beyond all others. They have gathered to evaluate the nature of that love. Shakespeare used animals to portray special human qualities. One of his sources was bestiary lore, while another may have been his awareness of this means in Oriental literature. The following lines from the poem show how Shakespeare grasped love and union beyond the Eros principle and described it at a level that is unmistakably hermaphroditic:

> So they loved, as love in twain
> Had the essence but in one;
> Two distincts, division none:
> Number there in love was slain.

The love-birds were dead before the poem began, and the nature of their love (in one of the lines the bard refers to it as "married chastity") is the subject of the poem through obsequy. This has to do with two major archetypal sources that Plate IX may activate, aspects of nonmaterial union and death. Scholars have been confused about Shakespeare's "sources" for the poem, as well as those for *The Tempest,* his last complete play. We would suggest the sources were inner ones, belonging to a Shakespeare who had moved into a new psychological stage. His vehicle, birds with qualities out of a bestiary, may have come through contact Shakespeare may have made with Persian literature. The Persian poet, Attar (1), wrote an epic, *Conference of the Birds,* some four hundred years before Shakespeare, which had qualities that parallel the poem.

If Shakespeare's *Sonnets* are viewed as passionate outpourings about the interplay between opposites within, some of the mystery about certain ones having been addressed to a specific woman and others to a particular man may take on a different dimension (whether they were addressed to specific individuals or not). They are surely laments about the movement of life away from youth, but the scope in the *Sonnets* lies around the *permanence* of the love he sang about because the addressee (male or female) *contained* him. In them, Shakespeare may have been working out the relationship between opposites in himself, apart from his conscious intent. Emily Dickinson may have done something similar. That is, she came upon the psychology of the union of opposites through her *Love Poems,* perhaps as a dialogue

between herself and the opposite within. We may see an essence of this in
her poem, *Emancipation* (7), with the lines:

> Two bodies therefore be;
> Bind one, and one will flee.

Still in his prime, Shakespeare wrote *The Tempest* at the time he left
London to return to Warwickshire, never to write a complete play again.
He died five years later at age fifty-two. The substance of *The Tempest*
comes from myth and fairy tale. Louis Wright (34), director of the Folger
Shakespeare Library, has written that no adequate explanation for Shakespeare's sources for *The Tempest* has emerged. He noted that the plot elements are common to romance and folklore and appear in many places.
For us, this means his sources were archetypal ones. *The Tempest* is really
a fairy tale, in which something that had been under an enchanted spell (perceived falsely) was released (Ariel). What Ariel represented became conscious. Then, through his archetypal powers, Ariel transported all those involved in the play onto a new psychological dimension. Shakespeare showed
us about his knowledge of man's nonmaterial destiny in this play, a flickering
glimpse that approaches the meaning in the *Prajna Parimita*. He understood
that one must be capable of true perception, and this is done through perceptions that reach beyond that veil the ego hangs over our awareness.
In perhaps the most profound lines in English, Prospero grasped *Sila* when
he said:

> As I foretold, you were all spirits and
> Are melted into air, into thin air;
> And, like the *baseless fabric of this vision*.[11]
> The cloud-capped towers, the gorgeous palaces,
> The solemn temples, the great globe itself,
> Yea, all which it inherit, shall dissolve,
> And, like this insubstantial pageant faded,
> Leave not a rack behind. We are such stuff
> As dreams are made on, and our little life
> Is rounded with a sleep.

The matter of a psychological, sacred marriage, a *hieros gamos,* may
mystify us. So does much that happens in our patients, especially if we regard what happens to them as experience, apart from symptoms *per se.*
Profound experiences, frequently of forces over which they have no control,
come to disturbed patients. Many of these experiences are unknown to
those who walk through life unruffled. Many a disturbed individual has to
face himself up against nature. Altered perceptions take him away from

---

[11] Italics are the author's.

the ordinary. Archetypal energy lies behind feelings of cosmic influence, an experience of transmigration into another body, and voices calling out of thin air. In some instances, the plates may stir thunder in a subject and we must listen for its echo. An array of astonishing experiences comes to those who fall under the power of archetypal energy and experience it through a negative relationship. Archaic sources may crack an ego and set an ancient god up in its place. Many find this view difficult to tolerate and often seek the security of disbelief or evade the issue through applying labels. We must be careful not to go beyond where data take us, but we must also learn to widen outselves about how we use it. In some instances, Plate IX may take us to a subject locked with his fate, and in others it may not. The substance to do it exists within the plate.

Our female subject provided us with the following images here:

1. There's a type of worm you study in biology, this is like the eyes of the worm, it isn't really a worm, it is just sensitive to light and dark.
2. Two pair of bruised buttocks, and fingers reaching out.
3. Two Negro heads [rejected on inquiry].
4. Two Merlin magicians, the whole figure of a Merlin with the dunce cap.

The "eyes of the worm" were seen in the central part of the blot (which were referred to as an area often seen as "a pelvis", and sometimes as a "death's head or skull"). This subject experienced that blot area in an origi-way way. Her percept takes us directly into a theme of stage in evolutionary development. One of the most undeveloped animal forms, a worm, able to do little more than distinguish between light and dark, as an image is opposite to a high form in psychological development. From what we know about the subject already, we would suggest that this image may carry meaning about how weak and inadequate the subject feels against her fate. However, be it ever so lowly, she has a quality in her that enables her to differentiate between light and darkness, between one form of opposites. She, herself, is in danger from the forces that may cast her in darkness. Her own eyes did not perceive the color the plate provides, though she was alert to color changes, since they gave the "bruised" quality in the central, lower red detail. From what we know about her, this image may pertain to the mother-child archetype, which we know gives her psychological trouble. She felt her own child held her back. Merlin, the archetype of the sage in Western tradition appears for her in a "dunce cap." We saw evidence on Plate II (bookends) how this subject previously connected "dunce" with the masculine side of life. It seems clear now that the subject probably functions psychologically to make the male feel inadequate. Dunceship renders logos impotent. Psychologically, the subject is probably not capable of containing the creative side of a man's energy. She would not be a fit subject as an inspirational partner. Merlin's alchemical cap connects him with interest in the great preoccupation of alchemists in the Middle Ages, that of turning lead into gold. Psychologically, this is a transformation. That which weights us down needs to be exchanged for a higher value. In this way, Plate IX carried our subject into contact with a need for change. If it requires magic (which is probably what logos power means to her), her chances of moving on are slim. If she can look through that aspect in her that distinguishes opposites (light from dark), at the simplest, nonlogos level (eyes of a worm), casting aside the rest of intellectual impedimenta (for her), she may not only survive, but progress, leaving instinctual obsessions behind. Can she perceive beyond the veil of the ego? If she does, is she strong enough to see herself as she is? Does she have the compassion for her own child that Mary shows in Pièta? What role does punishment play for her as she apprehends herself as a woman? These are some of the questions that her Rorschach experiences raise as she comes into contact with her destiny.

PLATE X

Many clinicians have noted that Plate X has a quality that enables it to summarize or pull together what has already emerged about a subject's psychology. If we look at it as a stage following that associated with the

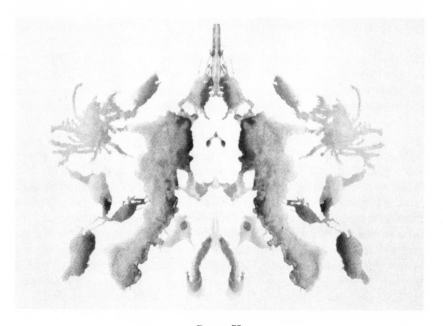

PLATE X

archetypal psychology of Plate IX, we would consider it as a means for observing the integrative functioning of the subject. The perceptual power of form and color tend to be balanced. There is no dominant perceptual push, vertically or horizontally, when the whole blot is considered. As a vehicle, it tends to provide a balance perceptually. This follows what may have been stress in subjects as color stimulated them on VIII and IX. If a subject has psychological resilience, and his color experiences have been powerful for him, Plate X may enable him to display the quality of his adaptation in the midst of bright color and fairly clear forms. Plates V and X may give a subject a psychological rest more than the others because of the relative ease with which percepts arise against rather definite form. Plate IX makes a subject uneasy when he has seen nothing, since it leaves him feeling inadequate, on the one hand, and pressured in himself to find something, on the other.

Plate X does not seem to have as much potential for archetypal energy as do some of the others. There are two pair of animals (upper green, and central, outer grey-green) which might be found on Paleolithic cave walls. One pair might be bison or bulls with horns, the other deer. Neither carries much perceptual power. On the other hand, because of the many life forms here, and a quality of figures evolving, or stages of basic development in creatures, patients or subjects open to inner processes sometimes experience "evolving life" for Plate X. There is an excellent perceptual hook for an image of "an amoeba" (one of the lowest forms of life), and one may see qualities associated with a variety of life forms, including animals, insects, humans, and seeds of trees or vegetation. Nature seems more prominent on Plate X than do human affairs. Perhaps the most common image for the whole of the blot is some form of sea life. Yet, life on the land is equally easy to come by perceptually. While, in addition to its color, its position as the last plate of the series may give it qualities because it does come last, archetypally speaking, it would seem equally appropriate as the first plate. It would be interesting to compare materials in subjects using it as Plate I, and then follow the series. We suggest that it has archetypal qualities associated with the source of life, or the *Sansara,* the Hindu notion of a vast wheel of life on which all living things turn. Every woman who has given birth has been a Sansaric vehicle. The foetus she carries goes through phylogenic stages. It is not her religion, but archetypal power that gives a woman pause as she ponders steps to alter nature's cycle in pregnancy. The cycle of life precedes the Paleolith *and* follows it as the archetype of the *eternal round.* As a sea-source, Plate X is like an archetypal pattern for the unconscious itself, the source of all things. It is nonspecific, it is general, integrative, summarizing, repeating, returning. As such, it may tell us little about an individual's psychological journey in life, though it may tell us much about

FIG. 22. "The Garden of Venus," by the American Negro folk artist Minnie Evans, 1965. Mrs. Evans reports that she paints images that spring to her view while she is awake, and that they pertain to events "before the flood." In this work, one is reminded of the Pleistocene, when nature experimented with a large variety of life forms, plants, animals, and human beings. Both in array of color and in the circular spray-like movement, similarities exist between the archetypal significance of Plate X and Mrs. Evans's work. Several years ago, the American composer Richard Rodgers first pointed out to the author a visual and experiential linking between the two. We have suggested that their archetypal connection pertains to their significance as life sources, mother nature, and the unconscious itself. Here, Venus is not the matriarch, a goddess in female form, nor the sensual goddess of love, but nature herself, the source from whence we came. Psychologically this is the unconscious itself, and we may see through this how the Biblical "paradise" was both a psychological state and nature's acres.

his flexibility. As with all plates, one may get any facet of a personal complex or persona problem. Many of our youths are beginning to concern themselves with man's place in natural patterns, and how his efforts may disrupt balance in nature. The tiny ego-consciousness against the whirl of multidetermined forms of life has an archetypal counterpart in something of the stimulus nature of Plate X. Reversed, a small figure suspended between the green seahorses may carry something of this in its significance for a subject. It may be a Space Age image. Plate X is not often potent as a source for symbol formation. There are very recessive blot contours for displaced sexual organs, and, upon occasion, archetypal energy does split perception and alter it. No particular consistency exists here around individual archetypal experiences.

Offhand, one might expect that Plate X would be just that one which pitted man against fate, if the plate activates something about the impersonal side of nature. Conscious logic would take us to such a conclusion, but subjective laws do not seem to operate as we would expect. One has to go through *the personal* to his experience with life forces outside him, not through the impersonal.

Usually, when one obtains general imagery here, and we do not see signs of archetypal sources in them, those images reflect something of a subject's mode of adaptation and the relationship he has to his instinctual energy. Through careful observation, one may see signs of laws of subjective consciousness at work. This seems to take place more around parts of images, than with a whole image in a given instance.

Since archetypal energy associated with sources or beginnings is feminine as an experience, one may find a relationship between Plate X and "mother nature," as an impersonal archetypal source of life. Through this, we may designate X as being inside the experience of life that is more feminine than masculine. It may take a patient (in a negative relation with matriarchal power) into the area of reproduction and his personal relationship to his fertility as an archetypal power.

Our subject reported the following images for Plate X:

1. Two spider crabs.
2. Two eggs with burnt yolks and burnt whites, fried eggs.
3. Seeds, you put them on your nose as children.
4. Two German pipes.
5. Horses that have just been shot. Blood, it isn't blood, but it looks like blood to me.
6. Two holes to hang it up by.

The subject uses the side yellow here, not the more central ones (which. as perceptual carriers, have a central "yolk" and are more frequently "eggs" than are the details she used). Whenever images that are statistically frequent for a particular blot area are displaced perceptually to a totally different area, even though there may be features in common between the two areas, some aspect of the *law of excluded awareness* may have been involved. When this is so, we may look to archetypal sources as an aid in explanation. While one may make a conclusion about an image as "obvious," without going to such a source, one is in danger thereby of losing objectivity. An egg is an image of the source of life. For this subject, the eggs have been altered on two accounts by the action of man. Using them for food prevents their natural destiny, and burning them destroys their food value. From her history, we know that this subject took steps to alter her life-giving function through abortions. We would suspect traces of the impact of her having tampered with the cycle of life at an archetypal level here. She is sensitive about fertility, and it continues when she reports maple "seeds." "German pipes" is a masculine image, bringing in the male side of experience. It is man-made, inanimate, and unconnected with natural phenomena. Smoking, in our time, carries the meaning of something detrimental to nature. We have already seen how her relationship to the masculine intrudes itself and disrupts her natural functioning. Finally, a natural creature, friendly and helpful to man (horse) has been shot. Violence from man has destroyed a natural beast and disrupted his cycle of life artificially. As an ending, the plate has two holes for hanging. This is a reflection of deanimating the plate and bringing it under her personal control. We may find this as another manifestation of her opposition toward a number of vital sources in herself.

In general, we may say that the subject is open to sources in herself which could aid her. Her main task is to redefine herself as a woman, and if she can accomplish this in a manner that does not defy archetypal energy that surges up, she may be freed to develop her relationships with others. Without this, the same archetypal influences may push her into despair.

REFERENCES

1. Attar, Ud-Din Farid. (1175 A.D.) 1961. The Conference of the Birds. 147 p. London: Routledge & Kegan Paul, Ltd.
2. Bachofen, Johann J. (1859) 1957. Myth, Religion, and Mother Right. 309 p. Princeton: Princeton University Press.
3. Boas, George. 1967. Preface to Myth, Religion, and Mother Right. 309 p. Princeton: Princeton University Press.
4. Bower, Gordon. 1970. Analysis of a mnemonic device. Amer. Sci., 58: 496–510.
5. Campbell, Joseph. 1968. Lecture series (Myth of Modern Man). C. G. Jung Foundation and Institute, New York.
6. Conrad, Joseph. (1902) 1958. Heart of Darkness. In: The Collective Unconscious in Literature. 141 p. New York: The Analytical Psychology Club of New York, Inc.
7. Dickinson, Emily. 1945. Love Poems. 61 p. Mount Vernon, N.Y.: The Peter Pauper Press.
8. Freud, Sigmund. 1952. (ed., Jones, E.) Collected Papers, Vol. IV. 508 p. London: Hogarth Press.
9. Giedion, S. 1962. The Eternal Present: The Beginnings of Art. 588 p. New York: Pantheon Books.
10. Haggard, H. Rider. (1887) 1966. She. 238 p. New York: Pyramid Books.
11. Harding, M. Esther. 1935. Woman's Mysteries. 342 p. New York: Longmans, Green, & Co.

12. Jarry, Madeleine. 1968. World Tapestry. 358 p. New York: G. P. Putnam's Sons.
13. Jersild, A. T. 1960. Professor of Education, Teachers College, Columbia University, New York. Personal communication.
14. Jung, C. G. (1952) 1956. Symbols of Transformation. In: Collected Works, Vol. V. 567 p. New York: Pantheon Books.
15. Kellogg, Rhoda. 1967. Analyzing Children's Art. Palo Alto, Calif.: National Press.
16. Kerényi, Carl, and Jung, C. G. (1949) 1963. Essays on a Science of Mythology. 200 p. New York: Harper & Row.
17. Leroi-Gourhan, André. (1965) 1967. Treasures of Prehistoric Art. 543 p. New York: Harry N. Abrams, Inc.
18. McCully, Robert S. 1964. Art of Ajanta and Ellora. Natur. Hist., 73: 53–57.
19. McCully, Robert S. 1963. Fantasy productions of children with a progressively crippling and fatal illness. J. Genetic Psychol., 102: 203–216.
20. McCully, Robert S. 1961. Human movement in the Rorschach materials of a group of preadolescent boys suffering from progressive muscular loss. J. Projective Techn., 25: 205–213.
21. McCully, Robert S. 1962. "The phoenix and turtle": an interpretation. Harvest (London), 8: 48–56.
22. Mellaart, James. 1967. Çatal Hüyük: A Neolithic Town in Anatolia. 232 p. New York: McGraw-Hill Book Co.
23. Milton, John P. 1969. Arctic walk. Natur. Hist., 78: 44–53.
24. Nefzaoui, Sheikh. (1394–1433 A.D.) 1964. The Perfumed Garden. 192 p. New York: Lancer Books, Inc.
25. Nelson, Richard K. 1970. Hunters of the Northern Ice. 429 p. Chicago: University of Chicago Press.
26. Neumann, Erich, 1959. The Archetypal World of Henry Moore. 137 p. New York: Pantheon Books.
27. Neumann, Erich. 1955. The Great Mother. 380 p. New York: Pantheon Books.
28. Neumann, Erich. 1954. The Origins and History of Consciousness. 493 p. New York: Pantheon Books.
29. Rorschach, Hermann. (1921) 1942. Psychodiagnostics. 263 p. Berne: Hans Huber.
30. Starr, Nina H. 1969. The lost world of Minnie Evans. Bennington Coll. Rev., 2: 41–58.
31. Ucko, Peter, and Rosenfeld, André. 1967. Palaeolithic Cave Art. 256 p. New York: McGraw-Hill Book Co.
32. da Vinci, Leonardo. (1452–1519 A.D.) 1959. In: Erich Neumann, Art and the Creative Unconscious. New York: Pantheon Books.
33. Wolff, Toni. 1956. Structural Forms of the Feminine Psyche. Zurich: privately published.
34. Wright, Louis B. (ed.). 1961. William Shakespeare, The Tempest (1611?). 89 p. New York: Washington Square Press.

SIX

Process Analysis: A Frame For Rorschach Data

Too often, Rorschach workers are expected to solve ambiguous diagnostic problems in a fashion that clears away the ambiguity and produces a definitive, preferably unitary diagnosis. This expectation may hold even though the individual who made the referral may have a flexible approach to nosology. This attitude toward diagnosis may not be realistic in terms of the actual inner state of the patient at hand. Ambiguity in projective findings may be an accurate reflection of the psychic states in which shifting trends may be confusing for purposes of nosology, but which may nevertheless accurately reflect conditions existing in the inner world.

The whole concept of diagnosis has imposed an artificial, perhaps dated encasement around Rorschach findings. It does not appear that the medical model from which the urgency for diagnosis stems can advance us much further in understanding either pathological or normal states in subjective consciousness. Through being able to catch a representative sample of the state of subjective affairs with the Rorschach, one is in a good position to study those data for many purposes. It is extremely valuable for teaching purposes, and for learning about how the inner nature of man orders itself. We are not simply making a plea for less emphasis on pathology. We question the applicability of a medical model to our data because of its self-limiting nature. It keeps us focused around symptoms and their treatment. Of course, no one denies the importance of alleviating symptoms, and Rorschach data can be helpful in providing information in that regard. Our point is that we have used our data too exclusively for those purposes. It has given us blinders, preventing us from examining what we have thoroughly. As the future unfolds, we are going to have to ask different questions apart from pathology. Rorschach material can have an important part in providing us with leads on many issues. Instead of producing artificial, temporary states of consciousness through drugs, we will need to ask what qualities does this individual have that keeps him frozen in the attitudes of yesterday? Can he change? If he changes, what attributes does he have, how far can he go? Is there a model appropriate for a state of psychological health? What is the criterion of growth and progress for this individual? Those are only a few questions that must be considered. We have little grasp of how to answer them through present sets, modes, and attitudes. Changes are taking place in those attitudes, and we must be prepared to make use of our data for the extensions they demand. It is through instruments like the Rorschach, when our eyes are cleared of bias or restrictive habits of thinking, that we may be enabled to extend our knowledge.

When consciousness is altered, as we find in psychosis or borderline conditions, we have an opportunity to see *more* in relation to subjective happenings. Men have long learned about themselves through studying the abnormal. Many individuals recognize and talk about borderline conditions, but do we have enough understanding about the *process* going on in such conditions? Frequently, we think of a borderline condition as one of transition, a state not an entity in itself, but something assumed to be moving between more discrete categories. That, however, is largely a theoretical assumption. Some individuals remain in a borderline state and do not show signs of external pathology or symptoms. When we find a patient in that state, it is unrealistic to pin a label on him, since we may not yet know where he is headed. He may stay where he is.

We need a way of looking at what is happening as Rorschach data form. The relationship between scoring categories provides us with important clues in that regard. However, process is what links happenings, and neither scores nor content alone provides us with a sufficient grasp of them. If we examine processes in those individuals who are open enough to illustrate them for us, we may be able to apply our knowledge elsewhere. Borderline states may provide us with the sort of data we need.

The nature of any given subjective process is elusive, and, like subjective consciousness itself, its manifestation is often momentary. It is seldom that a subject has any valid awareness about what has taken place. He is usually not conscious of the processes and hence is ignorant about them. We usually see subjects rationalize about their images or wax defensive or disclaim them. When a patient is known not to show psychotic symptoms on a behavioral level and then produces what we tend to call "bizarre" Rorschach material, we usually assume that repressed material has "emerged." Freud's libido theory has conditioned this assumption. There are, of course, frequent occasions when repressed material does emerge, but there are times when material that had not been repressed appears. We must learn to distinguish between them. What do we know about the conditions that allowed an image to emerge? If the material qualifies for a conventional definition of pathology, we indicate that ego strength was weak or defenses were loose and, hence, pathology popped out. So it may have been, but we have done no more than describe the condition we need to understand.

Because appropriate conditions were available in the Rorschach stimuli, symbols formed. Some symbols tell us that a pathological set of conditions released them and others do not. Both may look similar until they are examined against other data. A symbol may not be "repressed material," but a messenger reporting on the nature of an inner state. It is useful to look at the processes taking place, insofar as we can identify them, as a symbol appears.

If one wishes to understand the nature of processes in a Rorschach examination, the differences between this variety of investigation and other types of diagnostic evaluation must be considered. The author (2) has pointed out some of the crucial differences between types of evaluation elsewhere. Forer (1) gave cogent consideration to some of those qualities in discussing the problem of latency and Rorschach material. Rorschach tends to extend the range of stimulation from familiar experiences to unfamiliar ones. Interview techniques tend to focus on questions associated with a patient's formal adaptation to life situations. It is unlikely that symbols are provided with the conditions they require for formation in an interview. No formal questions are being put to a Rorschach subject about his life adaptation. Only vaguely formed ink shapes and colors provide focus and direction for perceptions and reactions in a subject. Cues or guides to response behavior are not forthcoming in the Rorschach situation. The subject must seek them within himself. The response field is relatively open when one looks at a Rorschach plate, whereas, in interview, specific questions tend to narrow the range of response possibility. This is not to say that interviews do not stimulate rich, illuminating, and highly important data. Yet, they do not ordinarily offer opportunity for certain kinds of data, especially symbol formation. The person interviewing has to infer symbolic attitudes when certain data emerge. It is an inference about material that is unconscious. In Rorschach, a symbol appears. The examiner then has to infer qualities associated with consciousness and adaptation from it. The two techniques tend to be reverse in how they gather data. Each is equally important and complements the other. To some extent, this is a restatement of what every clinician knows, but we must consider the difference in data sources when we apply them to questions. Much misunderstanding occurs because sources are neglected when individuals from different disciplines consider problems or diagnosis about the same patient.

A theoretical set may interfere with grasping crucial features of the process that takes place as an image forms. It is incorrect to view any Rorschach image as "latent" itself. Conflict, dynamic facets, and other manifestations of pathology may reflect latent qualities associated with material in the different sources that exist in the unconscious, but the image or symbol itself is not latent; it has come about. Peculiar associations are not in themselves material still existing in "deep layers": they have happened. A more appropriate question may be not is this bizarre material "latent" but, rather, what was the nature of the stimulus and a corresponding process in the subject when this kind of data came into being or no longer remained "latent"? In Rorschach, we have the advantage of watching processes occur without having directly influenced the proceedings. The examiner is careful not to give that patient any pushes in directing his consciousness. Awareness about an image, or conscious judgments made about it, are brought to bear by the subject *after* the image appears. As any examiner knows, a subject's own images frequently surprise him, and it is at just this point, the confluence between image formation and conscious reaction, that we get information about the *process* of interaction between subject and image. An analysis of this process may tell us a great deal about the relation between the conscious and unconscious worlds belonging to the subject. It should be apparent that, in Rorschach, we are dealing with somewhat different dimensions of psychic processes from those we obtain through other means of gathering psychological data. There are qualitative differences in the kind of data obtained. Neglect of this knowledge may lead to misunderstandings about a diagnosis arrived at by other means.

One way to identify events taking place within a Rorschach examination is to make what the author (3) has called "process analysis." The distinguishing feature of this kind of Rorschach analysis is its focus. It is an attempt to isolate some of the facets that experienced Rorschach workers tend to utilize in making interpretations. It is a particular kind of focus in the analysis of sequence through Rorschach. It is an analysis of the linking conditions that contribute to the nature of the sequence. Designating sources for subjective data aids us in analysis of them. To be sure, it overlaps with content analysis, but it is an attempt to isolate and interpret the process the patient uses in structuring and integrating "whatever emerges or becomes part of conscious awareness." To accomplish this, one must make defenses, dynamics, and other ordinary foci in Rorschach interpretation peripheral for the moment. We must change our usual sets, since they may obscure identification of the process itself. We focus on what an individual is doing at any one time and its relation to the whole, a subtle use of interpretation of interaction between subject and image. Instead of being purely visual, a symbol may be inherent in the nature of a particular process.

It is useful to describe a schema against which dynamic processes may move. This schema provides us with a frame for viewing patterns related to sources of data, and of identifying processes related to disturbance against those associated with adaptation.

One may conceive two planes, one horizontal and the other vertical (see Fig. 23). On the left side of the horizontal place at "A," we designate withdrawal, and on its right side, at "B," we designate adaptation. Axis "AB" designates a movement zone reflecting the degree of formal adaptiveness. Vertically, at "C," we designate conscious processes, and at "D," we assign unconscious sources. The "CD" axis provides for a pattern of processes associated with conscious sources or unconscious ones.

Movement in either disturbed processes or adaptive ones may occur anywhere along these axes; they may vary from one moment to another, or they may cluster in certain areas.

Plate I

Responses	Inquiry
It looks like it could be one animal combined together. It could be Siamese twins. It could be a bat, but I don't think so.	It just looks like two animals born together. I wouldn't know what kind. Well, it sort of looked like a bat because of the little wings up here (means usual hands, central projections). (Q—What about this part?—meaning the outer large Ds or usual bat wings.) I haven't the slightest idea, they could be wings for all I know. It's possible that each one is a bat (each half of the card); it's very possible they could be having intercourse, but I doubt it. (Q—Could this whole thing be a bat?) I doubt it, because the wings are too far apart.

Plate II

Responses	Inquiry
Two animals combined together with their beaks. They could possibly be having intercourse. Don't know what this is (top red).	(Q—What makes them look like that?) Well, the connections here (above) and here (below). Wouldn't know what kind.

Plate III

Responses	Inquiry
This could be a man and a woman, and I doubt if this would be the breast (center red). Or it could be two animals, but they're exactly the same. It's possible they could be having a relation.	Well, a man and woman that way. (Q—top red?) Don't know. (Q—Having a relation?) The connection down here, but the faces are too far apart. (Q—center red?) Breasts or could be a bow tie. It's impossible to tell if it's a man or woman.

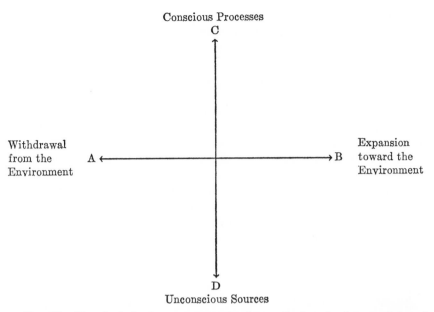

FIG. 23. AB axis designates a movement sphere reflecting the degree of formal adaptiveness. CD axis designates a sphere of movement between conscious awareness and symbol formation.

We will use a sample of Rorschach material from a patient to illustrate how we may use this schema. Plate I provides the stimulus for an easily perceived popular image. The subject experienced the blot in terms of what was combined and what was separate. This reflects an inner state in which she cannot separate conscious sources from unconscious ones. The ego has lost some of its judgmental power. Lack of differentiation within determines lack of differentiation without. The image is that of separate figures that are fused. The source materials for the responses to Plate I center within the angle formed by "AD" on our schema. The strength of those processes is shown by the subject's rejection of a more rational and far more conventional image, a bat. Inner movement has taken place from the unconscious, which tends to determine what she thinks consciously. She is not unaware of the obvious (form of a bat), but she rejects both the image and thoughts about taking it at face value. She actually tells us why it was not a bat to her, and her reasoning was determined by processes, *not* the nature of the content of the image. Forces that would not have occurred outside this kind of stimulus determined her experience. When she actually tried to separate her image into parts (could be two bats), her judgment evaporated and she got confused about what could be and what could not be the wings of the bat or bats. The process of trying to separate things threw her judgment askew. That became so strong that, when she was asked to respond to the obvious (large wings, side Ds), she failed to recognize it. Some quality that is archetypal in its strength of energy emerged around separateness and combination as symbols inside the process. When asked, she rejected the notion that the whole card could be a bat.

We have purposely left out any consideration of the sexual comments the subject made. An interpretation for "bats having intercourse" is rather easy to make in isolation. But by looking at the symbols inherent in the process of what happened, interpretation may acquire more scope. There is no question but that the patient has a complex associated with sexual differenti-ation. However, the symbol that emerged centered around the separation and combination as determiners of the *quality* of her perception. Intercourse be-tween the bats was not a symbol itself; it was a conscious deduction she made about two bats that looked joined physically. Sexual differentiation is shown against a larger problem of general differentiation between conscious and un-conscious worlds.

No movement of processes occurred that suggested any social concern or interest in outward adaptation. In substance, Plate I has provided us with the information that the patient is highly sensitive to a process related to things being combined and separated, that an image formed which contained an aspect of those forces in it (Siamese), and that those features within her were more predominant than her adaptive qualities connected with con-scious judgments.

Her response to Plate II shows us that the symbolization inside the process we isolated from Plate I continues to manifest itself. The blot contours are quite different, but we get much the same image as before, refitted to this blot. Bright color is present, and this can act as an emotional challenge al-lowing expression of concern or moving out to others (as well as the oppo-site), but the subject did not involve herself with it. The symbolism inside the process itself (image of how things are joined) continued along the lines of connection and fusion. Her consciousness lacks freedom to tolerate separa-tion. We may assume that separating the two sides of the blot was blocked by an unconscious state, and this determined the nature of the image. She is peculiarly sensitive to how her image is fused. When she reported "two animals," she gave us a popular image, which would fall inside the "CB'" angle on our schema, but qualities from the "AD" side contaminated what could have been adaptive. Neither the animals' positions not their activity was conventional. Sexual qualities again were not themselves the symbol that formed; they were attributed to the figures (through "AD" area sources) be-cause of the position observed (literal objective connectedness). Absence of separation means something sexual to the patient, but the symbolic vehicle was that of perceiving something connected, and this touches off an archetypal source that was shunted through a sexual complex. A lack of inner separation or differentiation became vested with sexual channeling.

Her responses to Plate III show us that the processes taking place in the subject are much more powerful for her than blot contours or her percepts. Experiences related to differences and likenesses, separateness and connections have become personal symbols for her. The strength of inner needs associated with those symbols infuses her images and logic. As with Plate II, she provides us with a popular image, people, but there are few other signs of "CB" area (adaptive) activity. She makes a conscious effort to make the two sides of the blot stimulus different (one male, one female), but doing so distorts the stimulus, since both sides are indeed exactly alike. The symbol message is that she cannot tolerate *awareness* of two sides looking exactly alike. This stems from lack of differentiation within, but this time she does reason about or question her own response. Consciousness made a weak attempt to assert itself through judgment, but when this happened, almost at once, her judgment became highly unrealistic (showing the much greater source-influence from "AD"), leading her to comment that the red center detail could be "a breast." That area is physically *separate* from the rest of the blot. Actually separating something from her image succeeds in separating the patient from realistic, conscious judgments. Red color, as a potential for a feeling response, might be experienced adaptively (bow tie), except archetypal influences altered the reality of her percept, leaving her with an image of breast. She cannot perceive her image realistically so long as she experiences the two sides as same or identical. We may readily infer that the patient has a homosexual complex which is displaced by flight into heterosexual fantasies. However, the nature of the process that goes on for her in Rorschach plays out the extent of a generalized lack of differentiation. This takes place not because of a sexual complex, but the sexual complex developed as a consequence of the differentiation problem. At this point, the patient is in danger of losing ego control, and the larger concern for her is separating what is conscious and connected with her complex, on the one hand, and her negative influences from archetypal sources, on the other. She is not separated from instinctual qualities, and in Rorschach we see these fused. The roots of her problem go back to the Paleolith. She has no power as goddess to rely on in her outer world, and she is being overwhelmed inside because of an absence of effective differentiation from her instinctual side. Her animals carried the symbol of her fused or undifferentiated instinctual life within, which was the root substance of her dilemma. Separation and connectedness as symbol experience touched off processes in the patient.

Archetypal influences led her percept from an image of a bow tie to the experience of the same area as a breast. Yet, an important aspect necessary to understanding this process includes her "*doubting*" that the center detail could be breasts. We must grasp the implications of that if we wish to understand something fundamental about the Rorschach experience. First, the image of a breast had to emerge; this happened totally *outside* any conscious intent on the part of the subject, and then and only then, ego awareness or judgment responded to the symbol. She immediately doubted its existence. A subjective process happened to her through laws that consciousness did not control. The image emerged despite any effort she may have made to suppress it. The image did not remain latent; it happened. What ensued was a fascinating process that owed its existence to laws separate from those applicable to conscious logic. In the first place, there are perfectly acceptable, realistic breasts on the figures of the blot, attached in an appropriate manner. We can see here a remarkable example of the archetypal significance of detached body members. Detaching them takes us to a different symbolism in our relation to them, a different psychological plane. The *subjective law of excluded awareness* has been at work. She was not consciously able to tolerate an awareness that the two figures were identical (either two females or two males). Their identical qualities were *excluded* from awareness. An essential condition for symbol formation developed.

Not only does the stimulus plate provide for percepts of breast appropriately placed on the human figures, the subject told us that she recognized the central red detail conventionally as a bow tie. *Despite* both of those hooks in the stimulus for rational thinking, the nature of the subject's percepts took meaning from different sources. Perceptual lines for the bow tie dissolved, and momentarily an image of a breast replaced it. The patient's need to see two figures that are objectively identical in form as different from each other (male and female) was powerful. The source for that need may have come partly from a personal complex about sexual differentiation. An archetypal source within flashed her an image of "breast." It was a communication that appeared inside subjective consciousness, because of the nature of the forces that came into play. This is *not* mystical, but a function of subjective laws. We would have to decipher the meaning of the symbol of breast, a universal symbol, inside the structure of this patient's psychology. Something connected with nurture and the functioning side of the female underlies the patient's sexual complex.

Something of the same process had happened before on Plate I. When the subject consciously attempted to separate the whole into parts (could be two bats), and when she was asked if usual wing areas for a popular bat could be wings, some *process* separated her from logic associated with objective consciousness and drew her into a different frame that influenced the nature of her percepts.

When this subject had been interviewed by another examiner with a goal of establishing a diagnosis and discovering complexes and dynamics, the interviewer got the impression she was disturbed, but he could not pin it down, and the impression was that her disturbance was not of psychotic proportions. She made appropriate responses to questions, and it was not clear how much her adaptiveness was impaired. Rorschach samples from her subjective state as she experienced inkblot stimuli helped us grasp more through analyzing subjective processes. The subject was in a precarious state, and her logic was not providing her with the structure to keep up her adaptivity. We can see that she had a great vulnerability for psychotic thinking under certain conditions, but a struggle was going on, and she exerted much energy around trying to separate out what was a product of her own consciousness and what was a function of what happened to her inside. Psychosis was not latent for her. Under the unique stimulus qualities of the Rorschach, in which outer adaptation may get removed, the extent of her disturbance became clear. However, a unitary diagnosis like psychosis would not be necessarily appropriate. We tend to define psychosis only for purposes of outer adaptation. We use it for making judgments about symptoms. This narrow use discriminates against Rorschach diagnosis and any patient's inner world.

Our schema may be useful for judging Rorschach data. It is, though, very general, and we must not leave out the possibility that any data may have a positive or negative influence on a given subject. Some individuals may show "AD" (unconscious sources) process activity and not be subject to either symptoms or disturbance. Some may show "CB" (conscious adaptation) activity and be vulnerable to psychological collapse. So long as we keep an open attitude about what data can mean for a person, and we seek to identify as much as we can about it, we move on in understanding ourselves.

REFERENCES

1. Forer, B. R. 1950. The latency of latent schizophrenia. J. Projective Techn., 14: 297–302.
2. McCully, R. S. 1962. Certain theoretical considerations in relation to borderline schizophrenia and the Rorschach. J. Projective Techn., 26: 404–418.
3. McCully, R. S. 1965. Process analysis: A tool in understanding ambiguity in diagnostic problems in Rorschach. J. Projective Techn. Personality Assessment, 29: 436–444.

SEVEN
Illustrative Case Materials

I. Jay Dunn (4) has pointed out that the history of emphasis in the field of mental health has moved into a third phase. The first phase, during the first part of this century, emphasized descriptive classification. The second phase, taking us nearly up to the present, has been focused around individual dynamics. The third phase, beginning in the sixties, has been focused around the individual as an integral member of society. Dunn noted that social psychology and psychiatry have been difficult to define because there is no uniform social theory of behavior. Community psychiatry represents an effort to apply knowledge that has come from an exchange of view from many disciplines. It is not clear what will result from the potpourri we have begun to apply at a grass roots level in America. Dunn emphasizes that people who are disassociated from each other are usually disassociated from themselves. The predicament that ensues is generally projected in demands for rational solutions, government programs, and social action to alleviate problems that cannot necessarily be solved by changing external conditions. Dunn notes that personal identity must must not be sacrificed for group identity.

We would suggest that archetypal laws influence both collective and individual behavior through structure. While the pendulum swings now here, now there, until we understand more about the laws of subjective consciousness, we will waste a great deal of human energy. Except in temporary conditions, like Hitler's time in Germany, archetypal energies associated with individual and group as separate varieties of human experience will continue to survive. This does not rule out that we may destroy ourselves in the meantime. The destructive energy collected by Hitler's movement is a clear example of how extinction may occur through man's own actions. In some ways that are collective, the youths of today, through clearing their percepts of particular chauvinism, and through intimate contact with youths of widely disparate cultural traditions, have been touched by their grasp of the archetype of destruction. A notion of "flower power" comes from the East. It is not understood in the West, nor is it likely to be in our time. An individual youth may carry none of this and may use the changing mores of youth to exploit personal needs, but collective energy is abroad today, and its effects may be wide, though they may be temporary.

In Rorschach psychology, we must be alert about how our technique may be used adaptively in a changing scene. The old way of diagnosis and delineation of dynamics may be over. This is not to say that their importance will disappear, but emphasis on them may, because either our grasp of what diagnosis is and what dynamics mean will widen or we will stay at an unproductive stage. History is not without unproductive stages, insofar as our improving our vision or grasp of ourselves is concerned. At present, considerable reaction exists about psychoanalysis and Freud's theories. Following Horney and Harry Stack Sullivan, the existentialists have widened our grasp. Carl Jung's depth psychology has a unique correspondence with many of the qualities that concern our youth of today. He has written on just those facets of human experience that have caught their fancy. Jung went to Africa and spent time with natives in remote places. He visited some of the American Indian cultures of the southwestern part of the United States. He spent the winter of 1937–1938 in India, talking with Yogins and searching through Indian art and thought. A number of illnesses afflicted him after his trip to India (at age 63). He has provided us with great wisdom and the perspective that is needed for the understanding of collective influences. He has warned against the dangers of Westerners getting caught up in the psychology of the East because we do not have a proper means of coping with Eastern experience. Archetypal structures are different in some respects for the different cultural traditions. Jung (9) made these points clear in "The Psychology of Eastern Meditation" (1943), and in an earlier paper (9) just before his visit to India, "Yoga and the West" (1936). Eastern psychic material may be destructive and dangerous to a Westerner, whose consciousness and archetypal influences are different. We will look at the case materials of a subject who was rent asunder by her experiences in the East.

All of these matters pertain to the way the Rorschach may be useful inside the changing scene. The individual must be understood in a different way and not solely against the old ideas of psychological pathology.

For those reasons, we are going to look at several individual cases in a way that is not traditional. The nature of a particular diagnosis is not going to be crucial, and understanding dynamics is not going to be as important for us as raising questions and looking at processes. The questions raised and the processes we focus on may help bridge the Rorschach with the changing scene. We do not expect to talk about group dynamics, since the Rorschach reflects them only indirectly. Our approach will remain with the individual, but, hopefully, it will take into consideration the changing setting for the individual looked at against the archetypal influences that have defined the human condition.

The author assumes that any student of the Rorschach method will obtain ample instruction and experience with the dynamics associated with Freud's libido theory elsewhere. This does not minimize the importance of those dynamics when they apply through the data that may pertain. Other authors have amply provided students with the nature of Rorschach correlates that pertain to nosology. By emphasizing theory and a means to grasp wider views about symbolism, we do not mean to devalue other kinds of interpretation and use for data.

We will allow the data themselves, in our case materials, to take us where they will. Selections of cases have been made around amplifying our point of view, showing how key cases may provide us with more information than might necessarily accrue with scores of cases in whom the facet we are interested in may be excluded, and how flexible the Rorschach is in molding itself around human psychology, no matter what facet of it may be uppermost in the consciousness of the cultural influences at hand.

We regret that it is not possible to present the Rorschach data for each case in a uniform way. The author did not administer the Rorschach in each case, and we have had to make do with varying degrees of material from inquiry. Scoring is not crucial here, since we have not been concerned with completeness in interpretation. The location of images has been made clear when it was possible and appropriate.

Case 1
A Stone Age record in a geriatric context

RORSCHACH

Card I

51 seconds

A woman . . . three women . . . (center, and two sides . . .) Pretty . . . Three women dancing, a devilish dance . . . they are dancing devilish dance . . . a fantastic story . . . saw once a person in the form of a cat . . . and he killed the person in form of cat . . . a devil . . . Diablo—devil . . . (a friend of his asked him to kill the devil) . . . he had magical powers . . . he still has magic powers . . . the devil flew to a tree . . . and he caught him, and they showed him the AMULET . . . started doing his magician works . . . he killed.

Card II

4 seconds

Here it is . . . this is it . . . the devil with the fire in his head and tail . . . only 25 words he said, and he disappeared . . . the devil was afraid of the words . . . (advises interpreter against the devil).

Card III

4 seconds

The devil again . . . you see that's it . . . the devil is afraid of him . . . they cooked a leg (on each side), after killed devil . . .

I will never know anything about this (tells interpreter . . .) He would like to teach me the magic words . . . and sayings . . . so I am able to do what he can do . . .

After he teaches me, I will be able to kill devil, and do things he can do. With those prayers . . . magic prayers, he can kill phantoms too . . .

He once saw a phantom . . . a big phantom . . . he was sick of something at that time when they called him to kill the phantom. However, he went there, and he saw the big one with seven children, and he took four different kinds of plants and threw it at the witch's neck . . . and she died.

And the witch told him that she will die, and he had to take care of the children or kill all of them . . . all of them were dead . . . she died . . . but then the children said that she wasn't dead, she was alive, so he again used his magic powers, and finally killed her.

181

Card IV

10 seconds

This is a different kind of devil ... it has ... spurs for horse riding ... (he is not speaking of this one in particular, but devil in general.) Devil is afraid of prayers in general, and magic prayers ... He knows a prayer called the "little our father" which is very dangerous for the devil ... he doesn't know of this one in particular but telling in general about devils. I can kill them if I learn the magic prayers ... Another story patient was attacked by mad dogs ... that seemed to be endeviled, maddened ... he was riding a horse, and he grabbed one of the dogs by the tail ... and rode away ... and he took rib ... from the dog ... from the devil's dog ... and killed the rest with the rib from the devil dog ...

Card V

3 seconds

He's coming back, but now he looks like a bat with horns ... (devil in form of a bat with horns) ... tells the same story about dogs again ... Same story in detail about dogs ... (refuses to stop with story).

Card VI

10 seconds

This is the oldest one of the devils ... he's good for nothing already ... he's too old ... "he doesn't blow anymore" (slang expression means "he's too old." If something is not good anymore, doesn't blow anymore.) These are the things you must learn ... so devils can't harm you.

Card VII

4 seconds

Another impersonation of the devil ... this is the wife of the devil, and this is the son of the devil. (Each D-2 separately.) She's pregnant for 14 months ... after the wife of the devil was pregnant for 14 months ... the devil in person came to him and asked him to see his wife and investigate and see what was wrong ... and offered 5000 pesos if he could do something. After using his magic powers he finally brought son to life ...

That's the way old men used to do ... now don't know about these things, work with machines, do nothing.

Card VIII

4 seconds

Now he's turned red ... and it has the legs outward, and (D-1) are the two children, and this is the magician (D-3) is the magic which he applied to the devils ... devil is small, because he's afraid of his magic powers. The devil promised him two cases of silver. The devil could give him two cases of silver but the patient wouldn't free him. There's no way for the devil to get out; he doesn't want him to get out ... he's already said all of his magic prayers ... so there is no way out for the devil.

Card IX

(Turns card on back.)

The devil is already dead. He would need two cases of gold to revive him. But the patient won't revive him . . . a great death. (Patient is pleased about devil's death. The Indian Basiliom Hermandez was his teacher.)

Card X

(Turns card over on back and looks at printing.)

He's dead. (D-11) (Turns card back.) This is dead . . . but reviving him in different forms, different ways. He's traveling in different direction, and taking different roads. Reviving in different forms and spreading in different ways . . . the old devil. Devil couldn't do anything against the interpreter because patient is protecting him.

The first case is a record obtained from a South American Indian, who shared the culture of the Caribbean Indians. He lived in a mountain village in the Andes of Colombia, near Monteria. Great age was common in the village, and individuals aged 110 years were documented. He claimed to have been born in 1789, which would have made him 167 years old at the time he was examined in 1956 at The New York Hospital-Cornell Medical Center,[1] during an 8-day stay at that center while he was being studied by geriatric experts. He was 4 feet, 4 inches tall and weighed around 85 pounds. He had no teeth, but little, if any, grey hair. He was vigorous, enjoyed smoking cigars, and drank much rum and coffee. Through an interpreter, he made it clear that he was in search of his sixth wife, and he wanted a fat one, who could support him. Medical officials at The New York Hospital-Cornell Center reported that he was "vigorous, alert, and observing." They stated that although his hands suffered from degenerative arthritis, "his bones and joints are in a condition that many a young man might envy." They noted that the most impressive thing about the subject was the condition of his blood vessels. Extensive tests failed to show any calcification. Hospital officials commented to the press that their examinations led them to believe that the subject "possibly may be more than 150 years old." He died exactly 1½ years later at a Catholic home for the aged near the place of his birth in the Andes.

At the time of examination, he was said to have been married five times and to have outlived all his wives. All of his relatives had long since died, and the last, a grandchild, had died 20 years earlier at the age of 80 years. He did not read. A man, whose age was 90, and who lived in his village, reported that the subject was considered to be a very old man when he was

---

[1] Permission to use this case was kindly given by Dr. William N. Thetford, who administered the Rorschach to the subject.

a boy. The subject himself spoke again and again of fighting in the seige of Cartagena, which ended in 1826. He spoke of a General Ayala, and of carrying messages for him; also of a Sergeant Alvana, who seems to have been instrumental in converting him to Catholicism.

At his home in Colombia, he was medically observed at the time of his death. He had been doing well until 3 weeks prior to his death. There was no dramatic disease; he started to lose vitality and activity and soon had to lie in bed, where he remained until he died. Urinary excretion diminished and disappeared 3 days before his death. An autopsy was carefully done by an expert in Colombia,[2] and his vital organs were shipped to the United States for study. There were electrocardiographic (EKG) tracings made of his heart action 2 or 3 days prior to his death and another at the end until no further electrical action was recorded by the machine. The autopsy findings were unremarkable as to any disease; there was some evidence for cerebral atrophy, but this was not extensive. Some of the usual changes with age were found. The autopsy physician had the impression of uremia as the cause of death.

Our chief interest in this record is not so much the subject's great age, but the nature of his experience as he meets each Rorschach plate's impact. Almost all of the content of his images and the narrative that accompanies them is outside the layered complexities of the contents of consciousness in Western civilization. The subject knew Spanish, and he had become converted to the Catholic Church around age 37, if his birth date was correct. Neither the Catholic Church nor Spanish culture had left much mark on his consciousness or on his subjective experiences. The nature of what he saw and experienced connects him with consciousness in primitive men transculturally. Possibly, 75 years earlier, his Rorschach imagery would have been more culturally adapted. Perhaps consciousness diminishes in a phylogenetic way past a certain peak. Whatever the case, and we suspect Western culture never touched him much, we are interested in his experience because of what it may tell us about the nature of a stimulus plate, given the qualities we may associate with this antique man.

Plate I provides him with a female trio, one median, and two laterally. Their dance is a devilish one, but the aesthetic impact for him was positive (pretty). The story he gave had to do with getting out of the power of a feline devil. This supports our notion of Plate I as having substance of matriarchal power, which may have a positive or negative effect. The subject is aware of the need for protection from something female.

Plate II provides the subject with the devil, perhaps the result of the dance of the figures on I, since he seemed to have expected a devil to appear, with "here it is," "this is it." Words are a result of thinking, and magic

---

[2] Dr. L. Salleg.

words, which recur in fairy tales, are usually symbolic of consciousness. Through *the word,* the power of the authority in his possession, the irrational attributes of his psychological energy come under conscious control. This irrational part seems to be a manifestation of his experience with matriarchal power. Subjectively, all his experiences through the Rorschach have to do with the means to obtaining power over an irrational element. That means is a supernatural one for him. As a simple archetypal condition, Plate II turns a male subject toward the task of separation from the power of matriarchal authority, and this subject's experience with this plate is not counter to the psychology of that task. Becoming aware (through words or thinking), frees a subject like magic, if the awareness belongs to the subject, personally. This was not the case for this subject; awareness came through rote repetition of twenty-five words, the gleanings from another's experience. The subject remains in the power of matriarchal authority.

Plate III continues the theme of a means to avoid negative power, this time of a witch, who represents, in masculine experience, a negative female power. For this subject, getting power over that negative force dominates how he views others and what his relationship to them is like. While he is not expected to behave in New York in the same way as in the Andean village, all newspaper accounts of his visit to New York showed him highly labile, belligerent, and combative. He punched male and female reporters alike, and, while being photographed with a blond who thought he might find it aesthetically pleasant, he socked her one and accused her of trying to steal his ring. In the beginning, there is the suggestion that the devil was being eaten, but the major portion of his response to the plate had to do with destroying the power of a witch. His behavior was influenced by the dominance of the way he experienced the negative side of the female.

Plate IV shows us that the subject does not use the concept of devils indiscriminately. He recognizes this one as "the devil in general," the one who stands for all the others in his class. He is a fully masculine one, who rides with spurs, and his power is humbled only when he feels influence from the Church. Here is the only brush the subject has with the Church inside his Rorschach experiences. A prayer, "little our father" is dangerous for devils, but the subject is careful not to commit himself as to whether this archetype of the masculine devil can be brought under control by prayer. He is awed by the presence in Plate IV, and he doubts his personal magic as a means of protection. All of this primitive man's subjective experiences for Plate IV had to do with the masculine side of life (dogs, riding, little father, God, and male devil). We feel this is an authentic experience of the plate around the archetype of masculine structure. How he functions through it includes the first sign of any humility in the subject.

Plate V takes him to the devil as bat. His world is populated with forces that would do him in, and his balance against it depends on his powers to combat it. Since we doubt that life for him in his village was a continual matter of fear about magic and devils (allowing for plenty of superstition and some magic), his subjective experiences through the Rorschach may have been atavistic, and they may have contrasted rather markedly with actual events in his mountain home.

Plate VI provides us with especially interesting perceptual discriminations. If Plate IV was a generic, nonspecific male devil, who stirred up awe in the subject, Plate VI is a specific one indeed, and he tells us about his psychological capacities. This is the oldest specific devil; he has become impotent. The subject himself was called the oldest living man on earth, and he was well aware of that. There is little question but that the subject gave us primary data about his own masculine energy and its level of functioning.

Plate VII becomes authentically feminine for him, stirring up a mother-son connection, and importunate qualities associated with a woman's overdue fertility. Something is long overdue about his separation from the mother. The subject's fears are related to a tremendous need for matriarchal protection. All the world is hostile without her nurture and protection. His own masculinity is fearsome and unreliable as a source. He is still inside the power of the matriarch, over 150 years after his birth. At the same time, he may have returned to an earlier stage psychologically. Perhaps earlier, he functioned better through Eros, though there is no evidence to support higher development. Matriarch, mother-son, and fertility, together with separation from the mother, all summate for him here. Presumably, the matriarch cannot free her child; she is caught in a continuous situation of hosting and nurturing. It requires maleness-in-general to disrupt the repetitive cycle. This is an authentic means to disrupt mother-child symbiosis. A bribe brings about the birth, and since this is an external means (not a personal one), separation is an illusion, since physical separation is not a psychological one. The primary interest here is the nature of his experience with matriarchal substance.

Plate VIII transforms, diminishes, and imprisons the hostile force that *devil* represented for him. The ego struggles to gain control over the force that is alien to it. Success is slender, since nothing shows the subject behaving outside a power struggle. He doesn't function through or with the feminine; he seeks to subdue her power.

Plate IX takes the subject into contact with "a great death," which suggests an archetypal one, beyond the individual ego. This seems to be a death for the devil-in-general, not a particular one. As "doesn't blow anymore" implied impotence, death for his masculine energy seals the fate for his ego. The ego would take no action to revive the devil if it could. This psychological state may be related to the subject's own death. When he was examined, there was no good physical reason to expect death soon. He appeared vigorous, and with much animal appetites, looking for a new mate. There is no affirmation of life in association with Plate IX for this subject. His own masculinity, which has been at odds with him, loses its life force here. His physical energy for life is not accompanied by enough psychological energy to sustain it.

Plate X shows the powerlessness of the ego to exterminate the forces that haunt the subject. As in a naturalistic Sansara, the forces become reincarnate, and on many levels and several dimensions for him. No need is expressed to seek protection from this multi-manifestation of what had frightened him before. Through this man's experience, we see the eternal return from the *great round*. The subject remarked that if it frightened the interpreter, he, the subject, would protect him. The psychological state wakened in him through Plate X may reflect a readiness to return to whence he came.

We have been able to glean bits of material from the Rorschach pattern in this subject that have collective application. While we can only conjecture about the nature of his personal psychology in the past, it looks as though he never got independent of matriarchal power. He has a false set of ego values which do not coincide with the means to cope with the power struggle that has him in its grips. Amulet, words, plants, prayer, bone (rib), and money were variously used to subdue hostile forces. The sequence of his images shows us that each is a temporary expedient. Some of the questions raised from the materials would be as follows.

Did he have five wives or five mothers? We know from his remarks that he wanted to be "taken care of and supported." He was not a febrile old man, but vigorous enough to assert himself aggressively. Yet, instead of wanting to be a sixth husband, did he wish to become an only child? Could the subject have lived out his ego values? At this point, did he have enough masculine energy to support his ego values? Left too long in the human condition, perhaps nature saw her neglect and called him in.

The materials in this subject's Rorschach are the stuff of fairy tale and myth. They illustrate how those media function to carry collective qualities. Wholly an assumption, we may guess that earlier, his Rorschach would have included much more personal material. It may mean that if we learn to prolong the state of life, through transplants or other means, the psyche will continue on a plane of involution in which the individual disappears and the collective in humanity is all that is left. His experience with Plate IX may have meant his own readiness to die. Should this psychology be tampered with through artificial medical means?

Case 2
Cracking the power of the ego: resurgence of the influence from an ancient archetype

RORSCHACH

Response   Inquiry

Card II

16 seconds

1. That's a little more difficult, it looks almost like something anatomical, curious looking. I just don't know what to think on this. First impression was not quite so immediate, it did have some sort of facial appearance, but then the red parts of it changed that feeling I've had. I never had any kind of test like this before. (Say whatever occurs to you.) Well, I suppose you are supposed to report some kind of sensation or impression, and that's hard for me to do.

W   F(CF,Fm)   At

2. Some kind of face. (Q) Looks sort of like a skull a little bit, as did the other. The red suggested something anatomical, something dissected out of an animal. Pelvis keeps popping in my mind, animal pelvis, but I guess it shouldn't.

W   F   At

1. Lower part of anatomy of some large animal. (Q) Overall shape, part of a living thing, or once part of a living thing. Color disrupts that, originally the color made it harder to decide what it is. The red could be blood that came from it, ripped out or dissected, and red is blood that came out. This is not new, a second look at it, oozing out, and a drawing, the red looks like a fluid and it drained symmetrically.

2. I was cheating a little. (Meaning cuts off all red.) I'd like to turn it, (v) now more like a skull with top part removed.

188

Card IV

6 seconds

1. Another strange one. Kelp you see in shallows, salt harbors, but so symmetrical. Does look like seaweed, but that's not helpful, I suppose.

DW   cF   Otendency

1. This curved thing with its shading made it look like Northern Lights (female area at top). A curtain-like effect, illustration, fold effect, kaleidoscopic color effect. The shading makes it look like that—that gives the effect, shading gives translucency. It looks translucent and like a fold. Shading.

Card VIII

18 seconds

1. Oh, we got colors this time, sort of bilious colors too. Looks like a couple of salamanders or frogs, tearing a piece of water vegetation as might be seen under water. Color scheme is interesting—on either side of the symmetrical axis of symmetry, each animal comes out of an orange area and is surrounded by pinkish area same color, and are touching green, blue-green projections with one foot and touching grey-blue-green with other leg, and other hind leg is more purple. I'm just describing the way it's designed, that's wasting it, but I don't know what else to do. Maybe I'd get better with some years.

W   FM(CF,F/C)   A   Ptendency

1. (Q-salamander) Fish-shaped, don't know what. (Q-color) Yes, somewhat. (Q-underwater) Color scheme.

Limits

(Patient was asked to look through the cards and see if anything reminded him of people. He took this quite literally and spent a great deal of time on each card.)

Card I

This looks like a witch-like person, creature perched on a rock, being reflected from a still pool. (Side D)-hat, cape is projection, and bottom is cloak.

Projections look like hands pointing—part of the witch. Still looks like a fox face though.

Card IV

This one, only thing here—this looks like a heavy man in overcoat with pack on his back, stooping under the weight of the load. He's carrying a cane or umbrella, it sticks out in front, but doesn't look right since nothing sticks out in back of him. It occurs to me, looks like an angel, mythical figure, looking down at a tome or book—or a witch with pointed cap with object in his hands, a winged being of some kind.

Card VI

Here again, this projection looks like somebody bending over with a heavy load on his back. (Q-kind of person) Heavily clothed. Two of them of course, one on each side. The Ghost of Christmas Past, from Charles Dickens. Looks like he, or it, is carrying some kind of burden on his shoulder or back, and a great big cloak spreading around on the ground.

The second case shows us something of how archetypal energy associated with an ancient image can become split from a murky depth and lodge in the multilayered consciousness of a modern youth. The dominant image in this subject might have appeared in the record we called "Stone Age." The image of vampire for this subject gained as much control over consciousness as did "devil" for the first subject. Both cases have to do with a male in a negative relation with matriarchal power. That power interfered with sexual functioning in both cases, but quite differently.

The subject was a young adult, unmarried, white male. The author (12) has published materials about this case elsewhere. It has no parallel in the annals of medical history. No known factors in his background would connect him with any special attitudes or exposure to the myth of the vampire. We have called the case one of autovampirism, though his vampiristic needs extended externally also. His earliest memory (age 3) was seeing a dog which had been hit by a car lying in a pool of blood. Another, around the same time, included his sitting on a child's toilet, and having his brother squirt water from a syringe at him through the keyhole. At 4, he remembered having a nurse place his cold hands on her neck after a winter's walk in a park. There were no unusual childhood diseases. Masturbation began at age 11 and became associated with drawing his own blood and a compulsion to see it as it was drawn. He developed a complicated means to achieve this. He punctured his neck veins, and by performing the Valsalva maneuver, he could make venous blood pour rapidly in a cup while watching in a mirror. In time, he learned to obtain arterial blood from his neck, having first used a broken razor to puncture a small artery, and later the carotid artery by the same means. He discovered that by lying on his back, he could catch the spray of blood in his mouth and drink it. Later, he learned to puncture the basilic vein in his arm and suck the blood directly. Masturbation began after having started the bloodletting, and reached ejaculation. This was accompanied by fantasies of taking blood from a young, smooth, hairless boy with prominent neck arteries. There was no fantasy of the other young boy's genitals, and the subjects of fantasy were never female. The frequency of these episodes was about once every 3 weeks. Masturbation itself was much more frequent and was accompanied by fantasies of sucking blood from the necks of young boys. During one period, around age 20, he found a young boy who would allow him to put his mouth on his neck for a short time.

He was known to have a congenital vascular anomaly of the right cerebral hemisphere.[3] This came to light in relation to the appearance of partial paralysis (not long before his psychiatric hospitalization). There were complicating hysterical qualities as well, and he made use of his physical handicap for secondary gain.

Before we look at the subject's Rorschach materials, some orientation about the significance of vampire in history may be useful.

The vampire has been a subject in folk tale, superstition, and myth throughout the history of man. Since it is generally thought to be a predominantly Slavic myth, and its pervasive recurrence in history is seldom

---

[3] Dr. Arthur W. Epstein of Tulane University pointed out to the author that primitive symbols sometimes appear with abnormalities in the temporal-limbic system. There was a suggestion of temporal lobe burst pattern in this subject's electroencephalogram (EEG), but it was not considered diagnostic. There is a growing scientific interest in examining violence against temporal lobe abnormalities.

An interesting parallel exists between a facet of the materials in this case and those of Sirhan Sirhan. His Rorschach materials were published in the appendices of Kaiser's (10) book on the Kennedy assassination. Sirhan Sirhan responded to Rorschach Plate IV with an original image similar to the one in this case. He said, "Hell, underwater plantations (meaning plankton), plant life, kelp. Like seeing through kelp, this depth thing here." Kelp is an exceedingly rare image, and its appearance on Plate IV raises interesting questions. As a form of life kelp symbolizes lack of development, and its passivity is almost its definition as it is buffeted about in ocean currents. It is the pawn of the whim of the medium it subsists upon, the sea. As an image, it represents the psychology of a wholly inadequate masculine structure, and an energy associated with helpless passivity. Like the subject in our case, Sirhan Sirhan may have also been inside the power of the matriarchal archetype. This may be the *sine qua non* for certain types of violence. Perhaps if not the only ingredient, it may be an essential one. The ambition psychologically in both subjects may have been to acquire power through the means of mother-right (to destroy), an illegitimate aspiration for a male (whose masculinity was too formless to offer structure of hope). Looked at this way, his zeal about who owned the earth of Israel, a powerful local archetypal force in the Arab world, took him psychologically into a region of mother-source, and his lability catapulted him into violence. Absence of masculine sources within further such a state.

Another facet may link the two cases. The author reviewed Sirhan Sirhan's Rorschach materials blindly, without any other data (the materials were copied and mailed to the author by a colleague) and the question of epilepsy as a factor in the picture occurred at once. In a most fascinating way, color threw Sirhan Sirhan into a powerful state ranging from imbalance to panic. It would be useful to acquire a series of EEG sequences on the man accused of shooting Robert Kennedy.

recognized, some attention to the historical perspective of the vampire image may be useful.

Some of the most venerable members of the pantheon of human gods were given to blood sucking in one form or another. However, the symbolism of the act may have no connection with vampirism *per se*. For example, a whole group of Vajra deities in Tibetan Lamaism are represented as blood drinkers, but their dripping flagons of blood merely symbolize the need for mastery over life. Yet, in the *Gilgamesh* legend, the oldest in recorded history, the vampire theme emerged and its qualities were as clearly described and gory as those of medieval times. The earliest known depiction of a vampire appears on a prehistoric Assyrian bowl (15) and shows a man copulating with a vampire whose head has been severed from her body. In India, the vampire theme can be traced to the *Atharva Veda,* and the *Baital-Pachisi,* or *Tales of a Vampire*, form an important part of the body of ancient literary heritage. In ancient Mexico, vampires were called Ciuateteo and were associated with women who had died in their first labor. The Chinese vampire, Ch'ing Shih, often described in stories of the T'ang Dynasty, takes origin from much earlier times and has a close similarity with the vampire image of the West. It would appear that a psychic counterpart necessary for projection of the vampire into myth has existed since earliest times and that it may be among the most archaic images known.

Joseph Campbell (1) has stated that European mythology and folk tale suffered from a comparative poverty until around the twelfth century, when works of Indian, Celtic, and Arabian masters of narrative found their way onto the European scene. Some of the most beautiful of the European tales can be traced to Eastern and Celtic sources. Indian story forms influenced the style and content of the works of Boccaccio and Chaucer. The vampire theme may have reached Western Europe through Turkey and the Balkans, having come from India.

The vampire myth caught the imagination of a number of the most influential literary minds of the past century. Goethe, Southey, Byron, and Baudelaire wrote about the subject, and it played an important role in John Keats's *Lamia*, and in Samuel Taylor Coleridge's *Christobel*. In *Justine*, the Marquis de Sade vividly depicted a character who takes lustful pleasure in watching the blood flow from the veins of his victims. Le Fanu and Thomas Preskett Prest were among those who brought the image to the popular press, while Bram Stoker's *Dracula* made the vampire a household word. Even so brilliant a scientific mind as that of James Clerk Maxwell was fascinated with the image and he wrote a poem, *The Vampyre,* in his 14th year.

Ernest Jones (8) described the vampire as "a nocturnal spirit who embraces a sleeper to suck his blood from him; he is evidently a product of the nightmare." Jones (8) discussed vampirism as a symbolic manifestation, and, using the psychoanalytic point of view, he has described and drawn together considerable information about the vampire myth in Eastern Europe. In his review of writings on the subject, he indicated that certain popularized figures described in the annals of sexual criminology as "vampires" were necrophiliacs. Several sensational accounts of criminal psychopaths in Europe in the nineteenth and twentieth centuries were mistakenly called "vampires." The *Encyclopedie Medico-Chirurgicale* records that Epaulard published a thesis (1901) entitled *Vampirisme,* written at Lyons in France. These case histories dealt mainly with criminal psychopaths and necrophilia, however, and may not be directly pertinent to the subject of this study.

We are concerned with a subject who showed overt vampiristic characteristics. This uniquely pathological drive was acted out on himself, while a similar drive toward others was partly contained. There is no parallel case recorded in the literature. When discussed at all, Fenichel (5) being an example, the notion of vampirism has been regarded as a theme in mythology derived from dream or fantasy.

The subject was studied during the period of a year's hospitalization. He showed a curious, unexplained cyclic mood swing, which was known not to have been due to medication. For a long period, he showed a 4-day period of elation, followed by 12 days of depression. He said that he noticed his deepest depression coincided with the appearance of the full moon. He reported not infrequent dreams of bloodletting, which created a pleasant feeling at the time, but brought about anxiety upon awaking. At least one known attempt to puncture the common carotid artery was made during his stay at the hospital. When describing his subjective attitudes during the bloodletting episodes, he reported that at one time he would feel a sense of peace as if being loved by someone, while at another time he felt as if he had subdued somebody who had attacked him.

Except for the period of elation, a sustained depressed mood was obvious during his hospitalization. There was no history of either heterosexual or homosexual experiences, nor of any use of alcohol, drugs, or tobacco. He was well aware of the abnormality of his behavior. He did have thoughts about self-destruction.

He was the fourth of four children, having two brothers and a sister. One brother was considered severely disturbed. Of the children, his sister made the best adaptation. He developed a craze for collecting flashlights about the time his bizarre fantasies began. By fourteen, his interest switched to guns, telescopes, and racing bicycles. His family was in the upper socioeconomic bracket. His sister described his relationship with his mother as "more like a lover than a son." The family was Protestant. Most significantly of all, the family showed a blindness toward the whole pattern. At times, he had to be hospitalized during puberty for blood transfusions due to anemia. Flimsy, untenable reasons were put forth by their son to account for this, which were unquestioned by the parents.

It is not possible to exclude organic facets in the overall picture. Against that, however, he was known to demonstrate a remarkable, highly circumstantial memory. He showed perfect recall for the nine Bender Gestalt designs. It is unlikely that any intellectual loss had occurred alongside any central nervous system damage.

His approach to the Rorschach plates was excruciatingly circumstantial and defensive. For this reason, we have left out some of his circumstantial details. We have included all his images that would be useful. His images during limits testing were often more pertinent than his first ones, because of his defensiveness and ego-screening.

His first image was that of a "face of a fox," and in limits the side images were a "witch, perched on a rock, being reflected in a still pool." Perceptually, fox head was the stronger of the two images. One may be alerted for a crafty means of dealing with negative power from the matriarchal world.

Most of the Rorschach imagery and his comments (apart from the material that appeared with limits testing), showed a psychological world in which the ego strained desperately to maintain control. His intricate defensiveness and circumstantiality reflect an effort to glue consciousness to extraversion. His efforts kept most of his images within the "CB" triangle, made up by the coordinates we described in Chapter 6 on process analysis. Yet, in spite of the energy spent in that regard, his images dipped into the zone "AD" momentarily, upon occasion, moving back again to "CB" processes. We may see an example of this as he responded to Plate II.

As if drawn along by primitive energy and its momentum, and in spite of his contrary conscious intent, something formless, but raw and primitive, emerged by the end of the inquiry about his imagery for Plate II. Interestingly, he not only stated that the red color represented blood, but he was alert to its state, that of freshness. It was blood that disrupted the possibility of *life* in the image for him. This links the subject's inner struggle with proportions between life and death. This is a subject who is forced to deal with his fate inside matriarchal powers. Without going through any of the later psychological stages, his is a struggle with destructive forces in a state of oneness, or lack of differentiation from matriarchal dominance. It is known that he had suicidal thoughts. A struggle between life and death is the basic motive in the vampire's search for blood. A need for renewal of life is concretized by extracting it from others, or, as in this case, from himself. The utter impersonal quality associated with matriarchal forces is made crystal clear here. The subject systematically endangered his own life. His own person was irrelevant to the force. While it is true that sexual pleasure was associated with his autovampirism, the fantasy image he carried was not a sexual one, but one associated with the availability of a tender, easy mark (beardless boy) for more blood from distended arteries. None of the materials from the study of this subject suggested more for his sexual development than of impulses created by puberty grafted on a primitive psyche, unequipped to move through sexual powering to higher psychological stages.

It should be kept in mind that the subject was fully aware of the morbidity of his desires and his behavior. He viewed the entire matter like having been caught in the web of a terrible curse. He was terrified of himself. Yet, consciousness and the desires of the ego were unable to pull him away from his struggle with inner power, though at the time he was studied, they kept him suspended, almost nowhere, against negative flooding of consciousness from archetypal sources.

When he was asked to write what sort of animal would he like most to be, he responded, "what really occurs to me is not an animal, but something that flies, maybe a hawk or bird of prey, or better, an albatross." Those reflections in the subject show the extent to which *contradiction* existed among his instinctual needs. His aspirations, even his ego ideal, are pulled into the pathos of his struggle. It is not farfetched for us to assume that the instincts of this subject were avian and, like the negative power of the matriarch, impersonal enough to prey on what came by, if survival demanded it. While the albatross was the "bird of good hope" to sailors, it had impunity, since to kill one would bring disaster. These qualities make it clear that the subject was extremely undeveloped psychologically, engrossed in autogratifications, tempered only by his intellect and the relentless struggle of his ego to keep balance. He was like the albatross in Coleridge's poem, *The Rime of the Ancient Mariner,* "It ate the food it ne'er had eat."

His imagery for Plate IV shows how formless his masculine structure actually was. Like seaweed, its essence was passively buffeted by the ebb and flow from sea-sources within. When he reported "Northern Lights" for the female area of this plate, the *law of excluded awareness* may have been at work. The symbolism is one of extreme remoteness and cold, impartiality in nature. Nothing there connects him with life and developmental potentials.

For Plate V he reported the image of a bat, as a bird of prey, coming in to pounce. Plate VI was a "bear skin," and shading was not used as texture. However, more was offered for Plate VI through limits. Plate VII yielded two images of dogs. This adds nothing archetypally, except possible instinctual fidelity inside the mother-world, which seems to have engulfed him. Plate VIII elicited images of very primitive creatures involved in destructive behavior. Plate IX elicited a "face of a cat," and Plate X, "mosaic tile colors." The Rorschach sequence does not provide us with any data much beyond those that reflect an enormously undifferentiated passivity pitted against predatory instinctual needs. This appears in a rigid, perfectionistic, compulsive context, through which his ego strains against any inner participation. He is so undeveloped that without the vigilance of his intellect he would be thrown into chaos. Classical signs of depression exist, and a paranoid obligato moves to the depressive accompaniment, but the ego has kept a semblance of power. There are psychopathic traits, and vampire, something that preys on others, is a psychopathic image. However, these diagnostic terms, though useful, do not carry us far enough in understanding more about this extraordinary state in a modern subject. Since the whole theme is from myth, we must look to myth for clarification.

The subject drew on two images which appear in Coleridge's *Rime of the Ancient Mariner*. He probably knew this poem, but that is less important than how the images carry qualities of his peculiar psychology. The point of Coleridge's poem was the nature of the split between forces of good and evil. That psychology dominated consciousness in this subject. He was split between the urge to express his subhuman needs in life beyond fantasy, and the wish to deny them and throw his energy in with upright morality. In Coleridge's poem, the albatross was a pious bird of good omen, who looked to desolate sailors as if it had a "Christian soul." The ancient mariner (suggesting that he carried archetypal energy through his antiquity), overcome by some inner force of evil, shot the albatross with his crossbow. The sailors hung it around his *neck,* "instead of a cross." The ancient mariner was caught then under a curse or evil spell, until his human compassion enabled him to overcome his insolent, egocentric impulses associated with evil and destruction of good. When that occurred, the albatross fell from his neck into the sea. This is the source of the saying, "albatross around your neck," meaning something that sacrifices the bearer for purposes outside his will. This subject was locked in a similar struggle. He was caught inside the archetypal forces of good versus evil, through the means of being under the power of the destructive side of matriarchal energy. His neck was his *bête noir.* He, like the ancient mariner, one who ploughed the same course in ages yore, was caught in a kind of "life-in-death" vise which would not let go. After destroying the albatross, the ancient mariner spoke words which rather starkly reflect a similar state in our subject:

> Fear at my heart, as at a cup
> My life-blood seem'd to sip.

Plate IV stirred an atmosphere in the subject similar to that in Coleridge's rhyme: sea life, dark wetness, absence of longed-for color, and the presence of primitive, primal forces of nature, totally impersonal. The subject had no masculine strength or energy with which to stand against the cold, impersonal side of matriarchy. His sister saw him as "son-lover" to his mother, but the subject was simply in her power. He was psychologically like the unborn child the subject in the previous case saw on Plate VII. Fourteen months had passed and he had not yet emerged.

It is interesting to note the contrast between the imagery in the subject's limits versus the original ones. This shows us how the psychological split in the subject carries forth to the difference between good and evil on other planes. Reality and unreality, the world of imagination and the supernatural versus the literal and the real were all tense contrasts for him. On limits, witches, angels, and ghosts appeared, along with male beings bent down with heavy burdens. He plunged into the archetypal world, through supernatural beings (figures who hold archetypal energy), the moment he was pushed a bit from his props and intellectual facade. His figure for Plate VI, the "ghost of Christmas past," being an association with Charles Dickens's Scrooge, carried the theme of good versus evil. Since experience transformed Scrooge, this may be a clue for our subject. In what way is cruelty preventing masculine growth in the subject? Is cruelty the only way he can feel masculine and separate from the mother? He is cruel to himself and toward others in his fantasy. As he lets his own blood, he holds his own penis, the concrete root of maleness. He told us he achieved two satisfactions from this psychologically, one being a sense of having overpowered someone who has attacked him, and the other one being a sense of peace as if being loved by someone. One was an extreme means of contacting some vague sense of masculine power in himself, against what we would suggest would be matriarchal power, and the other probably being wholly passive through having placated the destructive qualities in him stirred by negative matriarchal powers.

That such dark images like vampire which may cluster psychological energy exist in us is shown by this subject. Such behavior had been thought to exist only in myth. Something from the murky bottoms of the past clutched a modern man. Ideas about vampires have been with us since our images were first recorded. Was fascination with the macabre that which insured its survival and kept its form virtually intact since the dawn of history? Does its sheer atavism and destructively negative nature justify its survival? Is it simply man's means of contrasting evil with good? Perhaps so, but there are many vehicles for achieving those purposes, some of which are often culture-specific, but the vampire image has a strangely universal quality. Its importance may be more than we may see at face value.

Earliest mythology has associated the vampire with the destructive side of the feminine principle. There can be no doubt but that something destructive was at work within this subject's psyche, and the fact that it took the form of one of the earliest images recorded by man suggests that its history may add to understanding the subject. The negative side of the feminine is well known in the East. Neumann (15) has an entire book devoted to the origins associated with the feminine principle. He has numerous illustrations of the positive and negative sides of the feminine in the cults of many cultures. Typical examples include the cults of Kali in India, Hecate in Greece, Osiris in Egypt. Artemis Orthia, the powerful goddess of ancient Sparta, was known as the winged lady, ruler of the kingdom of the beasts. She, as well as Hecate, was not without highly negative traits comparable to vampirism. An ivory plaque survives from the eighth century B.C. (15), showing her strangling two large white birds by the neck. Mutilated beasts, from which "a member was cut off," were sacrificed to her. As ruler of primordial mysteries of the feminine, her role was intimately bound up with a sacrifice of blood, or she may have had the power to transform blood into milk. Neumann (15) has pointed out that the decisive moments in the life of the female involve blood sacrifice, since they include menstruation, deflowering, conception, and childbearing. Instead of offering healing and protection, and promoting growth (her positive side), the matriarch through her negative side may demand the bloody sacrifice of castration. There are parallels between some of the qualities ascribed to her and some of the behavioral effects apparent in our subject. Negative aspects of an archetypal source had threatened the life principle in this subject. Neumann (15) has called attention to youths not developed enough to resist the forces symbolized by an overpowering mother. Psychological flight from the dominance of destructive forces becomes self-castration, in that context. This, of course, is tantamount to capitulation. The frightening aspect of the power of the mother may get masked by an ostensible "son-lover" relationship, but the psychological price for this is a ban on sexuality for the capitulant. Our subject acted as if he was amidst such a ban. His identity became attached to the negative force from which he could not disentangle himself. Thus, he acted out the role of the destructive feminine, and, quite like Hecate, he sucked blood from young boys. We see from this how sexless the vehicle for archetypal power may be. This would not occur in a subject who was further developed inside his masculine structure. Being formless as a male, the subject could become a carrier for feminine power. Nevertheless, being a male, he used that power to attempt to define his maleness, which could not be accomplished. He was left suspended in a psychological void. We would call his condition a "Hecate Complex," if it had to be named or labeled.

The vampire image carries the symbol of the split between the animal and social nature in man. Stevenson depicted a variation on this theme in *Dr.*

Jekyll and Mr. Hyde. These are the conditions in extreme, when the beast in man snaps into consciousness and takes over. *Beauty and the Beast* is a fairy tale linking bestiality in men to their relationship with the feminine. There is something archetypal in women that can turn men into beasts and keep them in that state. Our subject became a passive carrier of negative archetypal power, and his personality stood in no kind of relationship to what it carried. When archetypal power takes hold, and its negative effects dominate, others apprehend it without knowing anything about the carrier or the source. It provides a psychological aura of stigmata. Our subject has this about him, leading his classmates at college to call him "ghoul."

Our means is not the only means to account for this subject's condition. What must we call him? Is he not indeed schizophrenic? If there is an underlying psychosis, where is the flood of archaic material the Rorschach is capable of eliciting? In a subject like this, we have wandered from the path of the known, and known explanations may not account for anything but surface features. Someway, the answer lies around archetypal sources. Intellectually, the subject was bright and advanced, but his psychological growth was at a symbiotic level with maternal forces. We know that his ego experiences were antagonistic to the negative forces that had trapped the personality. Ego energy was still active, but the power of the ego was cracked. Perhaps it takes more psychological development than he had to *project* negative archetypal forces into what we called paranoid schizophrenia. We would see this subject as not having projected the negative power, but remaining a passive carrier for it. There was nothing "latent" about his experiences; he had them full force, but he simply restrained his behavior toward others. Psychosis may require projection for us to recognize it, because our grasp of what it *is* is so limited. This is the reason why archetypal experiences did not appear through symbolism in the Rorschach plates. Primitive qualities, passivity, and predatory instincts had grown on a formless, insubstantial masculine latticework. Nothing else was present beyond his powerlessness inside matriarchal dominance. The subject's only hope was to find a source that would lay down more substance to support masculine energy. What both Scrooge and the ancient mariner lacked was *compassion.* Egocentric needs had led them into limited masculine achievements through prowess (skill in killing a bird and collecting a fortune). The subject might discover a basis of masculine structure around experiencing more through compassion. If he can develop a genuine sense of it through feelings, not his intellect, he is in a position to define something in his masculine structure. When Scrooge found compassion, a higher value replaced money. Nonmaterial values touched him for the first time. When the mariner expressed compassion, he broke the spell that had been cast on him. He diminished the archetypal power of evil. If the subject can discover the positive inside the symbol of the vampire, he may break its spell. It symbolizes more than primitive desire; it contains humanity's ever constant desire for the renewal of life. The blood of Christ symbolizes that in the sacrament of the Holy Communion. It was *compassion* that took Christ into his sacrifice. It may be a form of compassion that may free our subject from his compulsion.

Case 3

Loss of ego control and orientation: the impact of prolonged experience in the East on Western consciousness

RORSCHACH

Card I

2 seconds

Mars is going to collide, are you ready? I see two men dancing, with a woman in middle pointing out what is happening, crucifixion, dance of the spheres—geometric patterns, triangles. Open here and comes down. Bat-man —This is an ash tray, a pearl (center dot), me in the middle. The black is also evil, the forces of the id. Man's mind is a dark cavern, we don't know that much about it.

Card II

Oh now, peace, folded hands, but people trying to step on each other's toes, talking together over cigarettes. Red is Chinese—just the Communist worlds talking together. Peace ... Get out of Viet Nam. East is East and West is West and never the twain will meet ... Mark Twain ... There is a meeting place in the arts ... north, south, east, west ... points of the compass. Still two men with white spot. A rocket, they are trying to control the rocket, peaceful use of the atom.

Card III

Now we're sitting over a cocktail. Butterfly in middle. Dead foetuses coming out of the sky, attached to the earth below. Hands on two ovaries; butterfly coming out of the ovaries ... could be peace. A scepter coming out, the Indian sign for peace, Namaste over martini glass, butterfly coming out of martini glass. Could be women now, oh yes, women, 1921. This is what women have done for the world, created the wars, Helen of Troy, Joan of Arc, etc.

Card IV

I see dogs leaning up against the wall, listening to each other, very quiet. Two together make a whispering face of a dog.

Here's God here (female area) or whatever that force is keeping the dividing line set. Could be a clam, the pearl in the oyster. He could be a monk, could be Ganesh, creativity, an elephant.

Card V

Bat man. Could be butterfly, both working together. They crucified Christ on a cross, we don't care, evil squared, help. We are against the wall. Help the Beatles. She don't care, she do care, she don't want to be crucified. Free world and Communist world again, pressing up against one another. Also could be two men whose minds are pressed against one another and a jack rabbit on the cross comes out of their minds, his head is not there. Both have beards, goatees, could be women with one big and one smaller than the other. Siamese twins, masculine and female, Russian Siamese twins.

Card VI

A hide—a tiger skin. Here's God, here's creation in the form of a cat now, pretty sneaky, like roses (sings) . . . could be two submarines. "There are two springs . . ." (quotation from the Japanese.) Here are submarines, line is getting darker, storm clouds, off Saigon. It hurts my nose, things are pressing on my nose, my grandmother's glasses. She (grandmother) was a perfectionist, she died when I was in the Peace Corps. Aunt Elsie died too. Now getting back to . . . two ovaries here, scepter coming out, could be America and Australia—we may collide with Mars, there's space out here, outer world. This is the God of our fathers still looking out over the world in the form of a cat, God is the ground of our being, it was better when he was inside us, not out here.
(Plate reversed.)

Ship of State. Two men belly to belly, not that way . . . back to back . . . let's clean up the pig pen in our back yard, not others' back yards. Americans are jittery for war—Go, go-go generation, getting too fast. Machines, forced obsolescence, cars, death. Money doesn't always speak. Rorschach is all black (reads back) 1921, year after the war. Nepal is like Switzerland. My name in Nepali is Prakrati (means "image"). "Gita"—song Gita and Joli, two men in Tagore, first book I read that took me by storm. "I am Gita" Maya Nirvana, don't kill love, I didn't know what this meant. The customs of the country got me, the Communists were going to take Nepal in my dream. I had three dreams . . . three dreams . . . two about Chinese in Nepal and one about fighting in Viet Nam. I don't want them (Nepal) to have machines, it would be terrible for them.

Card VII

Oh, people talking, the barriers are getting smaller, gossiping, talking about gay things, could be two fairies . . . one has a darker mouth, could be Siamese twins again, Russian twins again, getting separated.

Card VIII

Color—looks like those of Picasso. Could be my insides, animals crawling up, Kashmir rugs, animal figures. Wall getting bigger again, colors in it. Separation, but unity too, beautiful colors ... Heaven on Earth really. Color of creativity and earth down here. I was created again with a man who opened the life force in me, and his sign is aquamarine, that color is something to me. My parents gave me pearls on my 21st birthday.

Card IX

If one controls cigarette smoking, comes creativity. Dancing colors, earth color here, light line between, they are blowing, the life forces of creativity are on the line, it's "Blowing in the Wind." Cigarette is the male principle, the female principle is the ash tray ... dancing colors.

Card X

Oh—the line is almost gone. Could be the destruction of the world, Chinese have just detonated an H-bomb. But controlled, but our milk may have radioactive particles.

Spiders being held by two women, they have a cigarette in middle, bashing their heads, still Siamese twins, heads separated by cigarette, spear, or scepter, the scepter should come between, it's the male principle—women caught, they run riot if men didn't control them, if men didn't push the right buttons, peaceful use of the atom, not harmful.

Beautiful shades, beautiful colors— you have a nice outfit yourself, blue shirt and green tie, has connection with Kennedy's death, Ireland. I have an aunt who is a leprechaun, still living. I was fighting with death until the 10th of May, now I'm fighting with life, that was the day I got my first apartment.

The materials obtained from Case 3 were recorded from a young, adult female subject. She was unmarried and had been brought up in an east coast state. She majored in American history in college. She had no record of earlier psychiatric illness, and her history prior to living in Nepal had been unremarkable. She had little knowledge of the East prior to entering the Peace Corps. Through their orienting programs, she was trained and sent to Nepal. She had not been a member of a hippie cult, nor had she been involved with drugs prior to her assignment in the East (nor is it known that she had any there). Her assignment occurred prior to the widespread attention that has been given to Kathmandu and Nepal as meeting spots for roving bands of hippies. She had had little awareness about esoteric Buddhist culture prior to living in Nepal.

In Nepal, one is surrounded by a multitude of strange forms of Tantric art and artifacts, and large numbers of images that would appear to be erotic to a Westerner, but whose meanings transcend the sexual plane for the Tantric initiate. Tantric art depicts physical union between male and female. It is meant as an hermaphroditic union between the two life principles. For a male, union with his feminine principle means embracing his creative source in Tantric Buddhism. Tantric art personifies the archetypal meaning we have given to the hermaphroditic plane. These art forms in Nepal take origin from Tibetan Buddhism. Tibet imported Buddhism from India, and it was blended with an earlier religion, Pön, which was daemonic in form. Certain yogic practices were brought in from India, and these ingredients have given Northern Buddhism a unique, highly esoteric quality.

The subject was transported to a theocratic state (the King is a Buddhic representative) from a democratic one, and a country which had been closed to all influences from Western cultures up to 10 years prior to her assignment. Tantric art forms have a close association with archetypal energy. Their sources are in the unconscious and they have been tapped and formalized by monks who used yogic practices and trance states to grasp the contents of their unconscious, which they have synthesized in art forms. Prior to a half-dozen years ago (the author visited Nepal in 1961) one literally stepped into a world of archetypal experience, a plethora of material entirely outside of ego consciousness, when one wandered through the streets and temples of Nepal. The subject arrived in Nepal when the scene was changing rapidly, owing to Westernization. One may note this in her lament about what technology was doing to Nepal. Anyone who has been there understands exactly what she meant. Materialism was replacing a human culture oriented to nonmaterial values. It is not easy to grasp the power of the impact of the kind of change that was taking place in Nepal from an armchair in New York or Kansas City. Our subject was pulled into it, and it smashed the power of her ego to retain control over consciousness.

We do not suggest that it was *only* Nepal that created her loss of orientation. From her comments, it is clear that a man she met in Nepal changed her concepts, and the nature of that relationship played an important role against what happened to her. However, the whole relationship was infused with Tantric Buddhism; it was the medium they swam in together, and she was unable to tolerate the power of the currents that surrounded her.

The subject's fluid associations, manic flights, and generally psychotic condition are easy enough to recognize. The importance of the case lies elsewhere. We may see through her experiences how powerful archetypal energy is. There is reason to think that the Western man who "liberated her" may have exploited her, whether it was done intentionally or not. Yet, we see how, through being opened to forces she did not know existed in her, she apprehended a great deal more than some Western scholars of Buddhism may have grasped. She, herself, was caught up inside awesome forces in herself. Through the collective side in her humanity, she understood a cosmic language. This means understanding through archetypal laws. It occurred for her only because the ego's power was unseated.

If we only look at this subject's materials as a salad of images and associations from a deranged mind, then we may not see that they differ from any number of psychotic records obtained through the Rorschach. We do not propose to interpret the subject's materials with an eye to her personal dynamics. It probably cannot be done, because she is open to a great deal that would not be present if she were not inundated. Certain trends are obvious, but the main point is that the welter of material here is a mixture. Some aspects of what the Rorschach caught in her may relate to her personal complexes, and some may not. These intricacies are difficult to untangle, and one runs a great risk of losing objectivity if one attempts it.

At times, archetypal energy tosses the subject's focus in awareness around like seeds on the wind. It is not she, the ego force in her, who selects what comes into her awareness. Open cases like this one show what the real ingredients behind Rorschach images (if their source is archetypal) are, and how a view of Rorschach images as being consciously selected percepts is a limited one. If one keeps an eye to this strange wind, one may even see how archetypal forces organize trends in her in the midst of apparent chaos. The chaos comes from the dissolution of logic as a perceptual and associational organizer. We can only note landmarks that pertain to her imagery. If a reader can immerse himself in her images, they may resonate apperceptions for him. If one is closed to such an approach, then the materials may remain nothing more than bizarre, incomprehensive data in psychosis.

Finally, this case may be important because the subject is, herself, caught in the magnetic influences that have grabbed the youth of today. What we called the generation gap is an *archetypal gap*. This subject's materials disclose why some behavior in youths is incomprehensible to adults. We are not suggesting that most modern Western youths have any more awareness about these matters than do many of their elders. This case is included to show the dangers involved, because youth has, in many instances, no means to withstand consequences that may ensue for them. It is naive to think that esoteric youth movements that have become common are fads or kids "doing their thing," and if you leave them alone they will come home wagging their tails behind them. When archetypal energy summates in collective movements, much may be at stake. Some may not be able to go back at all, even if they wish it. One may imagine that Timothy Leary would no more wish to teach at Harvard University again than would Harvard welcome him.

This case shows qualities that are influencing many youths today, but who may not be either psychotic or aware of what is influencing them. This case is relatively uncontaminated by the blasé, adamantine attitudes exhibited by youths who have lived in cultish, tribal conditions outside modern Western mores. She was not artificially propelled into sham reactions through drugs or forms of overstimulation. She fell into an archetypal world that her ego could not withstand.

Plate I shows that the subject has been exposed to disorienting forces that exist in the open stretches of the psyche behind the ego. Like a dreamer who dreams of himself inside some unreal experience, but sees himself there, the subject observed a dot in the middle of the plate which stood for herself to her. She is in the middle of whatever is happening. Here, the central figure is perceived as one with orienting power for her, she points the way, while forces whirl around her. This may be a clue as to the means of getting her balance back. Something in her matriarchal side is useful and seems to "know the way." We will see if this holds up as time goes along. The dot in center becomes a pearl and an ash tray, as well as where she sees herself. An ash tray is a receptacle for discarded objects, and a pearl is a precious gem. What is it in this subject that pulls her between such opposite values? The pearl is a psychological gem, because it is an animal product and builds up through stages like the developmental path in psychology. Buddhists ascribe a similar meaning to the pearl, and the subject probably knew that. Smoking has a very personal meaning for her, which will emerge later. This image may presage something of great psychological importance for her. How will she contain and be contained as a woman? Will her value, as she sees herself, be base or lofty?

Plate II brings nothing conventional to her. The contents projected onto the plate are simply a running summary of what concerns modern youth. Adaptation is a matter of no interest. Instead of everyday affairs, the subject is very much at home with the language of symbolism. She notes that both sides or figures are identical, and she uses that observation to project two worlds that are the same, Communist ones, talking together. They are not opposites as they talk, but the rest of her images here compare opposites. When she says that opposites may come together through the arts, she is actually noting that archetypal energy, which is the transcultural connector in art, links man together. In Nepal, she has been exposed to the strangest looking art that she could imagine, outside of a dream. When one first sees their theocratic art, one is dazzled by its beauty and discomfited by having no logical connections to make with it. In time, the archetypal sources in Tantric art get felt, even though a Westerner may not comprehend them. The same happens in Rorschach material in subjects open to inner processes. Strange images occur, and, while a subject may feel something of their power, the ego does not apprehend them and often disclaims them entirely.

Plate III brings up the nature of the power between sexual opposites.

Most of the Rorschach plates tend to serve as vehicles on which she hangs whatever comes to her indiscriminately, because she seldom needs any vehicle to enable symbols to form. She is living *in* symbols and has immediate access to unconscious sources. They spring into awareness. A scepter emerges, which becomes a symbol of masculine power to her. She perceives her own sex as having been at the root of all evil, caused all wars, and shown destructive qualities. She is in touch with the impersonal side of matriarchal power, and she is making an effort to define herself against it and masculine power.

Plate IV first snaps her away from disorienting forces, and she observes man's faithful, instinctual helpmate, the dog. This may mean that she has qualities, when she is not rent apart, which can be sources of inspiration in her relationship with men. Then, the female area is experienced (through the *law of altered visual perception*) as its sexual opposite. She sees God there, a symbol of patriarchal law, also a pearl, which is something of herself in her experience, and Ganesh, the elephant-headed Hindu male god of good luck, and a monk. This sequence is an array of opposites, which would have to combine psychologically to be useful for her. While it is out of her reach now, this subject may not be without resources for psychological growth, at such time as she regains her balance.

Plate V yielded much, and what appeared circled around archetypal power of separation and combination among opposites. "Russian Siamese twins," male and female, carries the theme of fusion (as distinct from union) between opposites. Fusion of opposites is their state prior to differentiation. It is a state like that which is called "polymorphus perversus." Union of opposites is a return through a totally different means. Fusion is transformed through psychological differentiation into union. Each opposite (male or female psychological energy) retains its identity inside union. Fusion is opposite to the hermaphroditic union we have discussed earlier. Psychologically, separation of opposites in her may require great risk. Here, we may have the core problem which took her into psychosis. Her Eastern experience, as well as her experiences with a man, a self-styled East-West Guru or teacher, opened her (physically as well as psychically) to awareness about her opposite within. She can *talk about* the masculine principle and the feminine one, but she cannot tolerate either with psychological freedom in her experiences.

Plate VI carries the theme of confusion on a symbolic level. God reappears, in feline form. It is useful to note the ease with which sexual contours take the subject to the nonmaterial side of existence. This happened on Plate IV also. The psychology of reversed symbols (male for female on IV and female for male on VI) occurs when there is no psychological separation between them. Cat-as-God goes back to the Egyptians, whose culture was precursor to our tradition. The Egyptians associated the cat with the moon, and it was the animal vehicle of Isis and Bast, two mother goddesses, who could nourish or destroy. As cat, Bast would nourish, but as lionness, she would destroy. The subject's relation to her matriarchal sources influences her function *beside the impact* of masculine energy.

It looks as if her allusion to colliding with Mars means the destructive impact in her subjectively when opposite energies collide with each other. This is important to understand, because it does not reflect merely psychotic ideas, but a condition in a subject who is genuinely afraid of something in her that feels like a cosmic force. Psychologically, *it is* a cosmic force, something from an unknown source that renders one powerless in front of its tangibly intangible presence. She understands the meaning of religious fervor being split off or excluded in Western religious experiences, and she has seen its power in the Nepalese people she lived among. Their directness and lack of self-consciousness are very poignant for Westerners.

In the midst of abstractions and symbolic discourse (learned through her Guru), she perceived physical contact between members of the same sex (males belly to belly), which she could not tolerate visually. She turned them around, a conscious procedure; she did not change the sex of one of them and make them opposites. We note this in particular, not because of its sexual meaning (which interprets itself), but because it is an ego-directed affair, not an archetypal one. Conscious awareness about the nature of opposites and inter-relation between the same sex is filled with a set of positive and negative charges for her. Then, she reported an immensely important bit of philosophy. She tells us here that she never knew what she meant when she said, "don't kill love," like her peers, until she grasped archetypally something of the force of life and loving. Holding a banner which read "Don't Kill Love" was a rote affair, an intellectual pretention, until she earned the grasp of what it meant. The price for that knowledge was her psychological balance. This is what Carl Jung has warned Westerners about in his essays on Eastern thought. Youngsters shout shibboleths, often without knowing the power behind what they advocate. Flower Power is not a puny mockery of violence. Its meaning is that of a new kind of experience, when there is a psychological union of opposites within. This is one goal in Buddhist philosophy, and some forms of Yoga are a means to it. Yet, it is really no more than a sign contrary to violence, until Flower Power is energized by archetypal union. Few Western youths are capable of the experience underlying the Eastern significance of Flower Power. Physical experimentation and tribal living no more provide the necessary psychological experience required to achieve it than would attending a Hollywood movie.

Plate VII shows us that the psychological experience through living and overcoming developmental tasks has not led to a differentiation between opposites within her for this subject. She has been opened to something she was wholly unprepared for, and it cracked the power of her ego to carry orientation. She is not psychologically capable of living through Eros or through psychological union. This is not a homosexual problem *per se*. She has been hurled psychologically against the meaning of separation and loosening opposites, which she cannot tolerate. Yet, she reported that the Siamese twins were beginning to separate. Does this mean she has actually been achieving personal psychological development? It is possible, we cannot know until the present psychotic episode subsides. Even if it only means she will be left open to development, some gain may accrue. It is a well known clinical fact that some people recover from psychotic episodes with further psychological development than was observable before, and without psychotherapy. This may be a function of what happened archetypally to them. Nothing accrues in many cases, so far as observable behavior is concerned.

The subject experienced Plate VIII inside its meanings about functioning, rather like the description we have given for it. She apprehends that functioning through genuine union is on another plane. This does not mean she is necessarily aware of anything like this. She speaks of "separation, but unity too," a language apropos of the hermaphroditic plane Shakespeare and Emily Dickinson spoke of for love. Because she is opened to inner processes and has been living in and against archetypal powers, she recognizes the authenticity of hermaphroditic union, but we see elsewhere that she may not have the means to achieve it herself. Much depends on what is retained in consciousness when she recovers.

Plate IX takes her into an archetypal condition associated with fate. A guess would be that the subject has been studying Yoga, and her Yogi has been stressing the importance of not smoking to her. She has, though, in a natural way, described for us the archetype of the female as the containing principle. The cigarette is the male principle, and the ash tray, the female principle. We see now something of why she was not psychologically prepared for the range of knowledge imparted to her. Something destructive, or unnatural (smoking) is the medium for experiencing a creative union. Only if the container includes her positive womanhood, and something of the Chalice, not an ash tray, is it possible for her to move along psychologically.

Plate X summarizes and repeats the primary theme in her materials. Her experience of her feminine essence is destructive and negative for her. She has a wide grasp, and she is possessed with hunks of the wisdom of the East, yet her own inner destructive forces hold her fate in balance. This subject probably has some positive qualities which may contribute to her function as an inspirational woman. She has been ripped through experience from the natural stage she was in and propelled onto another stage, which she could not sustain. She was overcome by the East. As a result, she lost her psychological balance and fell headlong into chaos. The main question raised here is how much positive and how much negative energy will be available to her when the ego regains power? Can she make contact with the positive side of her matriarchal substance? Can she reach the Eros principle through her nurturing structure? Presently, she is afraid of the positive side in the feminine. This must be overcome by her, or, despite all her erudition, she will remain in service to some form of masculine energy or outer personification, at the expense of development.

Transsexualism: obsession with the archetypal power of the opposite

RORSCHACH

Card I

∧ Not anything.
∧ < Any old way? >
16 seconds

1. ∧ The x-ray of the anatomy of some part.
      W   FK   x-ray

2. ∧ Hands.
      d   F   Hd

3. ∧ Looks like landscape, water, and rocks, not much, but slightly.
      WS   cF(C′)   N

4. ∨ Some sort of bird.
      W   F   A

5. ∧ That looks like a woman.
      d   F   Sex

1. The black and white and the center line.

2. The shape (?) with mittens on. (?) Just the shape.

3. Shape, white is the water, rocky coast. (?) The color is solid rock, roughness.

4. Just the shape. (?) It doesn't really look like a bird. (?) Just shape.

5. Shape. (?) Well, way it looks. (?) Well, a woman's breasts, the two bumps just that.

Card II

36 seconds

1. ∧ That looks like that animal out of mythology, looks like a unicorn, they're white though, and a unicorn only has one horn and this has two.
      D   F   (Ad)

2. ∧ Two people sitting, awful funny looking people, clowns maybe.
      W   M(FC)   H

3. ∧ ∨ Again it looks like rocks, an opening in rocks out to the ocean and redness as from sunrise or sunset.
      WS   FK(cF, CF)   N

1. The shape; usually white, it's the shape.

2. Looks like they're sitting, odd nonhuman heads. (?) The red color, a costume.

3. Well, the same texture here and the white space, looks like you are looking through, the color of sunset.

Card III

6 seconds

1. ∧ Looks like a Toulouse-Lautrec painting. These additional things are meaningless, perhaps party decoration.

  W   M(CF)   H   P

2 ∨ Trees, again like a landscape, drawn for Rudyard Kipling's "Just So Stories," a lane a cat walked down.

  DS   FK   N

Are you familiar with my case?

1. People with top hats. (?) Oh well, depends on how you look at it. (?) Do you want to take it apart? In general look like men. (? why ?) The tall hat in the Toulouse-Lautrec picture, head, slender, not wearing a dress, legs, jacket.

2. Grass, leaves, distance. Oh yes, a butterfly.

  (D   F   A   P)

Card IV

12 seconds

1. ∧ Looks like an inkblot. Don't put that down. A bear rug really.

  W   Fc   A obj.

2. ∧ A cow's face.

∨ Something starts out to occur to me, but it doesn't ever finish. No, that's all.

  D   F   Ad

1. The texture and the head and shape.

2. Shape.

Card V

16 seconds

1. ∧ ∨ ∧ ∨ ∧ Looks   like   wings, winged creature.

  W   F   A   P

2. ∧ ∨ I tell you frankly all of them look like anatomy, somebody's shoulder blades, lungs, or nervous system.

  W   F   At

1. Shape. (? sort ?) Bat. (?) Either flying or better, under glass on exhibit.

2. Shape.

Card VI

∧ ∨ I'm bored with this, aren't you?

  ∧   ∨   ⋯   ∧

43 seconds

1. ∧ Well, that almost looks like part of a totem pole, yes, though I haven't seen one recently.

  D   F   Emb.

Honestly, I don't see anything, maybe the next one will be better.

1. Shape.

Card VII

6 seconds

    1. ∧ Two women's heads there.   1. Shape.
         D   F   Hd

∧ ∨ > ∧ I'm sorry to take so much of
your time. I don't know what this (rest
of card) is.

Card VIII

15 seconds

    1. ∧ This looks like also a spinal col-   1. Shape.
umn and lungs maybe.
         DS   F   At

    2. ∧ Heraldic lions.   2. Shape.
         D   F   (A)   P

    3. ∧ It looks like somebody's insides,   3. Shape and color.
lungs, lower spine.
         W   CF   At

    4. ∨ This way it almost looks like   4. Color for blue water, mostly the
some water where you see the reflection   blue.
of things above, trees, etc.
         D   CF   N

Card IX

∧ ∨ We have them in color now, the
past few ones, that is. ∧ ∨ ∧
1 minute, 37 seconds

    1. ∧ Somebody's hands, thumbs.   1. Shape.
         dr   F   Hd

    2. ∧ ∧ > Again looks like a spinal   2. Shape.
column, but guess they all look like that.
           D   F   At

    3. Water plus reflection again, a stone   3. Shape and the texture and water
bridge.   color.
         DS   CF(Fc)   N(Arch)

Card X

3 seconds

1. ∧ First thought of the Eiffel Tower,   1. Shape.
but it doesn't really look like that.

     D   F   Arch

2. ∨ Looks like mountain climbers.   2. Shape. (?) Men. (? why ?) Big.

     D   M   H   I wish I understood what you mean,
broad shouldered, I guess.

3. ∧ Pawn shop sign.   3. Shape. Actually should have

     D   F   Obj.   three, and they're usually white.

I see the mountain climbers mostly,
the rest seems superfluous.

This variety of subject has been chosen for particular reasons. Transsexualism is a condition that is peculiarly symbolic of aspects of the psychology of our time. It was first described in modern times by Westphal (17) in 1870. The first female case was described in 1951 by Dukor (3). Yet, the whole matter is an archetypal one, and its roots began in the Paleolith. The "sorcerer" at the cave of Les Trois Frères provides us with qualities of an ancient analog. Men needed to define their own power apart from the power of their opposite. We see transsexualism as an extreme in the incompleted task of definition *through,* not against the power of the opposite. In one sense, transsexualism represents a state in which the ego defies archetypal power. Hence, it is a form of disturbance which bears on theory in archetypal psychology.

The author (13) has described one case for the literature. A female case has been selected because of what it may contribute to the changing role and psychology of womanhood in our time. The author was able to examine a number of these patients over several years at The Payne Whitney Psychiatric Clinic in New York City. All of these cases have a quality that links them together. An obsession to change the physical status of their sex literally excludes all else from consciousness. When we see that kind of condition, one may be sure that archetypal influences are at work. These individuals are not obsessed about sex, a matter that is confusing to the public. They are unshakably convinced that nature made a mistake, and their whole sense of purpose in life surrounds the steps they take to correct nature's error. One case in particular tends to typify the powerful influences these patients feel. The author studied a male subject who had had the conversion operation, and a series of subsequent surgical reparative and synthetic efforts. He was 37 years old. He had been married and was the father of three children, and he had obtained a doctorate in mathematics and had taught college math for a number of years. His logos functioning had been highly developed, and he had lived in a world of abstract thoughts. Yet, he came under the influence of something so powerful that he left his wife and children, gave up his profession, which had required years of preparation, and flung himself headlong into the archetypal power of the opposite within. These patients are not homosexuals who wish to alter the physical to replace pretense. Their chances for future sexual gratification are problematic in each case. The physical means to physical sexual pleasure is removed surgically. Both the heterosexual and the homosexual do not use a means to avoid sexual pleasure; they find it through the means available to them. Logic is displaced in the potential transsexualite, because an archetypal force has replaced full grasp about the consequences. All the psychic energy that is available goes into the ego's importunate struggle with nature.

The condition is becoming more and more common. We see it as carrying an abortive pattern inside the way opposites are being experienced collectively in our youths today. Also, it is becoming easier to obtain surgical changes. While Huelke (7) performed the first operation to alter sexual anatomy in 1949, the procedure did not become well known until Christian Hamburger's (6) case received attention in the popular press in 1953. Hamburger (6) reported that some 500 individuals contacted him about similar procedure for themselves after learning about his work. Most interested people know that anyone may obtain this form of operation in Casablanca, for a considerable sum. The operation is being performed in this country also.

Rorschach materials in these cases are a profitable means of examining what the individual psychology is in a given case. Some potential transsexualites temper the logic associated with what they desire through believing that they are hermaphrodites, both sexes and neither, and justify surgical correction on that basis. Shortly after Hamburger's famous operation, the author (14) had occasion to study a true hermaphroditic boy, with bilateral ova-testes, external male genitalia, and internal female organs. Few similar cases had been reported in the literature. His physical status came to light when he began to develop breasts at puberty. The author studied him over a period of a year and a half, having projective materials before and after two sets of operations. One removed the breasts, and 6 months later all female sexual qualities were removed surgically. The most astonishing feature in his materials was the stability of his ego and the absence of disruptive inner processes despite what was happening to him. He had been reared as a boy, he projected as a boy, and he carried on as a boy; and the surgical processes had little psychological effect at puberty itself and over a year and a half.

Most of the records and materials of transsexualites that the author has

seen are not representative of extensive inner chaos or marked psychological distress. There are some exceptions, but the trend seems to be otherwise. One might say the ego remains in power, but through being in service
to a particular archetypal force. That seemed to be the case with the subject who was obsessed by vampirism. The ego was impotent to carry the
subject's energy apart from the obsession, but as long as the energy fed an
archetypal source, the ego was not rendered powerless. In a general way,
Rorschach materials in subjects who are caught up in transsexual drives
are characterized by ego sources rather than archetypal ones. This kind of
condition furthers symbol formation, which may tell us about important
psychological correlates inside their transsexual drive.

A study of these conditions may enable us to look objectively at some of
the cult traditions that are springing up in our youths, particularly movements like "unisex" in which behavior and dress are meant to be indistin-
guishable between the sexes.

In most instances, though one may find genuine exceptions, the problems
associated with conditions like transsexualism, and other means youths use
to defy archetypal qualities associated with the opposites within, have more
to do with fusion than union. Denial of differences is the opposite to psychological functioning through them. Surgical alteration may have no influence on the nature of psychological energy and how it is charged between
opposites. The tragic case of the male transsexualite we described earlier
shows this. In no way that was surprising to the author, the patient killed
himself 6 months after he had been last examined, and he was getting expert
treatment psychologically the whole time. Further, he was a transsexualite
who had found a "mate" and lived with a surgically created "opposite" with
whom he was "compatible."

The subject of our study here was 32 years old and had never been married. There were no known congenital abnormalities at birth, and her
growth and physical development were considered normal. She had a sister who was younger than she. By age 5, she preferred male activities and
boy's toys. She became a "tomboy" and was in constant friction with her
family who wanted her to cultivate feminine interests. Her mother died
when she was 9, and she was sent to boarding school. Menarche occurred
at 14. She felt rejected by her peers, and after high school she worked on a
farm so she could dress as a boy. She denied any homosexual experiences;
she had lived among them for a time, wondering if she was one, but she decided she was not. Her desire was to obtain a conversion operation so that
she would be one physically and psychologically. At the time she was examined, she had had a mastectomy, and she was demanding an exploratory
operation to remove what she considered was an hermaphroditic physical
condition. She had been taking male hormones for a number of years, and

she had a dramatic appearance as a man. She was placed on a male unit when she was hospitalized for study. Physical examination led to the conclusion that she was indeed female genotypically and phenotypically. She rejected any need for psychotherapy, and she insisted that she was a male, despite the presence of normal female genitalia. At a later time, and in another setting, she obtained an operation converting her genitalia into a facsimile of her opposite. The procedure usually requires a series of attempts.

There were no distortions of Bender Gestalt designs, including those associated with male and female images (original and recall sets). Her drawings of both members of the human species were of excellent quality, showing no aberrations of body image. She drew a cat when she was asked to draw an animal, one that carries elements of female psychology. Using a projective question the author[4] has found useful for years, she was asked to write *three things that she considered were impossible*. She responded with:

1. "To square a circle."
2. "To change day into night or vice versa."
3. "To step across the ocean."

This projective question has an interesting psychological effect on a subject. It is particularly interesting to see what it poses in a youth of today, since many are convinced, almost expansively, that nothing is impossible. The question sets man against nature. A subject may view the request at a personal level or a cosmic one. It sets the power of the ego against the power of the unknown. It yielded the most directly pertinent data in this subject; it took her close to her problem. The importance of what she said shows the paradox of forms of solution. Inside the laws of conscious logic and in the physics of outer reality, her thinking is indeed valid. At the same time, she expects a change in outer reality, altered physiology, to correspond to her inner state, when all she grasps of it pertains to ego values and the laws of consciousness. At a metaphoric level, none of the three is impossible *psychologically*. Squaring a circle is symbolic of the union of opposites, which can be achieved through individuation. Newfound awareness psychologically changes the dark into light; what was unknown becomes known. Stepping across the sea acts to bridge two shores, and psychologically land separated by water may symbolize how opposites are bridged only through human experience. Has she the psychology that would support an inner change simultaneously with an outer one? Does anybody? How does archetypal structure stack the chances for her? These are questions that pertain in a vital way to her state. In the male transsex-

---

[4] The author is indebted to Dr. Mary David Rootes, at the time a fellow graduate student, who told him of attending a party where the hostess used the question as a stunt and entertainment. It is often a means to obtaining rich data in a simple way.

ualite who killed himself, there was no chaos, no schizophrenia in his materials; but archetypal structure is not altered by surgery. He destroyed himself and, in doing so, may have ruined the lives of his former wife and children.

An assumption that the ego has power to control a subject's perceptions is illusory in cases like these.[5] Subjects like this one are almost wholly in the power of a negative relation with autonomous energy associated with the inner opposite. As we have noted, when the ego is guarded about its capacities to control, symbols slip through somewhere. Nothing emerged on Plate I that might be directly connected with symbol formation. There may be an element of *displaced awareness*, as she left out the central human figure entirely but reported "breasts" not attached to anything. As the organ of nurture, and a symbol of the growth-producing function of the mother-world, it suggests that something in that aspect of the feminine went awry for her. She had already had her breasts removed. They were highly undesirable to her, as was her capacity to nurture or promote growth. "Hands, with mittens" may be of some note. Can she become conscious about who she is since her breasts are gone? Consciously, she complained that nature played her a dirty trick anatomically, since she, herself, knew she was a male. The hand seems appropriately connected with a search for who she is against the opposite. She grasps that her connection with an opposite, whatever it is, will define her. No one can accuse transsexualities about neglecting a search for identity, since they look harder and risk more than do most. It is subject to the energy associated with "wanting to know" and an incapacity to tolerate ambiguity or vagueness in solution.

Plate II yielded the most important image of the series, insofar as archetypal sources are concerned. Reversed, and for the female area, she reported "that animal out of mythology, it looks like a unicorn, they are white though, and a unicorn only has one horn, and this has two." It is noteworthy that both the vampire and the unicorn, each nonexistent in nature, occur as images in the *Vedas*. The medieval iconography of the unicorn appears in the fifteenth century tapestries in the Cluny Museum in Paris, with their illustrations of *La Dame à la Licorne* (2). We have shown the importance of analogy with this blot area and the nature of animal heads in parietal art. At Lascaux, an imaginary animal in the Great Hall of the Bulls has been called a unicorn. As a master artist, the creator of the imaginary creature with a great horn, drew this figure differently than the rest he depicted there. It blends into a horse directly in front of it, the horse's tail becoming the unicorn's foreleg (11). This shows symbolically

---

[5] The author knows of a converted transsexualite who is convinced she has borne two children. That they do not exist does not trouble her, since these percepts are not controlled by ego action.

the continuity between the inner or imaginary, and outer, or tangible animal (at an archetypal level). The strength of this image and the manner in which it imposes itself despite the logical evidence contrary to it (wrong color, wrong number of horns) point out that subjective laws were at work and the unicorn appeared as a symbol. The psychic source for it is archetypal. Is the unicorn, with a phallic horn, an image that pertains to penis envy in this woman, who is expecting surgeons to make one for her? There is no question but that she wants a phallic instrument that is entirely her own possession. One on loan would not do. The unicorn has archetypal significance, and hence its meaning symbolically is excluded to awareness through the ego. One could expect logically that the subject, because of her condition, might experience a symbol of sexual inversion here and, through the law of excluded awareness, indeed perceive a penis instead of a vagina. This does happen in subjects and for this blot area. Nothing of that order took place. In myth, which often carries archetypal data, the unicorn was associated with chastity and purity. No male could catch a unicorn in the hunt. Pursue as they will, success eludes all men (this capacity probably gave rise to the powers of a unicorn's horn for potency in men, during medieval times). Yet, in myth, this perceptive creature knows a maiden when he sees one and eschews those who have been down the Primrose Path. He lays his head only in a virgin's lap. This is symbolic of union through the Eros principle. The female functions to receive and contain the male's animal vitality and sexual energy; she tames the beast through a natural, heterosexual goal, in union. Like the breast, this image is one associated with the sustaining, not the destructive side of female nature. We would suggest the positive side of this subject's matriarchal energy was split off; she had lost contact with it. The symbol (as archetypal data) suggests that a solution for her would be regaining a relationship with that part of her she is determined to discard, the relational function in her female nature. Her relationship with a part of herself that belongs to her through psychic laws is negatively experienced. She cannot tolerate the "good girl" in her, and, since participating as the "bad girl" left her feeling empty (on her own account), the energy of her opposite got charged and took her to the forge, hoping perhaps that Vulcan, the god of ironmongers and protector of the cuckolds, would remake her. She was indeed in search of a mythological means, and she may have become a cuckold to herself.

Plate III suggests a continuation of the theme of virtue as opposed to easy virtue as being psychologically important to her (dance hall girls and Toulouse-Lautrec colors). There too she saw a storybook path, and open space, from Kipling's stories for children about the instinctual nature in animals. Since no cat is there, the feline side in her nature needs to be examined against the picture of her wish to disembody her feminine instincts.

Plate IV yielded two adaptive images, nothing disruptive. This suggests the subject has a capacity to function as a woman with men, not the reverse. If her archetypal structure had been masculine (which is impossible under subjective laws), then the images here could be used as evidence for masculine adaptation in her. That would be a contradiction in terms and a violation of the genetic code. Yet, it is archetypal structure she would need to satisfy her voracious demands. Finally, she was unable to formulate consciously an experience the plate gave her. When subjects experience that situation, it usually means the ego has crowded subjective experience. Something has challenged its powers.

Plate VI, after viewing it for a considerable time, "bored her." If her problem was a simple form of penis envy, on any plane, she certainly did not make the most of it with VI. Did the law of excluded awareness function to obscure the desired object from her view? The whole matter rests, isofar as the data go, with her relationship to her feminine core, and not on the psychology of inversion or envy, even though her behavior is powered and determined by energy from the inner opposite. What would this woman have done before Huelke (7) undertook the first surgical sexual alteration? Man himself created the vehicle (surgical change) that guided the daydreams of hope and enabled psychological energy to collect around a physical chimera. True, there have been artificial apparati men or women could use as dildos since ancient times, and self-castration does occur in disturbed individuals, but no hope of acquiring a flesh and blood male organ existed before in history. The significance of this in our time is its coinciding with a collectively shared psychological change in Western women.

It is noteworthy to observe that her Rorschach images are strewn with an impersonal quality in nature through the plates. Water, trees, landscape, and other images seem to accompany her lonely obligato of search for identity. Concern with how she can define her identity takes her, like parietal artists of yore, to an image of hands (Plate IX). She is related to a Paleolithic symbol through similarity in psychological search. Like those artists, this modern woman was willing to undergo extreme physical distress to discover who she was, and what she would be if and when she became her opposite. Yet, without breasts, she was no more than she had been. When one notes how barren her feminine potentials seem to her and observes unused qualities which could serve to relate her to men as a woman (this is closed to some frigid women), it is not difficult to see how suicidal depression may occur when the bubble of her expectations bursts. Subjects who drain color away from where it exists objectively on the plates, and who project it where none is, are opposites along a continuum of feeling-adaptation ("AB" axis on our process analysis frame) but may be equally in danger from depression.

Projecting color is a psychological longing for the feeling it brings, while draining color is a psychological rejection of it and feelings. This subject had to divorce positive feelings about her physical female structure and substitute negative ones, if she would tolerate their eradication. She has no assurance that either the same or different feelings will return to her after the operation. So on two fundamental accounts, the risk of suicidal depression runs rife in this condition.

One may argue persuasively that a subject in this condition is miserable anyway, and he might destroy himself quite apart from any hope an operation might give him. Further, if one can become more comfortable, regardless of whether full erotic satisfactions can be established or not, one's lot in life will be improved. The literature which exists around the psychology of the effects of physical change is too new to draw any firm conclusions. Some of the research appears to have been designed to confirm pre-conceived ideas. The relief of human suffering is surely the goal of us all, but if man is going to alter nature, he must become aware of the consequences, some of which may not fit his hopes. The author knows personally of a case of altered sex in which tragedy stalks at every turn around the life of the subject. Yet, as part of a careful, scientific study, in a highly respectable setting, the subject's operation has been considered a successful one in certain ways. While this is no criticism about the intent of those who carried out the experiment, we tend to forget that, when the experiment is over, life goes on for the experimental subjects, and what ultimately happens to them may be quite different from the nature of earlier findings which may have been appropriate to that stage.

In a more subtle way, the subject inverted color perception again on Plate X. Conditions that appeared around the image of a unicorn reappeared around her image of "a pawn shop sign." This image (wishbone area) has gold color, which is appropriate to a typical pawn shop sign, but the subject said, "they are usually white," and, while she noted only two of the usual three balls here, against two powerful odds (shape and color), she stuck to an image of "pawn shop sign." Empirically, one finds that this blot area sometimes carries sexual imagery, and there is perceptual rationale for them as testes or ovaries. Logically, with a missing ball, the contour could have taken the subject to sexual imagery of testes (since she wanted their hormonal power) or ovaries (since she desired a destruction of their hormonal power). None of this happened. A particularly important aspect of her Rorschach is the absence of wish fulfillment correlates in a subject whose consciousness was filled with one huge wish.

She had put her feelings, one of her functions common to women, in pawn. Something symbolic about whiteness is archetypally important for her. We have suggested that it is related to some value that exists around purity and virginity in her, though it may not be available to her conscious view. She herself might laugh at such a suggestion. Yet, looked at one way, genital alteration acts to insure eternal virginity for women (she said she had had only autoerotic orgasms prior to this time).

Female transsexualism is probably psychologically different from the male variety. It insures virginity psychologically, whether the subject is actually a virgin or not. We must be careful not to discard the importance of the virgin state in a young woman, simply because sexual inhibitions have been lowered in our tradition. It still carries archetypal power. Even though her conscious attitude may be blasé, all women come into some influence from that power, whether it be early or late in life. It is related to biological control in the species. This does not mean that a woman necessarily wishes to keep her virginity. Olivia Primrose, the lovable character from Oliver Goldsmith's *Vicar of Wakefield,* in whose path many a sister has tred, was enthusiastic, eager for adventure, and "wished for many lovers," but when push came to shove, she settled for Squire Thornhill inside wedded bliss. This is entirely outside male psychology. A male who keeps his virginity suspects he is not a man. The male homosexual is in search of his manhood. Heterosexuality is taboo for him because homosexuality is often powered by the archetype of the chaste side, the purity in motherhood. The homosexual does not hate women; he worships the mother goddess, placing her on a pedestal. This is why homosexual groups in the larger cities always have a mother-superior on call, somewhere in the wings. In homosexuality, a male's virility as it functions through Eros has been placed under a taboo by the power of the matriarch, and much of his life energy is spent in search of it. The male transsexualite is in the power of the opposite within, the feminine principle, which includes more than just the matriarchal side in womanhood. He denies his virility, his male energy; he is not in search of it; he is in search of the means to destroy it. This is a radically different psychology. Psychologically, he wants to be like a virgin woman. He has no wish to participate instinctually as a man (which homosexuality does not necessarily prevent). If men have any instincts, one exists around protecting their genitals from harm. The transsexualite has lost the energy that underwrites that instinct, if he was born a man. Women remain eternally ambivalent about their virgin state, no matter what they may say, while men simply do not want theirs. Ambivalence about virginity is outside their psychology. His potency and sexual behavior do not function to control survival in the species. Survival requires his action. We would tend to call the force behind transsexualism in a male the masculine psychology of reluctant virginity (even though it may sound like a title from Perry Mason). When a male feels himself not participating through his virility (whether he is actually a virgin or not), this can shake his male energies loose from their masculine structure and the ego experiences this energy as being displaced onto the opposite, recessive feminine within. The change in the state of energy may make the feminine appear as more dominant, and the masculine recessive. Protecting his genitals from harm becomes empty for him. This state lies behind a capacity for self-castration, which is observed in some disturbed patients. Little energy or power is available to vitalize masculine structure; so as a symbol for the inner impotence the external organs are discarded. Usually, neither the tranvestite nor the homosexual denies the organs of his birth or is willing to risk the loss of them as an erotic source. The former conceals them publicly but makes use of them privately, while the latter displays them publicly, sometimes in a manner worthy of a Madison Avenue source.

The major question for this subject is whether she can tolerate the consequences of what will happen to her. There is no warning from Rorschach data that she is now veering toward a psychosis or may collapse. Does this finding justify an operation? What wreckage will be wrought psychologically when she finds that her physical experience is one thing and the psychology of her feelings is another? Even if her recessive masculine qualities absorb most of her psychological energy, her archetypal structure is not altered. She will move into a world of strange bedfellows, and psychologically she is very likely to become a second class citizen. Much, not little, is at stake when man disrupts the Sansara and scratches at the surface of powerful forces. As a symptom peculiar to our time, transsexualism is likely to become much more important statistically and philosophically as time passes. The Rorschach is useful in aiding us in grasping its meaning for an individual and in learning about the condition against changes in the psychology of our tradition.

Case 5
The ego against fate in the adolescent world: a double homicide and a suicide

RORSCHACH

Card I

3 seconds

1. Butterfly.
Who makes these things?
2. Bug or mantis with claws coming out.
3. Rocket.

4. Lazy Susan—where you put food over here.
5. Dog with ear coming up.

1. Wings, body—shape of it.

2. Way it looks—claws up here sticking out, body—feet down here.
3. Ready to take off—like a space satellite. Launching platform—rocket in middle.
4. Looks like one—the shape— fancy decorations—food goes here.
5. Shape—leave out center part because no dog has a middle leg.

Card II

3 seconds

All remind me of bugs. (comment)
Don't put that down.
1. Genghis Khan.

2. Sea in the middle of big block of land.
3. Africa or S. America.

1. Bold, powerful. Crown, horns. Scarf around neck (maybe). Mostly the feeling—shape of the blot. Scarf would be down here—red scarf.
2. Like you see on a map—white part is sea—irregular shape.
3. Shaped like that. This one Africa —this one S. A. (Upper D's)

Card III

5 seconds

1. A bug or beetle.

2. Horseshoe crab.

1. Eyes, claws—mouth—way it's shaped.
2. Shape of claws—ready to close on something.

224

Card IV

4 seconds

1. A tree.

1. Weeping willow tree. This is trunk and these are branches coming down. Shape of a tree—branches sticking out up here.

2. A bug.

2. Whole mess a bug.

3. Head of a spear.

3. Shape of it—pointed spear—this is shaft.

4. Rocket taking off—exhaust down here.

4. Whole thing a rocket—this is main part up here and this is exhaust coming out down here.

Card V

5 seconds

1. Another butterfly.
2. Ballet dancer.

1. Shape of wings—body.
2. Legs—crazy costume. Body in middle.

3. New Zealand.

3. Shape of New Z. An island surrounded by water.

Card VI

2 seconds

1. Lazy Susan.

1. Fancy one—food goes here. Turn it up here. Twirling movement.

2. A glass.

2. Just this section here. Shape of a glass.

3. Definitely a bomb. Goes up into shaft and blows up.

3. Goes up into shaft and explodes. This part is another bomb blowing up in the background.

4. Grandfather clock or cuckoo clock.

4. Main part is clock and this part is swinging pendulum—but not swinging in picture.

5. Something with whiskers.

5. Just something—don't know—just the whiskers.

Card VII

5 seconds

1. Horseshoe crab.

2. A woman split in half—split personality.

3. A split cat dressed as a woman.

4. Lampshade.

5. Little harbors and coves.

6. Machine gun of the future.

1. Whole thing—legs—open part here is where mouth is.

2. Hat, arm, leg—same on both sides—looks like it was cut down the middle to make two women—split down the center and separated.

3. Way it bristles out reminds me of fur—puss in boots—top piece looks like hat. (Essentially same percept as #2.)

4. White space—shade, neck, base of lamp.

5. White part is water—other part land—like on a map. Irregular shapes of coves.

6. Two barrels—hold it here and it shoots up here. Shape of it.

Card VIII

5 seconds

1. Genghis Khan.

2. Skeleton bone of a hamster.

3. Beetle.

1. Colorful—power and boldness—crown here.

2. Whole thing—bones here—rest insides of body—red part the head—colors and shapes of it.

3. Just a gucky mess—nothing here (Reject).

Card IX

3 seconds

1. Genghis Khan.

2. Cannibal chieftain.

3. Mushroom of an A-bomb.

4. Headpiece of suit of armor of knight.

1. Helmet, iron guard for eyes. Cloak around him. (If I ever saw Genghis Khan I'd meet him and then beat it—would be afraid.)

2. (Same location as G. K.—preferred to see G. K.)

3. Orange and green are water mains breaking, houses falling, people crying.

4. Whole thing goes over head—here is place where face guard is—shape of it.

Card X

5 seconds

1. Fireworks. Something stuck in a machine gun and it twirls around and all this stuff is thrown off.

2. Star-Spangled Banner.

3. Genghis Khan. (v, S)

4. A beetle.

1. Something like you have on 4 July—hold it in hand and stuff shoots off—but this twirls around.

2. Colors—the feeling that they had when the Star-Spangled Banner was first written—rockets bursting, fighting.

3. Don't see him—just a representation of him—Can't explain it.

4. Whole thing's just a messy beetle —don't know why—just mess.

The increase in violence as the means to psychological or material ends in our society has been a concern to responsible people everywhere. There is much confusion about the motives behind violence, particularly on college campuses and in protests in the streets. When things turn out not to be what they seem, when descriptions for conscious motives do not hold up against behavior, archetypal energy has been at work. Collectively, men frequently act on the distortions in their perceptions and misperceive their own motives. It should be clear to everyone that neither college students nor black men are necessarily seeking exactly what they demand. When given what they insist upon, new demands seem to spring up immediately. Movements are usually propulsed through archetypal energy and where this energy may take them and why is not often available in consciousness. Leaders tend to be no more discriminating or informed than their constituents. While material gain is comforting when one has been deprived, if one is seeking something psychological, it does not satisfy. Forces opposite to one another are abroad in the land. When youths in cults or bands reject materialism and all other values associated with acquisition, they serve to hold a mirror up to our one-sidedness. Affluence must exist before it can be rejected. The opposite state exists for black men. They are engaged in demanding what they perceive as having been excluded to them. While rejecting exactly what blacks demand, white youths espouse the cause of the blacks. The blacks do not reciprocate because there is not enough energy left for luxury. They are linked not by goals, but by being two sides of the same coin. We are living in a time when those two sides are split off from each other, and violence is partially freed as a result, and may run rife. The search is not material; it is psychological. Collective values disregard the values of an individual and his difference from others. The black man is seeking respect for himself (given by himself, to and from himself, not directly from others), while white youths are seeking freedom from the

anonymous, impersonal forces created through overpopulation and affluence in our culture. Frequently, the means both groups use stem from the
false perceptions they have of themselves. This situation engenders violence.

With these aspects of the collective scene in mind, we have selected a
subject who is known to carry violence in his roots. Through examining
his psychology, we may learn more about the sources of violence, particularly since all of us feel a sense of danger lurking in life that did not exist
in such an uppermost way before.

This subject,[6] a male adolescent, was 13 years and 7 months of age at
the time of the Rorschach examination. Interestingly enough, that occurred
the day before the Russians launched their first Sputnik, opening the Space
Age. The subject lived with his mother and father and an unmarried sister,
12 years his senior. Their home was in an upper class community in an ur-
ban section of the eastern seaboard. His sister taught school and was under
psychiatric treatment. He was a quiet boy, who made good progress in
school. He denied any difficulties personally and disclaimed any feelings of
stress. His father devoted much time to a demanding, successful business.
His sister perceived that something was amiss in her brother and insisted
that he obtain expert psychiatric evaluation. Neither his parents nor the
boy's teacher agreed with her. His sister persisted, and the subject was taken
reluctantly by those involved to the school psychologist, who examined him.
Her recommendation was for treatment, which went unheeded. Except for
his sister, none of those responsible for him, including himself, could de-
tect any special need for guidance.

Exactly 1 year later, as far as could be determined, early one evening,
when his father was not at home, he took a gun, killed his mother, and then
killed his sister, apparently as she attempted to interfere. Then, he killed
himself.

A Thematic Apperception Test (TAT) was administered at the same
time as the Rorschach. Ten cards were given, and all except one of them
yielded nothing but short, cliché narratives. Card Six, which shows a son
and his mother in serious interplay, included two separate cliché themes.
In one, he said, "Either his father dies—or sister or brother—both are
shocked, her son has told her the news." The second theme was, "They
had an argument. The son wants to go into the army. His mother had two
other sons in the army and they were killed, so she doesn't want him to go.
He will volunteer anyway. He wants to make his mother happy, but he
also wants to do his duty to his country, so he goes." Both of these themes
are common ones for this card, but they show solid ego control and conventional adaptation. His membership in the clan of men and his country

---

[6] The materials of this case were made available to the author by Dr. Florence R.
Miale who, in turn, had been given them by a former student of hers.

took precedence over the natural anxieties characteristic to a mother. It was Card Eight, showing a boy, a gun, and a figure clad in white on a table, that produced the only personal reaction in the subject. He responded, "God! Oh, please—This kid in the foreground has a rifle—maybe is—maybe isn't. (what happened?) Somebody shot the guy on the table, and they're taking the bullet out. (outcome?) He'll probably survive". While we can never be certain, it looks like Card Eight suddenly caught a personal reaction to violence that literally frightened him. It jarred him. Yet, his ego disbelieved what came in view. All else in the TAT reflects ego control. It is conceivable that Card Eight made him aware of some form of smoldering violence inside that he had not considered consciously before. We would be inclined to think such was the case. While no one can say, we tend to doubt that the subject wove elaborate, hostile fantasies about destroying his family. Ego fantasies of a hostile nature about restrictive adults are common in all youngsters. They are not usually acted on. We will suggest from the Rorschach that the sources for violence in this adolescent were not ego or personal ones.

Adolescence is the time when the ego claims control over consciousness as the rightful heir. This is established through asserting dominance over the sexual energy which hormones have begun to produce. Through assertiveness by the ego and the way sexual energy imposes itself, opposites within get charged with tension. It is a time of crisis for every youth. Powerful forces, those that link man with survival, come into play. Energy has to be displaced from the familiar archetypes that sustained the child. Nurture, care-needs of all kinds, the state of having controls originate externally, the general welter of patterning all children share together, must be related to in a different way. The ego has to carry off some of the power held by the mother (if the adolescent is a boy). If he needs it, he may find the support from his father and the collective energy provided by his gang, in unseating matriarchal power. Nature sets up tension between sexual opposites within to aid in this task. Changed physical qualities make the changed state tangible.

Through an individual's fate, what has happened to him personally as he has moved through development tends to determine the proportions of the crisis for an adolescent. Certain qualities may have been tended in one child, while the same qualities may have been ignored in another. Through not having lived fully themselves, many parents' energies are often glued to furthering what they lacked personally through their children. This can be useful or disastrous, depending on the nature of the child who becomes the vehicle of unseen parental needs. If a parental need has archetypal energy in it, the parent may never be aware of what has happened. Most parents sense something of this in themselves when they weigh the awesome qualities of parenthood in our world today against the joys it brings.

While these factors about development are well known, much disagreement pertains when experts discuss the "crises of adolescence." Viewing those happenings against the nature of the archetypal power may be useful in grasping levels, degrees, and proportions of the crises. When a male child is in a positive relationship with matriarchal power, he meets newborn tension between sexual opposites differently from the son who has a negative relationship with matriarchal power. Permissiveness on the part of the mother forces the child into a position of power. Either a positive or negative relationship may develop as a result of it. It is as much unfair to a child as repressiveness. What determines positive or negative relationships depends on other matters, since both repressive and permissive attitudes may play on children with either a positive or a negative connection with the mother's power. There is no formula. Consistency toward a child's behavior helps orient him at the stage where he cannot discriminate through his own demands, which are never stable. What is permitted and what is restricted should depend on the nature of the child.

How the father in a family has been related to matriarchal power influences what is furthered in his son. Obviously, if a father still carries a highly energized matriarchal complex, his influence on his son will be influenced by his complex. This does not necessarily mean that the child cannot overcome these powers alone. It happens. Our point is, there is a welter of psychological combinations that a youth carries with him into puberty.

The pattern is wholly different for the girl. She does not go against matriarchal power; she uses whatever she has of it in becoming a woman. While her relationship to it may be positive or negative, her task is finding her own values outside of those handed to her. This need not be taken up at adolescence, though it may be. The great archetypes for her at the time of adolescence are those of appeal and lure. She comes up against the restrictive archetypal energy in the father, whose role changes because his daughter must be protected. It is the time when the young girl begins her cyclic life, and this loosens something in her mothering instincts. She begins to know that she holds the power of life, an archetypal experience totally closed to males. She must face some kind of relationship with her virginal state, and what is formed is a function of what has happened to her as she has developed. The male's sexual energies in adolescence take him into the world of masculine power, into sexual fantasies, into erotic reveries, but not to the power he has in nature as procreator. Possibly, that is a psychological task for males in the distant future. In adolescence, a male youth's sexual instincts tend to be primarily tied up with his personal sense of masculinity, his power, and his erotic drive. When these qualities are contained later through a relationship with a woman, he is freed from their urgency to function more evenly through logos and relational feelings. While an individual girl may be caught up in eroticism or fantasies about herself as an enticing image sexually, the major feminine power-push focuses on cosmetic appeal and physical qualities she has that lure. Because of her physiology, she more easily knows she is a woman, than a man does through his physiology. A male child caught in a severe mother complex may not be cheered by the appearance of hair on his face, but rather quite frightened.

Adolescence is, of course, more than these sketchy forms of psychological interplay, but the archetypal power structure in adolescence has a great deal to do with how disruptive adolescence is for the boy or girl, through the degree of crisis that those forces engender. When a severe disruption occurs, as between the pull from the power of the sexual opposite versus negative matriarchal power, all within the adolescent, he may have crisis proportions that we call psychosis. The only difference between psychosis in adolescence and in later life is that it happens when developmental tasks in life are different. Destructive archetypal forces, against which the ego crumbles, are the same for any age. When the ego dissolves, whether it be a newly formed one or one with considerable age, the same forces play over it. The prognosis depends not on whether it occurs at adolescence or not, but on the substance in the subject involved. An adolescent may achieve separation through a major crisis and move along in development. At the same time, he may not. The nature of his structure and the nature of the forces that are activated determine what happens. There are a wide variety of differences and combinations in structure and the nature of forces. These must be discovered for an individual if we would understand his inner state.

Looking through our subject's Rorschach imagery, one may see how frequently insects occur to him. This happens beyond what blot contours tend to elicit perceptually. This reflects a weakness in structure, such as might carry instinctual energy and forcefulness in projection of the personality. When a subject shows images that constellate power as sheer force, and the structure for instinctual power is correspondingly weak, trouble lies ahead. This was the case in our subject. His was a passive-aggressive pattern, but it is up to us to discover, from the data, what makes this subject different from a typical passive-aggressive adolescent, since he later destroyed others and himself. A passive-aggressive condition of powerful proportions does not generally take the individual to the extreme, as happened here. Was it a psychosis set in a passive-aggressive context? There are qualities about his imagery which are autistic. That is to say, the form of the blot contours did not matter to him, since he was under the compelling sway of inner images that imposed themselves. Since they repeated content, they tended to be perseverative. There was nothing latent about them; they emerged frequently and with force. Yet, his behavior did not show any kind of aberration outwardly, prior to the terminal episode.

Plate I provides us with two insects, two inanimate objects, one of which was original, and an alive animal. The central detail was experienced as a "praying mantis." Does this offer us any definitive information about his relationship to the matriarchal world? In its attitude of prayer, it is supplicant. It is useful to man, but the female mantis eats the male in its life cycle. These are positive and negative qualities, but we cannot necessarily suppose that those qualities in the insect stood for corresponding archetypal power in this or any other subject. We are on safer ground when we use its identity, man's view of it, that of a *praying* insect. This attitude is ascribed to the mantis because its feet look supplicant through the position they characteristically take and hold. We may tentatively accept this attitude as psychologically important in our subject. Prayer symbolizes something personal that is longed for, even if we pray for someone else. We may assume that the subject carries a deep sense of weakness against the strength of matriarchal power. The fledging ego seeks something from the mother and is not up to its usual business of turning the subject outwardly. What is it the subject needs? Does the "lazy Susan" mean he wants nurture? It is just as reasonable to expect him to want power, since a rocket powerful enough to be launched into space follows the mantis. We doubt that the subject welcomes any passive longings that his images might imply. The rhythmic alternation between his passive and aggressive images shows us that whenever nurture needs or an experience that connects him with a dependent state occurs, power images arise in their place. Unlike some boys, his is not a problem of longing to remain inside the nurturing aspect of the matriarchal world, despite his having powerful nurture needs. He is a rather passive carrier for an interplay between archetypal energy associated with power drives, on the one hand, and passive energy, on the other. Some subjects are consciously aware of longings to be protected by a mother and are not hostile to those longings. Our subject is not caught in passive-dependent forces. We do not know how his ego will impose itself against these forces that plague him. The chief clue lies in two images, "praying mantis" and "Puss in Boots" (Plate VII). This separates him from the usual passive-aggressive state, as well as does the autism in his images. Autistic images impose themselves; they arise through subjective conditions and its laws, not through conscious fantasies (though one may find connections between them). We suspect from the first plate that his ego is not playing much of a role, and the struggle is played out *on* him, at his expense; yet it is a familiar struggle in adolescence, so much so that it is archetypal, defining the state in some respects.

Adolescence is a time of initiation. We have suggested that Plate II has qualities which may stir initiatory archetypal activity, should it pertain in the subject's psychology. Plate II's color, and much less its form, yielded an image of a power-holding image, that of "Genghis Khan." This twelfth century conqueror plundered north China, north India, and subdued what is now Iran, Iraq, and part of Russia. His name means "the great lord," and his hordes were known for their cruelty. It is natural for an adolescent boy to be interested in glamorous power figures from history, and it might be easy to come to a notion that this subject's power fantasies fed on the impersonal cruelty ascribed to Genghis Khan. Perhaps that was so, but the data do not support it. Later, he expressed fears about Genghis, should he meet him (his comment on Plate IX). It is most likely that the subject was familiar with Genghis Khan's history, and in some way that knowledge resonated with the psyche in this subject. We know that the subject attempts to conquer through power in its cruelest form, a year later. However, we must be careful not to come to an understanding of the subject through false means. We do not believe that Genghis Khan was a favorite figure in this subject's fantasies. It was an autistic perseveration, an image that imposed itself on the subject's perceptual field outside his intent. It was an image formed in subjective consciousness and faded as quickly as it emerged.

We would interpret this image on Plate II as representing the proportions of power his ego *needs* to sustain initiation and separation. It is not likely to attain it.

Plate III is absent of relational qualities. He doesn't have much energy available for others. We would guess that if he were asked about the figures here, he would see them readily and conventionally.

Plate IV sets a dysphoric mood. A tree tends to mean roots, something that goes down deeply and is substantial. A family tree shows what one's genetic roots are like. His personal image is of a tree that seems to weep as it bends down toward the mother-source that supports it. For this family group, *he* makes their destiny. Even though his father escaped, he destroyed the male heir in himself. Their tree of life became a tree of death, a state of continual mourning. We do not mean to put destiny into the image. The question it raises psychologically for the subject is, where are his masculine roots? Because the image that follows was a power image, with destructive implications, we may assume that the weeping willow was experienced as something feminine or passive for the subject. It is characteristic of his psychology. The weeping willow is under more earth-dominance than sky-dominance. It moves with the mood of the wind and does not carry the strength of an oak or pine. We see here something that suggests that his sense of power may have its roots in the matriarchal world, and that it may not at all represent masculine power. Power may be masculine in his daydreams, but the means to which he may have to resort to acquire it (power) may be hooked to matriarchal power. He, as a male, lacks the archetypal structure to find power through the matriarch. That may be a fundamental key in the dilemma of forces that play on him.

"A spear" was perceived for almost the whole blot, though it excluded the female area at the top. Since that female area sometimes does carry the perceptual lines appropriate to a spearhead, and his arbitrary designation does not, the *law of excluded awareness* influenced this image. It is a weapon of the man who is outside conventional social mores. It probably welled up to oppose the dysphoria and feminine qualities in the tree. The stark contrasts that play over him keep him from defining himself as a male. What ego forces exist to power the rocket and control it and handle the spear and control it? Among these unusual images appears his usual bug. Weakness is pitted against power, and the roots of some of the power may have nothing to do with male power. Almost any kind of image that occurs to this subject takes him some way to an opposite. The rocket is an opposite to a spear, though they both may be used for destructive purposes. One is completely simple, the other highly complex. The contradictions within, symbolic of death-locked power between opposites, will take the subject into destruction.

Plate V brings in the first full or complete human figure in a life-like state, "a ballet dancer." The sheer contrast of a ballet dancer among his power images is important. One would not expect him to report such an image at all, since it is not common in the imagery of adolescent boys, especially if they are desperate about defining their masculine status. It is followed by "New Zealand," the land where aborigines dance a different one from the movements at Covent Garden. At every turn, an opposite springs up in his imagery. The highest form of civilized dance, the ballet, not a place where a man is likely to find his firmest sense of masculinity, appears against an opposite, the site of man's most primitive state (New Zealand). Wellington is about as far from New York or London as you can get. They are geographic opposites. Which pertains to his ego's path, the polished or the primitive? His ego does not function in relation to either; it does not stand opposed. For this reason it is caught in the middle of *alternating opposites*. Two sides of the same coin are split from contact, split apart, and this releases alternating forces that buffet him in a predictable rhythm. Like the surf at a beach, power and weakness continually wash up after each other. That state seemed to characterize the whole of his inner psychology at the time of examination. What element is there to control the rocket or the spear, the primitive or the complicated, the civilized or the savage? We are beginning to see that his sexual energy does not take him outwardly any more than did his opposition to his needs for mother-nurture. He is a passive prisoner of destructive forces, suspended in a power struggle.

Plate VI offers little that is new. He is not in a position to project masculine energy into life. The passive side pops out; the strength of what keeps him suppliant, on his knees to mother-nurture, alternates with destructive power. His sense of masculinity insofar as ego power is concerned is "something with whiskers," an image related to his condition. His identity is formless, but whiskers are there. His structure is too weak to sustain the powerful forces of adolescence in a male. The clock continues a sense of the rhythmic swinging back and forth of the forces that sway him. How long can he remain the passive carrier for this intense struggle?

Plate VII tells us more about what proportion of energy is necessary or required to split or separate from matriarchal power. "Puss in Boots" takes us to the world of the marvels of cat-power. The subject wants things done for him, comforts created magically, on the one hand, and supreme power, on the other; nothing much lies in between. Behind the split woman lies magical instincts. Instead of overcoming the negative control masculine power can have, as Jack does in the *Beanstalk*, this boy wants the power of the mother goddess for himself. Separation and tension between sexual opposites, both archetypal pulls in him, do not take him out to others. He is interested in autogratification. Nothing relational in his images has appeared. Plate III was devoid of human experience. The rest of the images on Plates VIII, IX, and X are mostly repetition of what has already emerged. This shows the intensity of what is there, how little it is influenced by other stimuli, and the lack of substance outside these forces. Plate IX included an image which has a kinship with initiation, the head piece from a knight's suit of armor. It is the interplay of the other forces (shown in his images) on the blot that prevent his earning knighthood (destructive ones). The status of knighthood offers an independent means of moving out toward his opposite sexually. Plate X takes him back again to the emotional need for independence (fourth of July), but we see this as the need to break away emotionally from the proportions of the struggle in him, *not* from mother-power or fear of the opposite. It is a vast, dramatic display of the power his ego needs to get free of the play of opposites inside him. Independence can come only through destruction. A machine gun is the means to get the brilliant display of independence going. This turned out to be his way in life.

In looking back at this record, we have the total advantage of knowing the outcome. It can but color our view. Our interpretation was not meant to be one which delineated his sexual dynamics, the nature of his defenses, or to discover a diagnosis. All of that can be done. It was to illustrate the condition inside subjective experience when a subject is caught between the destructive power of archetypal opposites. We have no doubt but that the subject was much concerned about controlling his sexual impulses; but, if he killed his mother because of some incestual guilt which got too great for him, we do not have much data that support such a conclusion. We do not maintain that it cannot exist, but if it exists in the data here, we have misinterpreted it.

Caught in the bleak space between the split-off sides of a personal, psychological coin, the power of those forces battered him constantly. We doubt that this subject lived in a world of conscious, destructive fantasies. One face of his coin showed the features of the matriarch, and, if he had any fantasies about her at all, it was *she-in-service-to-him,* not the reverse. He wanted the magical energy belonging to she-who-must-be-obeyed; he wanted to reverse an archetype. It led to destruction. He would take over her magic by force, and get hold of the source of eternal nurture. The other face on his coin was formless, but one might discern whiskers. The formless masculine swirled with power, but there was nothing to contain it. Nothing was present to further the growth of ego power. He sustained the battle for another year after his Rorschach examination. Our guess would be that, when he was almost 15, he got confronted with an experience in life, maybe after school, probably with a girl, though it may have been a boy. Not necessarily sexual, though that may have been, something about the nature of his total impotence flashed into consciousness. Everything and nothing became obtainable simultaneously. He was shattered by some confrontation with his feminine side, hidden behind the empty, grandiose proportions of his need for power (to define himself). Something about the feminine spelled dissolution to him. It was in the mother-world or he would have included his father in the melee. He destroyed his source, his own mother, and ruthlessly his sister who had grasped his struggle, and then rubbed out the intolerable confrontation he had had in himself, through personal destruction.

This is, of course, conjecture, but it is based on the data we had, though it came cold, a year before, and from a second-hand source. The crucibles for violence were there, and it is through the psychological means in a subject like this one that violence emerges onto the social scene.

Was this a latent psychosis? Many of his images fell inside the "AD" angle in the axis we have described. We would say that the conditions for a psychotic break were present at the time of the original examination. He was like an accident waiting to happen, but it may not be accurate to call that a latent condition. His was not a state in which ego defenses were yet to crumble; they were little in evidence on the Rorschach, though his capacity for outward adaptation was shown in the TAT. We would propose that his acts of violence were not due to sudden psychosis or collapse, but to an intolerable inner experience which came at the time. He may have been psychotic for some time, noticed only by his sister. We do not know. From the data at hand, can we determine whether he could have been helped and the violence prevented? Probably he could have been helped, but preventing the violence is another matter. No one can say. When opposite sides are split, violence is no longer contained. It had come to that state. The author knows no more about the case than what has been presented here. Insofar as life and reality are concerned, looking at these materials without further information keeps us enough to the unknown to speculate more broadly. This does not necessarily mean less accurately. It is the means to understanding the archetypal side. Ego data get in the way. We need factual data when we deal with the personal dynamics of the boy in relation to his family. Our purpose here has been to look at the materials against a broader perspective, though it may not have been accurate in regard to all the personal details in the life of this subject. This mode enables us to catch what is collective about a subject's experience. Paradoxically, it keeps us more to an *objective* grasp. Life details about a subject often pull us in the wrong direction.

We have looked at five cases against such archetypal forces as we have been able to identify. We have tried to keep to our definitions and to remain consistent with subjective laws. All were unusual cases, but all afforded special kinds of information. We have deliberately kept away from conventional interpretation to demonstrate other forms of approach. We have used conventional means when they seemed appropriate, but our goal has been to link Rorschach behavior with a wider range of experience than conventional means have allowed it. We have approached symbols through the intrinsic and the universal, not through a specific theory. We do not mean for our theory about Paleolithic sources in Rorschach stimuli to stand up everywhere on every account. We have attempted to keep to empirical observations and to deal with Rorschach symbolism against a means to objectivity. In our search to broaden the scope of the Rorschach for ourselves and others, many details have gone unattended.

REFERENCES

1. Campbell, Joseph. 1956. (Commentary). In: Grimm's Fairy Tales. 864 p. New York: Pantheon Books.
2. Cirlot, J. E. 1962. In: A Dictionary of Symbols. 400 p. New York: Philosophical Library.
3. Dukor, B. 1951. Probleme um den transvestitismus. Schweiz. Med. Wochenschr., 81: 516–519.
4. Dunn, I. Jay. 1968. Social and community psychiatry and individual social consciousness. J. Anal. Psychol., 13: 146.
5. Fenichel, Otto. 1945. The Psychoanalytic Theory of Neurosis. New York: Norton.
6. Hamburger, Christian. 1953. Transvestitism: hormonal, psychiatric and surgical treatment. J. Amer. Med. Ass., 152: 391–396.

7. Huelke, H. 1949. Ein transvestit; der fall Heinrich, B. Kriminalistic, 3: 91.
8. Jones, Ernest. 1931. On the Nightmare. London: Hogarth Press.
9. Jung, C. G. 1958. Psychology and Religion: West and East. 699 p. In: Collected Works, Vol. IX. New York: Pantheon Books.
10. Kaiser, Robert B. 1970. R.F.K. Must Die. New York: E. P. Dutton.
11. Laming, Annette. 1959. Lascaux, Paintings and Engravings. 208 p. Baltimore: Penguin Books.
12. McCully, Robert S. 1964. Vampirism: Historical perspective and underlying process in relation to a case of auto-vampirism. J. Nerv. Ment. Dis., 139: 440–452.
13. McCully, Robert S. 1963. An interpretation of projective findings in a case of female transsexualism. J. Projective Techn. Personality Assessment, 27: 436–446.
14. McCully, Robert S. 1958. A projective study of a true hermaphrodite during a period of radical surgical procedures. Psychiat. Quart. (suppl.), 32: 1–36.
15. Neumann, Erich. 1955. The Great Mother. 380 p. New York: Pantheon Books.
16. Summers, M. 1960. The Vampire. 356 p. New York: University Books.
17. Westphal, C. 1870. Die conträre sexualempfindung. Arch. Psychiat. Nervenkr., 2: 73–108.

EIGHT
Overview

Our main effort in this book has been to apply a psychology of archetypes to the Rorschach method, and to deal with symbolism through its universal significance and intrinsic content. In this way, we have attempted, along with the existentialists and others in recent times, a different means of approaching Rorschach data. Our focus has been more on how the psyche may work than on delineating particulars about an individual's dynamics. We have wished to show the Rorschach as a means of taking candid shots showing how ego consciousness *reacts* alongside influences from sources we have called archetypal. How the ego reacts to material from personal complexes, and how it displays its defensive patterns, are well known. The dimension of Rorschach experience we have described tends to illustrate certain unique qualities that the Rorschach provides. We have suggested that an individual's mode of perception is crucial in understanding his personality structure. While individual dynamics may influence that mode, the mode itself is as important as dynamics. We have defined differences between male and female perception and apperception, while noting their similarities. The importance of *Erlebnistypus* has been noted, since the manifestation of internal forces peculiar to an individual takes that individual into his fate. It is a quality outside of the particulars of dynamics and the stresses of symptoms or complexes, though it may pertain to them. As inner and outer have been grasped against the frame of inkblots, we have not merely implied that each is part of the other or that the whole is greater than the sum of its parts. While those may be important relationships to remember, our position pivots around the idea that different laws pertain to each, whether or not they be parts of the same whole.

Gordon Allport (1) was one of the first critical thinkers who called attention to the limitations in projective techniques. He asked if what the subject himself thought had no meaning for interpretation. We have addressed ourselves to answering that question, at least in part. It depends on what aspects of Rorschach experience one is talking about. When symbolism and data with archetypal imprinting emerge, then, under our definition, the subject has *no* awareness of what his own symbols mean. Allport (1) noted that the Rorschach examiner became busy tracing a subject's images to his past, while the subject was busy thinking about his future. It would seem to us, as it did to Joseph Conrad, that yesterday, today, and tomorrow are nothing for humanity unless they are in the psyche. We maintain that Allport's criticism is a valid one, but we must not use it for the wrong purpose. Looked at one way, it can take us through a path back to where we started. One must not ask more of the Rorschach than it can give. The Rorschach experience does not provide a set disclosing those contents of consciousness that are presided over by the ego; it tends to show how the ego behaves inside a particular set of conditions. While it is extremely important to get a subject's associations about his images, if the image is a symbol that emerged from archetypal sources, the subject may have no more idea about its meaning than anyone else. Free association to the symbol does not necessarily bring in the central scope contained in the symbol, though it may provide other information about the subject. It is important to note the source of Rorschach material, and to be wary about a subject's own idea about what it means. Much too often, a subject repeats what knowledge of a particular theory has conditioned him to say. Our "Stone Age" case record is important in that regard. What he saw was unconnected with taint from any modern theory. None of the conditioned overlays of our tradition seemed to have influenced him, or those influences had been mostly lost through time. At the same time, a subject who is genuinely open to inner processes may grasp something of his own symbols through being in touch with something of his own myth.

When Rorschach data are used only to diagnose a condition or ferret out dynamics that lie behind symptoms, particulars in the data may lie fallow and never be used meaningfully for the subject, or *returned* to him. Just as with a dream image, an examiner and/or therapist may use a Rorschach image for a therapeutic encounter. While some workers do this, we need much more of it. Through amplification of an image, analyst and subject may be taken through it into an exciting *encounter together*. This way, the material is restored to its rightful owner, the subject, who learns how to claim what he had thought was not his own.

Eugene Minkowski (5), at the London Rorschach Congress in 1968, spoke movingly about how he used Rorschach images with his patients. He called this the *XIth* Rorschach plate. Minkowski (5) also called for a classification of the Rorschach under the mantle of anthropology. He used anthropology to mean personal contact, a term he preferred over "existentialism." Like Minkowski, one tends to see the term as an arbitrary carrier for a hybrid mixture. In the author's view, the existential movement concerns itself with an important aspect of archetypal experience, namely, man himself against fate. Paleolithic man had to consider himself against fate as much as we do, and it links us psychologically. We can only applaud those existentialists who have extended meanings in interpreting Rorschach imagery. Rawlings and Messina (6), at the same congress, demonstrated an existential means for grasping Rorschach data. We have suggested that Plate IX has special significance for man and the sources in him that pertain to the meanings in his existence.

We would wish to make a distinction between kinds of encounters for a subject involved in the Rorschach experience. How the subject experiences the examiner is one thing, and how he experiences his images is another. The personal impact of the examiner on a subject may be important or unimportant to the subject. "Over-relating" and imposing oneself or one's impressions on the subject during the inquiry may disrupt inner processes. A therapist or examiner must avoid a heliocentric view of his importance to the subject. At times, an examiner may intrude at points when a subject is absorbed by an inner drama. There are some subjects who rely heavily on interplay between themselves and the examiner during the Rorschach. This may be highly useful for the subject. In the final place, we agree with Minkowski that there should be an XIth plate experience for the subject, in which examiner and patient go together into an encounter with the subject's images. What was taken from him may then be restored to him for his own benefit. Naturally, this can take place only when an examiner is in a position to do it, and when a subject is ready to absorb it. If the Rorschach examiner is not the therapist, someone else may do it, if he is properly qualified.

An examiner may be as innocent as his subject about the meaning of an image as they approach it. Preconceived notions about an image topple objectivity. The examiner may or may not play a role in what emerges for a subject in the Rorschach experience. We see encounter in the Rorschach experience as one between *man and himself*. A man who does not communicate with himself, or is not in contact with his inner resources, can say very little to others. Ours has not been a view of the Rorschach as a carrier of a wide range of the content of consciousness. Yet, by watching closely what happens *in consciousness,* ego activity, we may obtain a dynamics of the present, as the ego bends or stands firm against what emerges before it from unconscious sources. One often finds a subject whose inner drama is powerful, yet one sees little of it in the subject's behavior in life. Nothing external corresponds to the proportions of an observable inner crisis. It is a subjective encounter, with few outer traces. Through observing the drama, we gain knowledge about what fate has in store for the subject. Sometimes it means a crisis may be imminent. If the crisis is based on material from archetypal sources, intervention in it should be appropriate to the nature of the forces involved. There is no pat formula for intervention. Through intervention, one may impose ego values against forces that are inappropriate to them. In such instances, intervention may become intrusion. We may become circumspect about personal crisis through examining Rorschach materials. Often, the Rorschach experience provides us with a view of a rehearsal, preliminary to a later outer drama.

A central thesis in our discussion of symbol formation has included the means by which well defined sexual contours in the stimulus qualities of the plates set going archetypal activity. We have referred to subjective laws that influence or determine the nature of a symbol. Why do sexual contours have potent power in symbol formation? Perhaps more than any other facet in mankind, the shape and nature of reproductive organs link men with other species. The energy attached to this linking no doubt predates the first glimmers of consciousness. We have suggested that archetypal energy guided men prior to consciousness and that something about the nature of consciousness itself displaces awareness of archetypal activity. We suggest that it is this aspect of the energy associated with sexual archetypes, and not merely a pleasure principle (and the deviations that get attached to it inside sexual expression), that is powerful enough to activate its own roots. As a means to survival, sexual energy must have played a powerful role inside natural selection in evolution. Another important quality which may pertain to the import of sexual images, apart from the erotic, centers around the fact that a sexual symbol *defines* its opposite. Sexual union combines opposite parts. When the two parts are brought together, they become more than each was separately. This meant survival phylogenetically in earlier times. Thus, we are saying that it is not the presence of a personal sexual complex that controls subjective laws which are associated with symbol formation. The presence of a complex may be illuminated through the symbol without one's having determined how the symbol came into being. Usually, when archetypal energy is activated, the image is split from the instinctual plane inside man's complicated visual cortex.

It is not necessarily a move toward objectivity to take an eclectic approach about Rorschach material. The authenticity of life may come to any individual from any school of thought. Yet, eclecticism may mean taking no position at all. That was not true for Hermann Rorschach. He was careful to choose features from the theories of others that he felt pertained to his method, and he eschewed explaining his technique through one theory. Yet, he fully grasped the importance of his technique's not being dependent on how a particular theory is regarded at a particular time. Jung avoided developing a specific theory, partly because he never claimed his psychology was a complete one. He was fully capable of devising a theory, but his humility kept him away from it. Particularly in the United States, Rorschach's method has suffered because it has been generally regarded against

Freud's libido theory. Through that, a tremendous body of research grew, but it has about come to an end. It has been milked dry, though many valuable insights about certain areas of behavior have accrued.

It may be useful to look briefly at Jung and Freud against the future of psychological theory. Those two giants have been compared endlessly, but let us look at them outside the contents of what they said or how they differed personally. This way we may get another view of them, permitting a broader evaluation. Great ignorance pertains generally about Jung's work. Many workers have thought that Freud trained Jung, and that Jung followed Freud's theories for many years, and that something rather petty and personal between them led to their break with each other. Jung has been lumped in with the "psychoanalytic movement" and is generally thought to have been a part of it, with some minor differences. Nothing could be further from the facts.

A comparison from the field of astronomy may clarify what we mean. Freud, like Galileo Galilei, was adapted to his times, and the contributions of both of those giants among men were easily intelligible to the general public. Galileo's observations could be applied at once to the instrumentation which had just become available through the work of Dutch innovators in optics. Similarly, Freud's theories had immediate relevance to the emerging theories of social science. Jung, on the other hand, like Johann Kepler, provided us with empirical data not easily intelligible to the general public, and the instrumentation to measure them is yet to be devised. (Nevertheless, it will be done.) The answers Jung sought did not emerge from the experimental techniques available. The importance of Kepler's observations, while his work was known and published, was not fully appreciated until much later. Sir Isaac Newton made them the cornerstone of his new concepts and laws of the universe. Kepler's ideas contained all that was necessary to account for gravity. Though contemporaries, neither Kepler nor Galileo tended to combine or coalesce their contributions. If they had, the true nature of the force controlling celestial movements would have been immediately obvious.

It does not necessarily follow that if we pooled Jung's and Freud's ideas a full understanding about subjective laws would emerge. Jung has not excluded Freud's concepts from his empiricism. Gerhard Adler of London, perhaps one of the most original living thinkers among Jung's followers, addressed his thoughts to such a combination recently at a Congress in Zurich. He rejected the notion that, through a marriage between the ways of Jung and Freud, the means to a new theory would emerge. An Isaac Newton is yet to arise for psychological theory.

It would be an error to perceive this book merely as an application of Jung's work to the Rorschach. We have excluded some of Jung's concepts that are central to his model (such as anima and animus). Jung had no theory to apply, though his model of the psyche is a theoretical one. We have used a number of Jung's concepts to widen the scope of the Rorschach as a means to understanding. We have used the approach Jung took to symbolism. A number of Rorschach workers, especially those who have had some contact with Jung's work, have been doing this for years. This approach to symbolism was understood long before Jung, but Jung was the first to apply it to materials obtained from mental patients.

Jung applied what he found in studying archetypal material to a developmental view of a psychology of life. Ericson has done a similar thing with a developmental model. Yet, Eastern sages understood stages of psychological development long before the Christian era; only the context was different. The stuff of the psyche that holds out invisible threads that link all men is not new. It has been and will be. Any Westerner who thinks that it was Freud who liberated mankind, so that it could be freer around its sexual impulses, should read the volumes of the great Chinese classic, *The Golden Lotus*. Fanny Hill might as well have stayed on the farm, milking in Shropshire, if she, in her endlessly repetitive exploits, would think herself competitive with Golden Lotus.

A chief purpose for us has been to catch hands with Rorschach's dream about how his technique might lead us into understanding remote epochs. We have used the materials of a remote epoch to aid us in understanding ourselves. When prototypal ideas that grew into this book were presented by the author (4) in London, 1968, André Morali-Daninos and David Kadinsky were kind enough to note our effort as a means to connecting several disciplines.

Louise Bates Ames (2) has commented recently on how a particular theory and its historical course should not pertain to the viability of the Rorschach. Like Ames, we have been much influenced by developmental processes as a frame for viewing Rorschach material. We would like to see new work done on Piaget's theories using the Rorschach as a means of investigation. A developmental frame has been highly useful in the study of history. Gibbon, Spengler, and Toynbee have freely used developmental concepts in their grasp of man's interactions with himself.

It is useful to view consciousness as a developmental process that continues. We understand very little about just what factors go into widening the range of consciousness in an individual, and what determines the focus inside consciousness. Something operates outside of the will of the subject. Education may or may not affect the range of awareness. Our view of cultural bonds tends to be opposite to that of Arbuckle (3), who holds that man's self transcends cultural laws. We would agree that the conscious contents of a particular person may become free of cultural dogmas, but we do not believe that man is outside of nature. It is consistent with experience to note that culture influences width in the scope of consciousness. There may be psychological laws that govern the awareness range a cultural group holds collectively. We must not be prejudiced by thinking our form of awareness and its width is the ideal one, nor should it be used as a general gauge for measure. We have a confused notion of intelligence in the West. The scope of awareness is seldom included as a measure of intelligence, yet it is a crucial one. The Wechsler scales do not begin to approach it adequately. There may be a normal curve of distribution for range of awareness, as well as for verbal facility and the acquisition of knowledge. The nature of the scope of awareness in a given tradition may be an important means through which nature ensures survival. Our current binge in the West, that of "everything for everybody and as quickly as you can," may go contrary to nature's laws and provide us with diminishing returns. It was nature, not man, that set up the normal curve of distribution. Nature's way is seldom democratic. One means of studying the range of awareness in a culture may be to study that culture's aesthetics. What does it matter to an ignorant, poverty-stricken, homeless wanderer in India that a particular sage has reached a state of clear perceptions? When similar experience is projected into art forms, the ordinary person may be connected to archetypal sources through them. The source is nourishing for him. So, we have discovered recently, are dreams. What the Indian may not have as regards his portion of the economy is a wholly different matter.

How did the black man tolerate the bleak poverty of his cabin during the period of slavery in the United States? He saw the white man's opulence and swept and scrubbed it. Opulence was not in focus in his range of awareness. It had nothing to do with how bright he may or may not have been. There was in him no similar energy attached to the aesthetics of the white man. The need for a different aesthetic is recognized in the black world today, and those who are in it are busily widening the range of awareness and developing a separate aesthetic. This is valid at an archetypal level, though not necessarily valid for an individual whose adaptation has become fixed through the effects of relations with whites.

To be sure, a particular black, while still a slave, may have dreamed enviously of a master's possessions. Yet, it seems doubtful that black men would have been so complaisant if those dreams had been widespread. The collective energy of the blacks was attached elsewhere. A hundred and fifty years ago, the blacks were caught between losing the outer frame (their African setting) which had been appropriate for inner experience, and assimilating strange new frames. Yet, their local archetypes came with them and continued to influence them. The interplay among these subjective forces existed apart from the world and materialism of the whites. It was not the focus in their awareness, nor was the level in awareness appropriate to what impinged on them from the outside. The story of Joseph gives us a clue about how a connection with archetypal experience alters personal enslavement. When Joseph was sold as a slave and was taken to Egypt, he moved into a much more complex culture. At such a time as he was able to grasp the meanings in Pharaoh's dream, which is to say, demonstrate a superior relationship with archetypal material and symbols, his psychological state changed. His slavery, the part of him that was in service to someone else, was freed, and he was given charge over his former masters. This enabled him to influence his own culture through preventing its extinction later. It may have taken the state of slavery to push Joseph into a widened grasp, through contact with his intuition.

The power of older archetypal pulls had to subside before the black man's awareness about himself and his relation to his altered state could change. The rugged conditions he faced in his African culture equipped him archetypally for the rugged conditions of slavery.

Local archetypal powers between whites and blacks are obviously in flux in the United States today. Effects extend throughout the world. It is important to note that how the black ego responds collectively to conflicting archetypal powers within his subjective experience is seldom grasped by the blacks consciously. The conscious attitudes of both blacks and whites about each other seldom correspond to the archetypal motivations behind behavior. A particular Rorschach record may sometimes reflect the whole scope of what burns groups of men into white or black heaps. The black man did not leave his inner nature behind when he was transported here. His condition had not been "primitive"; it had been different. The Romans found our ancestors painted blue and in trees, when they landed beneath the cliffs of Dover. The men they found were men-in-nature, not men-against-nature (as the Romans were); the latter condition is one which the Judaic-Christian culture has furthered. The Chinese were fully aware of what conflicting archetypal powers were in store for them when Western contact was made with them for trade. The Peace Corps girl (Case 3) grasped a similar fate for Nepal. A Western youth usually has a narrow range of awareness against the participation of an Eastern experience. He may get a kick out of the novelty without grasping anything of its meaning. This is not because of ignorance about cultural differences. He is not open to the nature of the experience. One can acquire a head full of information or facts about Tantric art and not know anything about what the experience means. Even with several degrees, a sitar, and a copy of the *Dhammapada,* a Western youth cannot, through intent, grasp what is closed to him. He may use drugs to break the barrier, but, without an experienced scope, he usually has little to take back with him to keep after his trip.

One of the dangers inherent in the various fads associated with group experience is ignorance about archetypal powers. Who knows what terrors ensue when a member of a group experience suddenly cannot assimilate direct confrontation with the power of the opposite within? Instant psychotherapy and group games may be found not to have linked us any closer than we were before. We do not suggest that some of the far-out group experiences do not have positive effects for a person. There is, though, an analogy for us in the religious group experiences of the campground meetings of the last century. Through religious fervor, individuals were sometimes struck to the ground by archetypal power. This may have sobered a sinner, who then behaved differently ever afterward. Perhaps that is the origin of the expression, "he got the fear of God put in him." In any case, the point we wish to make is that these are forces which we have little grasped, but apprehending them is not new. When they have been approached at all through serious scientific study, they were viewed through ego values. Through mutual assent, cult leaders acquire power. One may be certain that archetypal forces influenced the gory conditions of the Manson case. Widened knowledge about the Rorschach as a means to studying archetypal influences is one of the goals of this book. At a time when so much money is being spent by governments to repair social ills, we continue not to have a viable social theory. The question that should concern legislators who provide the funds is not whether basic research should be done, but what is the *range* of grasp in those few professionals who decide what research will be supported. We may find the material means to cure social ills without the knowledge to identify where the range in the sickness lies. Incomes and social benefits, while desirable for other reasons, do not themselves alter psychological laws. We have attempted to illustrate a means the Rorschach may serve to enhance our grasp of the power of social forces.

We have stressed the importance of Rorschach's blots in extending our knowledge about a general theory in psychology. It has been too long in the service of a single theory, and too embedded in a medical model. Its usefulness in an applied science, that of alleviating symptomatic conditions, is indeed a high cause. Nevertheless, this has led to neglecting other potentials that exist in Rorschach data. Our goal has been to refocus attention to neglected aspects of the materials it provides and to turn those data toward theory.

At the moment, considerable professional energy is being used in conditioning techniques in treatment. This coincides with a need for a means accessible to greater numbers of individuals. Yet, the focus in it is not toward theory, but toward application inside the psychology of symptom formation. Our major point is that if the techniques of psychology are going to be applied to large groups, we need to understand more about the laws that determine collective behavior. Group dynamics have been studied in great detail in the last decade or so, but most of the studies have been set inside the contents of consciousness and assessed against ego values. The Rorschach is a means by which we can study and learn more about the archetypal forces that influence group behavior. Reconditioning may change habits, but archetypal influences are not a matter of habit. Their energy has been collected and sustained through common group experiences over long stretches of time.

We believe that the Rorschach method of investigation has usefulness for other disciplines. Archaeology, philosophy, and history are good candidates for apprehending data through it. Philosophers tend to talk to each other more today than to the society in which they live. Except through education theory, philosophy has become aloof in a time when its contribution is needed more than ever. Philosophers have the advantage of not being influenced by models that have been lifted from other fields. We could see a study by philosophers, well versed themselves in the Rorschach method, making new discoveries through it for their field. We hope that we have contributed in a small way to paleoanthropology through the means we have used to look at Paleolithic art. The correctness of our interpretation is irrelevant. Sociologists and anthropologists have used the Rorschach technique in some of their research. Yet, those two disciplines tended to use the technique when the libido theory was central in research in other cultures. Those studies sounded the death knoll for the universal aspect of the Oedipus Complex. While establishing cultural norms for Rorschach material may be a serious problem, it is not insurmountable. We suggest the Rorschach as a means of communication *between those disciplines in which its use seems applicable.*

In the *Tao Te Ching,* the slender Chinese book of archetypal wisdom, one may read, "To know when one does not know is best, to think one knows when one does not know is a dire disease." We must get beyond disease, beyond faulty perception, if we would find a Western form of *Sila,* the fragrance that surrounds a clearing in our perceptual grasp. We see the Rorschach as a means toward that goal.

REFERENCES

1. Allport, Gordon W. 1953. The trend in motivational theory. Amer. J. Orthopsychiat., 23: 107–119.
2. Ames, Louise Bates. 1970. Projecting the future of a projective technique. J. Projective Techn. Personality Assessment, 34: 359–366.
3. Arbuckle, D. S. 1965. Existentialism in counseling: the humanist view. Personnel Guid. J., 43(b): 558–567.
4. McCully, Robert S. (1968) 1970. Archetypal qualities underlying the Rorschach experience. Rorschachiana IX. Rorschach Proceedings VII International Congress, London, N.R. 53: 985–992.

5. Minkowski, Eugene. (1968) 1970. Le courant anthropologique et le test de Rorschach. Rorschachiana IX. Rorschach Proceedings VII International Congress, London, N.R. 53: 985–992.
6. Rawlings, Sam, and Messina, Robert. (1968) 1970. Existentialism and the projective techniques. Rorschachiana IX. Rorschach Proceedings VII International Congress, London, N.R. 53: 963–970.

APPENDIX
A Commentary on Adolf Eichmann's Rorschach

Ritzler's (1978) article, "The Nuremberg Mind Revisited," prompted this writer to re-examine the Rorschach protocols of 16 Nazi leaders published in Miale and Selzer's (1975) book *The Nuremberg Mind*. The book includes Adolf Eichmann's Rorschach in an appendix. The nature of Eichmann's record struck me as worthy of attention in its own right.

Miale and Selzer, basing their view on certain traits in the Nazi records, concluded that the Nazi leaders were not psychologically normal or healthy individuals. *The Nuremberg Mind* has had a controversial impact and stimulated several experimental studies of the same data. Harrower (1976) designed a blind analysis study of 8 Nazi records and included control group protocols. The ambiguity of her findings led Harrower to remark, "It is an over-simplified position to look for an underlying common denominator in the Rorschach records of the Nazi prisoners" (p. 350). Ritzler (1978), using Rapaport's scoring method, submitted the Nazi data to statistical analysis. Analysis of these data led Ritzler to state, "we cannot be satisfied with Miale and Selzer's interpretation of the Nazi as highly disturbed individuals—at least in the psychiatric sense. At the same time, we should not accept Harrower's conclusion that the Nazis are no different from the man next door" (p. 353).

It is noteworthy that an application of techniques lacking in the Miale–Selzer approach failed to provide definitive clarifications. Perhaps one reason for this depends on the kind of set one takes to Rorschach analysis. Miale and Selzer searched for a clinical denominator. Taken alone, diagnostic labels are unlikely to account for the complex parameters Hitler used in selecting leaders for his grandiose schemes. There is no historical precedent for the Nazi Rorschach materials. The Nazi leaders were hardly a random sample from the varieties in human nature. Harrower's techniques would be appropriate if we had a more precise criterion for comparison. Blind Rorschach analysis is useful for verification, but perhaps inappropriate for discovery, which involves unraveling of puzzles in human nature. Neither control groups nor quantification, singly or in combination, represents a sufficient challenge to the problems of verification in this instance, when there are so many unknowns. Mixing Nazi Rorschachs with samples from other groups of subjects may be useful, but when there are no fully justified comparative data, results are bound to be inconclusive. If there existed Rorschach records from leaders of the French Revolution—Robespierre, Murat, Mirabeau, and above all, Madame La Farge—a justifiable control group would be comparatively available. Blind analysis yields little when an analyst has almost no idea of what variables to consider. Disturbed or not, these men *led,* and there must be other useful ways of considering these data, ways offering a fuller understanding of these highly selected, influential men.

When I looked back over the Rorschach data of these men, 4 records stood out as particularly challenging. This is not to say others were not interesting, but the 4 chosen ones struck this writer as the sort of accounts that would pique the curiosity of any experienced Rorschach analyst. Three of the records included those given by Hans Frank, Minister of Justice and Hitler's administrator for Poland; Hjalmar Schacht, the wily and brilliant Nazi economist; and Baldur von Schirach, the Reich youth leader who married the daughter of Hitler's personal photographer. The spontaneity and rich variety of imagery in these 3 records alone argue against the Nazi prisoners as a group of guarded, depressed individuals, unwilling to reveal themselves due to having been on trial for their lives. Several records were flat and guarded, but that quality was not characteristic of the group as a whole.

A fourth, but different sort of record, struck this writer as the most interesting of all. This was Adolf Eichmann's record (reprinted here). While Miale and Selzer had discussed Eichmann in another context, his record was included in an appendix to show its comparative nature with a record of an American community leader. The authors had done little with this record other than fit it into the broad categories designated in their study. The manner in which Eichmann organized his percepts inadvertently revealed his personality structure perhaps far more clearly than he himself had thought. This does not mean that Eichmann's nature was obvious, but it means that he left his psychological fingerprints on his record. Harrower (1976) included Eichmann's record in her study, designating it a sample of a "normal personality" among the Nazi officials. Harrower apparently defined normal as absence of obvious psychiatric disturbance. This failed to take into account various intriguing and subtle ways Eichmann reacted to and organized his imagery. Ritzler (1978) judged Eichmann's record "a rather banal, commonplace protocol." He omitted it from his statistical study for that reason and because there was no inquiry. Had Eichmann's record been overlooked because authoritative opinion about the man himself had been so pervasively accepted or unquestioned? This commentary is less an interpretation than an effort to show that a close study of Eichmann's percepts reveals him as a complex man. The commentary strives to avoid clinical technicalities with an aim to enable readers unfamiliar with the Rorschach method to grasp the reasoning which concludes that Eichmann was no simple, ordinary man.

KARL ADOLF EICHMANN'S RORSCHACH
Card I
1. ∧ Bat, from a collector or a museum, with spread-out wings.

Card II
1. ∧ Two brown bears pressing against a glass, hats on their heads which are blown away as in dueling. Even the snout is drawn on the left one, and the ear on the right one. Very

clear bear ears. Quickly drawn with sketching ink.

Card III

1. ∧ ("This is also a humorous sketch.") Two very polite dandies tipping their hats to each other, greeting each other very formally; there are even patent leather shoes there.
2. Two clowns who want to do their best, masked; white collars at the neck.
3. The red could be an eye-catching stage decoration in the background.

Card IV

1. ∧ A stretched-out cowhide, stretched for drying, or already treated. It is also trimmed —the forepaws and the rear. The head is very badly drawn; the backbone well drawn; it also goes well toward the side.

Card V

1. ∧ Bat—much better than the first one.

Card VI

1. ∧ Also a skin, but the head part doesn't fit—also a skin of a wild animal.
2. The head part like the head decoration of the Aztecs (upper D).

Card VII

1. ∧ Outlines of continents, if I cover the lower part.
2. ▽ South America down to Tierra del Fuego; Caribbean Sea with Brazil, Argentina, Chile.
3. ∧ Again a humorous drawing; two dancing elephants, trunks raised, eyes slightly indicated, standing on one foot.

Card VIII

1. ∧ A leaf chewed up by insects, pressed for (display in) herbarium; the color shading would look different in a fall leaf, but there is a leaf in Argentina whose color is similar.

Card IX

1. ∧ A coat of arms (covers half); above is the helmet, heraldry in the middle, drawing below—but one side must be covered.

Card X

1. ∧ A colored drawing from botany, a flower with pistil and stamens.
2. > A detailed drawing of stamens, drawn for a better view for school use.

Karl Adolf Eichmann was born in Hitler's home town of Linz, Austria. He was a middle-level Nazi official. He personally administered orders conceived by higher officials. As head of the "Office for Jewish Emigration," he was responsible for an organization Shirer (1960) described as "an agency not of emigration but of extermination and to organize the slaughter of more than four to six million persons" (p. 351). There was nothing abstract about his duties. Eichmann escaped from an American internment camp in 1945 and remained at large until he was located and brought to trial in Jerusalem in 1961.

Insofar as a theory of Nazi personality is concerned, the Eichmann trial had a more widespread effect on social philosophy than did the Nuremberg trials. This

was largely due to Hannah Arendt's (1964) personal study and report on her observations of Eichmann at his trial. This led to her widely influential proposition of the
"banality of evil." Evil, according to Arendt, often thrives because of the banality of
quite ordinary men. Eichmann struck her as a prime example of this. Arendt's view
was strongly supported by Stanley Milgram's (1974) famous experiments on obedience to authority.

Arendt described Eichmann as a trite, trivially ordinary person who would not
have slept at night had he not obeyed orders. She noted that he not only obeyed
orders, he obeyed the law. Arendt remarked that half a dozen psychiatrists certified
Eichmann as "normal" and that Eichmann, in her judgment, was an average, normal person. (I. M. Kulcsar, the psychiatrist who administered the Rorschach in person to Eichmann, told Michael Selzer that *no other psychiatrist but himself* ever
examined Eichmann professionally. Therefore, at least in this instance, when Arendt
stated categorically that "half a dozen psychiatrists certified Eichmann as
'normal,'" she was either misinformed or *unjustifiably* added incorrect data to
strengthen her personal thesis. The State of Israel guarded Eichmann like a hawk,
and he appeared at the trial in Jerusalem only inside a bullet-proof glass
encasement.) Most people have tended to accept this view of Eichmann, particularly
since Milgram's experiments lent it credence. Contrarily, Eichmann's Rorschach
struck me as a very unusual one by any standards. Merely reading it activated my
autonomic nervous system, sending cold chills up my spine.

Prior to Eichmann's trial, the State of Israel asked Kulcsar to examine him to
determine whether Eichmann might break down under the stress of trial. Kulcsar
administered several projective techniques to him, including the Rorschach. None
of this material was used or mentioned in evidence.

Eichmann's successive comments about his images suggest that he perceived the
Rorschach as a sort of test of his aesthetic or artistic sensibility. An ordinary man
does not perceive in that fashion, command the vocabulary Eichmann had at his
disposal, nor make careful, precise appraisals of nuances in a concerned manner.
Eichmann may have had artistic training, but his manner of proceeding alongside
odd inconsistences led me to conclude that he organized his percepts via a
characteristic mental mechanism. Does his aesthetic set and odd sudden attention to
details processed by artistic scrutiny hold up under logical analysis?

Several examples removed from context portray the flavor of his paradoxical
judgments: the popular bat on Plate I qualified by "from a collector or a museum"
(he did not say butterfly; who collects bats? This may seem a harsh judgment, but
we wish to show that it was often in moments of *precise* specificity Eichmann
managed to give himself away); "Even the snout is drawn on the left one, and the
ear on the right one. Very clear bear ears" (the snouts and ears are drawn identi-
cally on right and left; what, then, is the purpose of his remark?); "dandies . . . there
are even patent leather shoes there" (Eichmann lets the examiner know he is keenly
aware of nuances; is this perceptual acumen or his patterned way of justifying
everything he reports?); "clowns who want to do their best, masked; white collars
at the neck" (either "clowns who want to do their best" is a projection about the
affective state of the clowns, a feature not inherent in the blot, or, perhaps more
likely because of the vivid coloring in this plate, Eichmann passes judgment on how

well the clowns have made themselves up *to look the part.* From normative data we know these remarks are highly original as qualifiers and uncharacteristic of an average person); "cowhide . . . already treated. . . . also trimmed. . . . The head is very badly drawn; the backbone well drawn; it also goes well toward the side" (is this man a tanner? an art critic? If this tendency is merely a compulsive trait, why did he focus in some instances on nonexistent differences between identical blot areas?); Plate V, "Bat—much better than the first one" (yet, presumably the "worse" bat on Plate I belonged to a collector or museum; the point is that Eichmann's qualitative comments are opportunistic, and often when he makes them his judgment is inconsistent); "leaf . . . pressed for . . . herbarium; the color shading would look different in a fall leaf, but there is a leaf in Argentina whose color is similar" (note the *uncommon* care with which he commits himself to color. Rorschach colors have to do with the quality of feelings for the emotions of others); "coat of arms . . . but one side must be covered" (why must one side be covered? What real advantage? Eichmann appeared to wish to create the impression that his keen sensibility was easily offended); "A detailed drawing of stamens, drawn for a better view for school use" (is this entire plate sideways solely stamens?). It struck me that these detailed comments based on seemingly aesthetic criteria combined the ordinary with the unusual, the former tending to overshadow the latter.

The way Eichmann processed his percepts suggested a cagey person at times given to a peculiarly unnecessary accountability. In some instances, his justifications cannot be checked without specialized knowledge. This mechanism struck me as a form of deceptive-forthrightness. Characteristically, he noted and described one thing in a fashion that called attention *away from* something else. This occurred with ordinary and unusual imagery alike. No ordinary mind does this as successfully as has Eichmann. He operated mentally as a magician does manually; when by design the audience looks where it is intended (off-center), the trick has come off when attention returns to the act. If this observation about Eichmann is correct, he would not be expected to show an obviously identifiable psychiatric disorder. His record shows him capable of garnering enough imagination to specialize in looking quite ordinary: like one of those clever men in detective novels who collects vital data by virtue of having personal characteristics which appear ordinary to others, while his real nature goes unnoticed. Is this mere speculation, and have we drawn too much on a knowledge of this man's known acts? Let us examine Eichmann's response to Plate II in some detail. This image is remarkable in its own right, with or without knowledge of the subject.

Two brown bears pressing against a glass, hats on their heads which are blown away as in dueling. Even the snout is drawn on the left one, and the ear on the right one. Very clear bear ears. Quickly drawn with sketching ink.

This image shows the ease with which Eichmann's percepts flowed from the commonplace into the idiosyncratic (giving us perhaps the essence of Eichmann's psychology). Bears do not wear hats in nature, nor do they duel. First, he reported what he saw, then what he imagined. This transition enables an analyst to distinguish which is which, a feature not always clearly discernible in Rorschach work. Observers unfamiliar with the Rorschach seldom realize that a Rorschach analyst proceeds with a background of normative data, that is, knowledge of what is *commonly done* by subjects. Taken alone, this is not the criterion for "normalcy"; rather, it represents an average manner of proceeding. When Eichmann reported "bears," he gave a commonly found percept. To that extent he linked himself with what an average person does with this plate; from then on, nothing he saw, said, or imagined had much in common with average, ordinary, or expected perceptual behavior. This does not necessarily mean that Eichmann was not normal. It means his percepts shift abruptly from usual to very unusual indeed. Whenever this occurs, a subject leaves psychological fingerprints on his record. These imprints are samples from his personal world. By definition, a banal mind lacks the capacity to transform what is ordinary into the unusual. Eichmann's imagery looks ordinary at first glance, documenting his capacity for ordinary adaptation. At the same time, his personal or imagined material reveals complex mechanisms and fantasy, fragments from an inner world sharply contrasting to his outer facade. Quite remarkably, Plate II sampled facets from his imagination directly related to the very issue society held against him: violent destruction of life!

Years ago, Piotrowski and Abrahamsen (1952) demonstrated a relationship between certain psychological traits and Rorschach animals, when the kind and quality of behaviors visualized were incongruous with the natural behavior of the species at hand. Data of this variety enabled them to predict successfully classes of antisocial acts in known criminals on blind analysis. Odd or unusual combination animal–human images (both in form and behavior) link empirically with psychological traits found to recur. Put another way, this kind of image tends to reflect *individualized* attitudes toward impulse control, raising a question about completeness of socialization in particularized areas.

Eichmann's popular–original image for Plate II suggested that *this subject would channel his impulse life or aggressions in a highly unusual or idiosyncratic way.* This image drew me to review his record carefully; I found it remarkable, having been given by a man on trial for his life because of his relationship to destructive violence. Insofar as the theme of violence is concerned, this image showed there was nothing trite or trivial about the way Eichmann's fancy flowed; he perceived this issue in a way *special for him.*

These bears (Plate II) participate in two kinds of behaviors totally unrelated to each other: they press against a glass one moment and blow each other's heads off the next. From normative data, we know that he saw both actions in a highly individualistic fashion. It is particularly interesting to note that *the way* Eichmann reported the activity envisioned leaves the violent action itself almost unnoticed. Further, incongruity between the two different behaviors little troubled Eichmann. He felt no urgency to account for the *action* in his imagery. No spontaneous accountability was applied to violence when it occurred in the imagination of a man who was at great pains to account for almost everything else he reported! Having reported violent action, Eichmann then devoted 25 of the 43 words spoken for Plate II to aesthetic concern about the quality of the plate as a drawing, carefully noting left–right differences when none exist between the specific details he chose to discuss. The sequence—first pressing against a glass, then dueling—suggests an inner state of *partitioned violence.* His remark "very clear bear ears" reflects the certainty for Eichmann that the figures were indeed bears (and not, for instance, human beings). Transition in this image suggests that partition around violence *dissolved easily;* abrupt change in action went unnoticed by the subject. Perhaps this is a clue about how this man was able to put into effect orders few other men could obey.

Dueling is a uniquely human concept with inhuman consequences. Its nature is based on a prescribed code, a gentleman's agreement to do violence in a certain way. It delivers justice over to brute force in the name of honor. A form of "civilized" revenge, the dueling code enabled individuals to take public law into their own hands and give vent to violent passions. A version of the law of talion, the duel aims to disguise violence by diverting attention to procedural appearances. Does not this image disclose that Eichmann's personal relationship to violence resembled features associated with the dueling code?

His choice of language and description is unusual. Appearances were emphasized over the action at hand. Did Eichmann mean hats were blown away, heads blown away, or heads with hats blown away? It is not precisely clear. The manner in which he envisioned this moment of violence shows a highly individualistic, almost fastidious quality. Eichmann was not one to call a spade a spade. While absence of an inquiry (ordinarily, an analyst would ask questions of the subject to clarify any ambiguities) is regrettable, in this instance it may be an advantage. It leaves us only with his spontaneous imagery, enabling us to see what he accounted for and what he left open, when left to his own devices. Did the red color influence the kind of action in this image? Quite probably (color was used on all other colored plates!), yet on his own, Eichmann made no reference to color or blood. Mention of blood would have emphasized violence. There was no reference to weapons. Dueling may have been a quaint way of referring to fighting, but the hat-heads were *blown* off. That quality suggested dueling to Eichmann, together with, we surmise, the unmentioned bloodletting.

An ordinary man with a banal position on violence would not have handled this plate in the fashion that occurred to Eichmann. He fantasied violence in a peculiarly personal way. Once violence sprang into his imagination, he used mental gymnastics which created a particular effect. The net result made violence *appear* trivial. This rather adroit achievement was accomplished by the fastidious way he droned on about appearances. Eichmann understood the psychology of trivia as camouflage. No one can say whether Eichmann's manner of structuring violence attracted him to his loathsome post or, once he was assigned to it, its impact on him was greater than he himself supposed. According to Shirer (1960), one of Eichmann's subordinates stated under oath that just before the German collapse, Eichmann announced that "he would leap laughing into the grave because the feeling that he had five million people on his conscience would be for him a source of extraordinary satisfaction" (p. 978). Eichmann's Rorschach shows mental mechanisms which make such a statement believable. His final remark on Plate II, "Quickly drawn with sketching ink," completed his shrewd mechanism of diverting attention: the sketching ink might have been spewed from a squid. This camouflage apparently worked very well. A number of professionals took the camouflage to represent the man, and a societal theory was built on this as evidence.

There are other features in Eichmann's record which are not commonplace. His botanical images include a great deal of specificity and fragments of illogic, enabling us to see his mechanisms repeated in so neutral an area as the plant world. The Argentine leaf on Plate VIII was perceived in two incongruous ways: first, "chewed up by insects"; then, "pressed for (display in) herbarium." This leaf's integrity was violated by insects; the next moment it passed muster for display in a museum. Is this a beautiful rare leaf or one chewed up by insects? An inquiry might have clarified these two different perceptions, but taken as is, his manner of processing images is noteworthy. A first impression, which hints of violence, was transformed into a more aesthetically acceptable one described so meticulously that there could be no mistake about Eichmann's knowledge about the flora of Argentina. Again, his choice of language is interesting: "the color shading would look different in a fall leaf." In fall foliage the leaf would look different? Yet, its color here is similar to that of a leaf found in Argentina; color seems to identify a particular leaf. Is the present color spring or summer foliage? Again, he shows a slippery evasiveness to emotion in others.

While an inquiry would have clarified the ambiguity, Eichmann omitted doing so himself. In the midst of great specificity about a leaf native only to a distant land, he diverted attention from the precise way color was integrated in his image. The net result was a kind of deceptive-forthrightness. His use of color includes an almost unnoticed idiosyncrasy, not dissimilar to the way shading was used on Plate IV. (Shading as texture—in, say, animal skins—reflects sensitivity about others' needs. Here we doubt that he used texture, but shape only, and it stretched or full of tension.) The significance of these observations lies in the impression that usually when Eichmann was technically precise about one aspect of an image, he left another, more important, aspect open or imprecise.

Unlike the man next door, Eichmann reported none of the popular responses Plate X usually elicits. Instead, he produced a great deal of specificity about the reproductive system of flowers. A second image (whole Plate, sideways) appeared to Eichmann solely as stamens. This is an uncommon set of percepts, quite apart from interesting symbolism. Images like this show *poor perceptual form* or shape and invariably reflect some problem about the reproductive apparatus. Miale and Selzer remarked on the unusually high number of botanical images in the Nazi records and linked them to an undeveloped human relatedness. Might these images not reflect purpose or need? In this instance of the Nazis, perhaps the statistically unexpected botanicals reflected a need to dilute or neutralize something else—exposure to the unsocialized side of unfettered aggression.

In some instances, nature imagery on the Rorschach may symbolize a compensatory mechanism, at least in some subjects who have an unusual or individualized relationship to their own inner violence. For instance, this writer (1978) reported on a series of exposures of different editions of inkblot stimuli to a subject who murdered his parents and tiny brother. A striking and consistent set of botanicals emerged in the series. These images contrasted with a personality geared to abject violence. The subject was untutored and uninterested in botany; his multiple flower images surprised him as much as they were statistically rare in normative Rorschach data. This striking finding, which held up over a 7-year period retest, called for a psychological explanation. Regarding them as compensatory symbols was an empirical conclusion.

This in no way means that botanicals invariably have this Rorschach connotation, but that in some instances they may reflect a compensatory function against violence, given a particular alignment of psychic variables. Heinrich Himmler had a magnificent botanical library and was considered to have been a fine botanist. It is noteworthy that Eichmann repeated a botanical focus similar to that found in several higher Nazi officials. This feature itself may *not* represent a common denominator peculiar to the Nazi leaders. Yet, it may reflect a common need-trait, in the sense of a psychological means of diluting other, importunate hostile forces which tend to impinge on conscious contents. While bakers tend to see bread in ink-blot stimuli, what does it mean when nonbakers also see an excess of bread images? This is the psychological issue here, and it centers around the fact that some Rorschach images are logically determined and many others are not. The Rorschach analyst relies on normative data from which to make psychological observations. In any event, we are suggesting that, in the case of the Nazis, the statistically unexpected botanicals in their records may represent a compensatory diluting function which contrasts with their outwardly blatant unethical practices, an activity that dominated Eichmann's lifestyle.

Curiously enough, General Wilhelm Keitel, himself a Prussian officer trained within a particular code and one who issued inhuman orders contrary to that code, reported an unusual or original botanical for Plate VIII: "Dandelion bud prepared on a slide and enlarged" (inquiry: "colored drawing of a microscopic slide projection with natural colors in a botany book"). This image suggests an odd preoccupation for a military man. His precise specificity of the bud variety resembles Eichmann's description of the Argentine leaf, in the sense that it represents a psychological mechanism stimulated by color. Note that, when questioned, Keitel stuck to the notion that the bud was in *natural* colors, yet there is little actual color on Plate VIII that one could ordinarily connect with a dandelion. Like Eichmann's leaf, color integration has a slippery, elusive, inappropriate rationale which cannot be readily checked or might be easily overlooked. Keitel's dandelion may be another example of deceptive-forthrightness. Neither man questioned his own color judgment in these instances, offering insight into their respective characters.

This commentary attempts to show that Eichmann's Rorschach perceptions were, in several respects, not ordinary or what one might expect from the man next door. His record enables an analyst to examine Eichmann's way of processing violence when it occurred solely in his imagination. The manner in which he structured his percepts makes it possible to trace repeated patterns in his mental mechanisms. Certain percepts disclose facets of his inner world which contrast sharply with the outer facade attributed to him. In some instances, he altered objective reality to suit his notion of how reality should be. When this occurred, he automatically drew attention elsewhere. This was accomplished in a deft, scarcely noticeable fashion. These features are uncharacteristic of an ordinary, banal mind.

The author recognizes that prior knowledge of the identity of the subject of this study influences his analysis. No apology is made for that fact. In this instance, our aim was discovery, not verification. The purpose was to discover more about what this particular man may have been like, and a byproduct has been to see that Eichmann was not so commonplace or ordinary as was generally supposed. A notion of "the banality of evil" may have great merit. However, on the basis of normative Rorschach data, Eichmann's manner of processing his percepts, and certain of his images themselves, leaves in question the validity of his having fit Arendt's proposition, much less having qualified as the prototype who formed the basis for it.

REFERENCES

Arendt, H. 1964. Eichmann in Jerusalem: A Report on the Banality of Evil (Rev. ed.). New York: McGraw-Hill.

Harrower, M. 1976. Rorschach records of the Nazi war criminals: An experimental study after thirty years. Journal of Personality Assessment, 40: 341–351.

McCully, R. 1978. The laugh of Satan: A study of a familial murderer. Journal of Personality Assessment, 42: 81–91.

Miale, F. and Selzer, M. 1975. The Nuremberg Mind: The Psychology of the Nazi Leaders. New York: Quadrangle/The New York Times Book Co.

Milgram, S. 1974. Obedience to Authority. New York: Harper & Row.

Piotrowski, Z. and Abrahamsen, D. 1952. Sexual crime, alcohol, and the Rorschach test. Psychiatric Quarterly Suppl., 26: 248–260.

Ritzler, B. 1978. The Nuremberg mind revisited: A quantitative approach to Nazi Rorschachs. Journal of Personality Assessment, 42: 344–353.

Shirer, W. 1960. The Rise and Fall of the Third Reich. New York: Simon & Schuster.

List of Illustrations

Abbreviated descriptions are given, including site of origin and sources of photographs (P).

1. CRETAN MOTHER-GODDESS. Mural at Knossos. P/Neumann.
2. GODDESS OF LAUSSEL. Dordogne, France. "Prehistoire de l'Art Occidental", A. Leroi-Gourhan. Editions de Mazenod, Paris. P/Musée d'Aquitaine, Bordeaux, cliché, J. Vertut.
3. MARBLE MOTHER-GODDESS. Çatal Hüyük. P/Mellaart.
4. BELL-SHAPED EARTH-GODDESS. Boetia. P/Neumann.
5. MARY PETTY CARTOON. May 3, 1952 cover, *New Yorker Magazine*.
6. SPEAR-THROWER. Paleolithic. Musée de L'Homme, Paris.
7. CIRCLE-IN-STONE. Paleolithic. P/Giedion. Photo by Achille Weider.
8. RECLINING FIGURE. Henry Moore. In coll. Gordon Onslow-Ford, Mills Valley, Calif. P/Courtesy of the sculptor.
9. FAMILY GROUP. Henry Moore. P/Courtesy of the sculptor.
10. GREEK VASE. Sixth century B.C. P/Jung.
11. BISON. LASCAUX. P/Leroi-Gourhan. Mazenod, Paris. Photo by J. Vertut.
12. SORCEROR. Les Trois Frères. P/Ucko & Rosenfeld.
13. CLAVIFORM SIGN. La Pasiega. P/Leroi-Gourhan. Mazenod, Paris. Photo by J. Vertut.
14. BRACKET SIGN. Le Portel. P/Ucko & Rosenfeld.
15. SIGN VARIETIES. Paleolithic. P/Leroi-Gourhan. Mazenod, Paris.
16. IBEXES. Paleolithic relief. P/Leroi-Gourhan. Mazenod, Paris. Photo by J. Vertut.
17. GILGAMESH. Assyrian relief. P/Jung. Courtesy of The Metropolitan Museum of Art, gift of John D. Rockefeller, Jr., 1931.
18. DRAPED RECLINING FIGURE. Two views. Henry Moore. Edition of 2; Time-Life Building, London; City of Cologne, Germany. P/Courtesy of the sculptor.
19. TAPESTRIES WITH BIRDS. Town coll. of Freiburg. P/Jarry.
20. HAND PRINT. Paleolithic. P/Giedion. Photo by Hugo Herdeg.
21. FERTILITY FIGURINES. Cycladic. P/Neumann. Photo by Alison Frantz.
22. GARDEN OF VENUS. Painting by Minnie Evans. Coll. R. McCully. P/Medical University of South Carolina.

Index of Sites

1. ALTAMIRA—Discovered in 1879 at Santillana, Santander, Spain. Inventoried by Abbé Breuil in 1902.
2. CASTILLO, EL—Discovered in 1903 at Puente Viesgo, Santander, Spain. Pictorial inventory published by Abbé Breuil in 1912.
3. ÇATAL HÜYÜK—Situated on a plain in southern Turkey, discovered in 1958, excavations that continue were started in 1961. Neolithic town, first form of urbanization, 5880 B.C.
4. COVALANAS—Discovered in 1903 at Ramales, Santander, Spain. Catalogued by Abbé Breuil.
5. FERRASSIE, LA—At Le Bugue, Dordogne, France. Excavation begun in 1902.
6. GARGAS—At Aventignan, Hautes-Pyrénées, France. Known for centuries. Cave-bear ossuary and hands outlined in red and black discovered at end of nineteenth century.
7. GRÈZE, LA—At Marquay, Dordogne, France. Excavated in 1904.
8. LABATUT—Aurignacian rock shelter at Sergeac, Dordogne, France.
9. LASCAUX—Discovered in 1940. Inventory undertaken by Abbé A. Glory, not yet complete.
10. LAUSSEL—At Marquay, Dordogne, France. Excavation begun in 1909. Fine stratigraphic sequences and figures in low relief.
11. MARSOULAS—At Marsoulas, Haute-Garonne, France. Excavated in 1883–1884 by Abbé Cau-Durban. Paintings discovered in 1897.
12. PASIEGA, LA—At Puento Viesgo, Santander, Spain. Discovered in 1911. Pictorial inventory by Abbé Breuil.
13. PECH MERLE—At Cabrerets, Lot, France. Discovered in 1922, new parts discovered in 1949. Entire decoration inventoried by Lemozi.
14. PETERFELS—At Baden, Germany. Site of rich finds of stylized fertility figurines carved from lignite.
15. PILETA, LA—At Benaojan, Malaga, Spain. Discovered in 1911. Very vast, only parts catalogued.
16. PORTEL, LE—At Loubens, Ariège, France. Cave known for a long time prior to discovery of paintings in 1908.
17. ROC DE SERS, LE—Rock shelter found at the foot of a cliff at Sers, Charente, France, in 1927. Highly reliable dates.
18. TROIS FRÈRES, LES—At Montesquieu-Aventès, Ariège, France. Gradually opened from 1912 on by Count Henri Bégouën and his three sons. Abbé Breuil published extensively on the findings from this site.

Index

Beast, 87, 93, 150, 198–199, 219
Beatles, The, 143, 202
Beauty and the Beast, 199
Behn-Eschenburg, Hans, 28, 29–30, 46
Behn-Rorschach inkblots, 28, 29–30
Behn-Rorschach Versuch, 47
Bell shape, 80–81, 251
Belly, 89, 202, 208
Bender Gestalt, archetypal sources in, 34–
    35, 121–122, 138, 194, 217
Bender, Lauretta, 34, 46
Bennington College Review, 167
Bible, The, 16, 54, 58, 164
Binswanger, Ludwig, 2
Bird, 57 (fn.), 64, 86–87, 129, 147–148,
    159, 195, 196, 199, 211, 251
Birth, 16, 57, 63–64, 89, 93–94, 101, 154,
    163, 186
Birth control, 134, 135, 137
Bisexual, 39–40, 64, 94–95, 98, 102, 120,
    125
Bison, 34, 61–62, 64, 68, 79, 87, 89, 92,
    111, 117, 122, 133, 138, 150–151,
    163, 251
Black color, 71 (fn.), 80, 87 (fn.), 89,
    153, 201–202, 211, 250
Black race (*see also* Negro), 74, 105,
    118, 128, 134, 137, 227, 245–246
Blacky Pictures, 34
Bleuler, Eugen, 3, 6
Blocking, 119, 152
Blood, 64, 79, 99, 150–151, 165, 188,
    190–198, 200
Blum, Gerald, 34, 46
Boas, George, 133, 166
Boccaccio, Giovanni, 192
Body, 34, 99, 102, 117, 160, 161, 217,
    224–226
Boeotia, 80, 251
Bollingen Foundation, The, 133
Bone, 63, 64, 67, 78, 89, 93, 106, 128,
    134, 150, 154, 187, 226
Bookends, as Rorschach image, 99, 161
Boomerang, 120–122, 138
Boots, as Rorschach image, 108
Borderline condition, 31–32, 33, 39, 42,
    153, 169, 177
Boss, Medart, 2
Botanical images (Nazi Rorschachs),
    258–259
Bower, Gordon, 75, 166
Bracket sign, 120–121, 138, 251
Breast, 68, 78, 80, 86, 87 (fn.), 105–107,
    120, 133, 138, 172, 175–176, 211,
    215, 218, 219, 220
Breuil, Abbé, 115, 250

Britain, 93, 96
Buddha, The, 51–52
Buddhism, xi, 15, 52, 57 (fn.), 96, 153,
    203–204, 206, 208
Bug (*see also* Insect), 224–225, 234
Bull, 57, 68, 79, 87, 88, 108, 117, 133,
    163, 218
Bulletin of the Menninger Clinic, 9, 22
Bulls, Great Hall of the, 218
Burckhardt, Jakob, xii, 131
Burghölzli, 3, 6
Butterfly, 99, 119, 123, 151, 201–202,
    212, 224–225
Byron, George Noel Gordon, Lord, 192

Campbell, Joseph, 75, 166, 192, 237
*Carl Gustav Jung, 1875–1961, a Me-
    morial Meeting,* 9
Castillo, El, 155, 250
Castration, 68, 198, 220, 223
Cat, 137, 140–141, 181, 196, 202, 207–
    208, 212, 217, 219, 226, 235
Çatal Hüyük, 80, 87 (fn.), 250, 251
*Çatal Hüyük: A Neolithic Town in Ana-
    tolia,* 167
Caterpillar, as Rorschach image, 110, 113
Catholic (*see also* Church), 100, 183–184
Cave (*see also* Parietal art), 34 (fn.),
    34–35, 48 (fn.), 59–60, 62–63, 64,
    66, 67–71, 75, 76, 82, 87, 89, 94,
    96 (fn.), 96–97, 115, 117, 120,
    150, 155, 163, 214, 250
Celtic, 192
Chalice, 156, 209
Chaos, 12, 137, 196, 205, 210, 216, 218
Chardin, Jean, 46
Chastity, 141, 159, 219, 222
Chaucer, Geoffrey, 192
Chevron sign, 35, 62, 89
Chieftain, psychology of the (*see also*
    King), 65
Child (*See also* Daughter; Father;
    Mother; Son), 11, 20, 24, 34, 51,
    55, 56, 67, 75, 94, 102, 112,
    118, 134, 136–137, 144, 150, 156,
    161–162, 186–187, 197, 219, 229–
    230
China, 17, 54 (fn.), 88, 135, 192, 201,
    203, 233, 244, 246, 248
Ch'ing Shih, 192
Chivalry, 135, 141
Christ, 51–52, 99–100, 120, 137, 200,
    202
Christian (*see also* Judaic), 4, 52, 54,
    96 (fn.), 96–97, 120, 129, 153, 196,
    244, 246

Recent and New Titles from Spring

THE LOGOS OF THE SOUL   Evangelos Christou

This book is an essay in the clarification of first principles. It attempts to think through a fundamental logic for psychotherapy and to separate this logic from those of the natural sciences and philosophy. Includes an addenda of illuminating excerpts from notebooks and letters, as well as an editor's introduction by James Hillman. Reissue of edition out of print since 1981. (iv, 104 pp., ISBN 202–X)

THE SELF IN PSYCHOTIC PROCESS   John Weir Perry

The case of a young housewife diagnosed catatonic schizophrenic demonstrates the interpenetration of collective symbols and individual processes as they come to light in "breakdown" (Part One), and extends knowledge of the psyche by elucidating symbols of the Self (Part Two). This second edition includes a new preface by Dr. Perry, together with the original Foreword by C. G. Jung, scholarly apparatus, illustrations, and index. (xv, 184 pp., ISBN 509–6)

FACING APOCALYPSE   D. Miller, R. J. Lifton et al.

Newport, Rhode Island: a group of truly original minds meets to give contour and features to "the end"—to face apocalypse. Each approach—D. Dolci's peace activism, D. Levertov's poetry, N. O. Brown's reflections on Islam, J. Hillman's invocation of Mars, M. Watkins's work with inner figures, W. Giegerich's demonstration that the Bomb is the *mysterium tremendum,* etc.—*imagines* the nuclear devastation that menaces the horizon so that it can reveal the shock of its meanings. (195 pp., ISBN 329–8)

THE CREATIVE PATTERN IN PRIMITIVE AFRICA   Laurens van der Post

Valuing story as "the most precious container of the spirit of 'primitive' man," Sir Laurens van der Post shows the profound potential in the African psyche for creative adaptation to the cosmos. Months spent patiently among Bushmen before they became acquainted with whites allowed that intimacy and trust necessary to receive their precious stories. The theme and the author reawaken in our contemporary lives a primordially religious sense of belonging to the world and its beauty. (40 pp., ISBN 405–7)

ANIMA AS FATE   Cornelia Brunner, preface by C. G. Jung

First translation into English of a 1963 Jungian work by a respected Swiss analyst. Part I explores the notion of the anima in the work of Rider Haggard, particularly in his novel *She,* but also provides background and a psychological evaluation of the author's life. Part II traces the development of the anima in a series of dreams that a middleaged physician experienced. (xv, 276 pp., ISBN 508–8)

EGALITARIAN TYPOLOGIES VERSUS THE PERCEPTION OF THE UNIQUE   James Hillman

The author goes beyond typology (Part One) to the revelation of character in faces—the physiognomy theories of Lavater, Darwin, Szondi, and Gestalt (Part Two). Part Three presents a theory of imagistic perception, seeing people and events as images, and it draws upon Imagist poets (H.D., Pound, Williams) for showing a way to regain an "animal eye" so as to perceive each individual in his or her uniqueness. (59 pp., ISBN 404–9)

ISBN prefix: 0-88214–
Spring Publications • P.O. Box 222069 • Dallas, TX 75222